Wicca

Wicca:

The Old Religion in the New Millennium

Vivianne Crowley

Thorsons
An Imprint of HarperCollins*Publishers*

Thorsons
An Imprint of HarperCollins*Publishers*
77–85 Fulham Palace Road,
Hammersmith, London W6 8JB
1160 Battery Street,
San Francisco, California 94111–1213

Published by Thorsons 1996

10

A catalogue record for this book
is available from the British Library

ISBN 1 7225 3271 7

Printed and bound in Great Britain by
Creative Print and Design Wales, Ebbw Vale

To my initiators who have walked the way,
to Chris with whom I make the journey
and who wrote the chapter on the God,
to those in many lands with whom we have danced
the Spiral Dance
and to the Wicca who are and who are yet to come:

Blessed Be.

Contents

Introduction

Over the past 40 years, many books have been written about Wicca. At Imbolc 1989, the first version of this book was published. Since then, Wicca has been rapidly evolving. New generations have been initiated into the Craft, many of them coming from countries whose first language is not English. My husband and I have spent much of our time teaching Wicca in England and overseas. The students who have passed our way have become our teachers. In seeking to answer their questions, our own understanding of Wicca has deepened. The time was therefore ripe to take another look at Wicca in the light of what we have learned.

This has resulted in changes from the first edition. The Wiccan community's understanding of its own history has evolved and a newer and clearer picture has emerged of the enduring Paganism that underlies European culture. Our understanding of the processes of inner change has also evolved. As each of us travels on our own initiatory journey, our understanding of the path which we have walked evolves. We can look back and ponder our own journey. We can watch those whom we initiate and train grow and develop. This does not mean that I now have all the answers. As each year passes and the turning wheel of the seasons unfolds the mysteries of life and death, I learn still more.

I wrote in the last edition that there are difficulties in writing about Wicca. No book can ever fully capture its essence. Wicca is not a religion or Craft that can be taught through and learned from books. It is a living, growing system of thought, belief, ideas, knowledge and experiences, each part of which is built upon the next. It is also essentially an oral tradition. It is only in recent years, with the development of literacy, that Wicca has been recorded. Wicca is still something which we must learn from others, by observation and by doing. A book can only be a shadow of the reality. This is why, in Wicca, our ritual books are called *Books of Shadows*.

Another difficulty is our oaths. The words of the oath of the first initiation bind us to secrecy. Wicca is a Mystery religion and if the Mysteries are to effect inner change, they must always contain elements that we cannot understand; elements which confound but also tantalize the conscious mind and force it to work on them until realization comes. The power of the Mysteries lies in maintaining their ability to mystify. If too much is explained about a mystery, it is rationalised and becomes a product of the finite conscious mind, not a product of the infinite unconscious.

When writing about Wicca, we must balance the desire to reveal where the Mysteries can be found, so allowing greater access by a greater number, with maintaining the essence of the Mystery. The decision about what should or should not be written must be a decision for each individual; but the decision is made easier because the true essence of Wicca cannot be expressed in words. The world of Wicca is the world of what is sometimes called *Dionysian truth*. This is truth that is intuitive and non-verbal; truth which is communicated through symbols and myth. Words and books cannot convey the full essence of this truth. Whatever we write cannot therefore convey what we can only experience by being in Wicca, working its rituals and participating in its myths.

There are, however, other difficulties in writing about Wicca. One of the beauties of Wicca is its lack of dogma. This allows Wicca to evolve. The danger of writing about Wicca is that people will accept too readily what we write and will not seek to find the answers, and more importantly the right questions, for themselves. Another danger is the egotistical one of writing about Wicca because we believe that our view of Wicca is the *right* one. Any book about Wicca can only be the personal view of the individual priestess or priest who writes it. It will contain truth and error, good bits, excellent bits and bad bits. It will please some of the people some of the time and none of the people all of the time. Other, and sometimes opposing views will be equally valid and right for those who hold them.

So why write at all? I write because I believe that Wicca has important messages for the world today. These messages are not just for those who decide to follow a Wiccan path, but also for all those who are concerned about the fate of our planet and ourselves. Wicca speaks to those who honour the Gods of our ancient past, because they hold the keys to truths that will guide us through the darkness of the future. Wicca speaks to all those who believe that the Gods are within us all and also in-dwelling in the Nature that our species seeks to destroy. Wicca speaks to those who believe that a purely masculine Deity is only part of the mystery of the Divine: that the truth is found in both God and Goddess. Lastly, but not least, Wicca speaks to those who are on the quest to draw nearer to the Gods.

Our task as walkers on the Wiccan path must be to rehabilitate the beliefs of our ancestors and to let the truth and beauty of Wicca shine forth through the murk of the misunderstandings of others. We must put Wicca in the context of what we know about humanity's spiritual aspirations, so that we can see the shape of the child which has been brought forth. Wicca can then take its true and special place amongst the religions and spiritual paths of today, a link between the past, present and future – the Old Religion in the New Millennium.

1

Wicca Today

What is Wicca?

Wicca is the religion of Witchcraft or Wisecraft which is at the forefront of the Pagan revival. Wicca has many strands. It is a religion worshipping ancient Pagan deities. It is also a Mystery tradition to help us grow in understanding of ourselves and hence nearer to the Gods, a system for developing and using psychic and magical powers, and a body of natural lore which is often called natural magic.

Wicca is called the *Old Religion* because it is based on the religious practices of our Pagan ancestors. Wicca worships Goddess and God using those symbols found deep within the psyche of humanity. Their antiquity and universality give them a power that more modern Gods will always lack. This is not the worship of devils, as sensationalist newspapers and those who should know better seek to claim, but the worship of two of the oldest forms of deity – the Great Goddess and her consort the Horned God.

In Wicca, although the Divine is seen as ultimately One, within the Divine we see a duality. The Divine is energy; energy is movement and change. Where there is movement and change, there is active and receptive, ebb and flow. The Divine is therefore seen as male and female, Goddess and God. Within different covens and traditions the emphasis on the Goddess and God may vary, but all traditions believe that for wholeness our image of the Divine must comprise both male and female. To worship either aspect alone will produce imbalance.

The Goddess is often depicted as triple and in her aspects as

Virgin, Mother and Wise Woman or Crone is associated with the waxing, full and waning aspects of the Moon. She is known by many different names. She is honoured variously as Aradia, Arianrhod, Bride, Cerridwen, Diana, but beneath her many faces we find the enduring essence of the Divine Feminine; that which is mysterious and paradoxical, ever the same but ever-changing.

Wicca and the other Pagan traditions are the only religions that worship the Goddess. The Gods we worship embody ideals to which we aspire. If we are to realize the fullness of our human potential we must worship both the male and female aspects of Deity. Many women today are hearing the spiritual summons within them and are seeking to enter the Christian priesthood; but what part can a woman play in a patriarchal religion that denies her the title of priestess? The Goddess orientation of Wicca is also important for men. If men are to find their own inner wholeness they must practise a religion which recognizes the inner feminine that leads a man to his spiritual destiny.

This is not to diminish the importance of the Horned God, for in this image is a key to the understanding of human nature. This ancient Deity which is animal, human and God symbolizes that to which humans must aspire; the three aspects of our nature integrated in harmony. Like the Goddess, the God is worshipped by many names as Herne, Cernunnos, Karnayna; but all of his names have the same root – *hornèd*. His image contains the essence of human perfection. He is no remote dweller in some insubstantial heavenly realm. He is hooved and in touch with the world of Nature, but his horns are a sign of Divinity, for they reach to the stars.

While Wicca provides signposts for those who wish to find it, it is not a religion that seeks to make converts. It does not offer a form of exoteric religion that is suitable for the many, but a spiritual discipline and path which is the way of a few, albeit an increasingly large few. This is because Wicca differs from other religions in the status of its adherents. Wicca offers not entry into a congregation of followers, but initiation into the priesthood of the Mysteries. But what is a Mystery religion? Carved above the doors of Mystery temples were the words: *Know Thyself.* This is also one of the aims of Wicca. The Pagan mystery religions were systems through which their initiates came to understand the true nature of reality and also their own inner nature: who and what we really are. Through exposure to teaching, ritual and symbol, the doors of perception were opened; the windows of the soul were cleansed; and unto the initiate were revealed the mysteries of the Gods and of their own inner psyche: all they were and all they had the potential to be.

In offering entry to the priesthood, Wicca offers a spiritual training which develops our self-knowledge. We come to an understanding and awareness of our own spiritual needs, so that we can in turn facilitate the spiritual growth of others. In explaining this spiritual growth, I refer often to the theories of the Swiss psychologist Carl Gustav Jung. Jung sought all his life to come to an understanding of the Divine. The son of a Christian minister, at an early age he rejected orthodox Christianity and sought through the study of Western and Eastern mysticism, through Gnosticism, Alchemy, Taoism, Hinduism and Buddhism, to find the answers to the eternal questions of humanity: who and what am I and what is my place in the scheme of things? Jung's psychological theories were strongly influenced by his study of occult, mystical and alchemical texts. They are therefore compatible with the esoteric view of humanity, and are indeed partly derived from it.

As a religion, Wicca offers what all religions offer: a philosophy of life, a sense of the place of human beings in the cosmos, an understanding of our relationship with the plant and animal kingdoms of our planet and home, and a form of worship through which we can participate in the mysteries of the life force and fulfil our needs for shared human activity by doing this with others.

As well as entering a priesthood, those who enter Wicca are also initiated as Witches. Witches practise what is known as *the Craft*, a tradition of wisdom and ancient lore. The word *Witch* is a difficult one, full of negative connotations. Recognizing the fear that the word conjures in the minds of many ordinary people and reading the excesses of some Christian fundamentalists and the tabloid press who persist in equating Witchcraft with *black magic*, it is a word which it might be thought tempting to discard. However, most Witches think this would be a mistake

3

and an affront to those of our ancestors who died for their beliefs.

People come to Wicca by many routes. Some come seeking the ancient faith of Goddess and God. The Gods may have spoken to them in dream or vision; or it may be that they have visited sacred sites, read of Pagan deities and come to feel and believe that the Way of the Wise is their way. They are seeking to enter a Pagan mystery tradition both to worship the Gods and to grow nearer the Gods through inner evolution and change.

Some come to the Craft from Witch families, having been raised in one of the family traditions. Others come to the Craft having had psychic and mystical experiences. They may come from other religious backgrounds, or from no religion at all; but often they will have felt since early childhood that they were Witches. Yet others discover the Craft through chance contact with a Witch, from reading a book or article, or from a television programme. By whatever route people come, they tend to share a common feeling of having *arrived home*. They experience a sense of *déjà vu* when hearing the rituals. Learning the Craft is really a re-learning; a remembering of something ancient that is buried deep within their psyche.

Traditionally, Witches are considered to have special powers, but most people who enter Wicca have no more ability in clairvoyance and magic than the average person; nor is this necessary. The average person's capacity is more than ample once he or she learns to use it. Most of us do not use one tenth of the capacity of our minds and much of Wicca is about developing and training the mind and spirit.

Wicca honours the Divine made manifest in Nature and many who have turned to Wicca have done so as the result of a deep commitment to *green* issues. Wicca considers that the focus of many religions on non-material reality has had unfortunate effects on what is seen by Witches as the representation of the Great Mother – this planet, our Earth. Wicca teaches us to value our planet because it is sacred soil. It is not ours. We do not own it. We inhabit it by the grace of the Gods and we must honour it, care for it and reverence the life force manifest within it. Wicca teaches us that we must respect our environment.

In Wicca, the Gods are honoured at eight important seasonal festivals or sabbats throughout the year. At these we reverence the ever-changing life force through the changing cloak of the seasons. The Gods are also honoured at monthly Moon rites called esbats. The word esbat is thought by many to derive from a French word meaning frolic[1] and both esbats and sabbats are joyful occasions. Wicca honours its Gods but, like our Pagan ancestors, Witches believe that our religion should be a celebration of the life force. Wicca also teaches that we should not fear death; for Wicca teaches reincarnation. We will live not just once, but many times. Life is considered to be a journey of many stages, not just one. Death is not the end, but a new beginning.

Like other religions, Wicca accepts that there is a non-material as well as a material reality, but it does not believe the non-material is superior to the material. Matter is not regarded with horror and the emphasis is on the joy of the flesh rather than the ascetics' view of flesh as sin. This is not to say that Wicca is hedonistic, but rather that we are followers of a middle way. Our time in physical incarnation is a gift from the Gods. However, we must also seek spiritual growth that expands our consciousness and allows us to live on levels beyond the physical.

Wicca is a religion that looks to the good in human beings rather than to the evil and seeks to bring out that good rather than dwelling on people's faults. It does not seek unrealistic sainthood, but rather makes the best of what is there. It does not divide people into the chosen and the damned but sees people as being in different stages of struggling towards the same end – that of unity with the Divine.

Wicca does not lay down a set of rules by which to live. Since life decisions are rarely black or white, the onus is on us to make decisions between various shades of grey. This moral sense is developed by seeking to adhere to certain basic ideals of love, joy, truth, honour and trust, and making decisions which are most in accordance with them. There is no book of rules, but there is one meta-rule by which we live our lives.

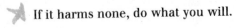   If it harms none, do what you will.

This is no easy morality but a difficult one which makes us scrupulously examine the motives for what we do.

5

Although Wicca has a strong ethical base, it has little dogma. It is a living religion which belongs to the present and, in Pagan philosophy, that present is ever-becoming, ever-moving. Since the present is not static, nor is Wicca. In Christianity, Islam and other Religions of the Book based on revelations of one person at a particular point in time, the dogma tends to become fixed. Once some authority figure has made a pronouncement, it becomes very difficult for the religion to evolve to meet new circumstances and needs that present themselves as the human race and the societies we create evolve.

Although much has been written about Wicca in recent years, it is primarily an oral tradition. Witches learn from the more experienced through formal teaching and by watching and learning from what they see their elders do. Covens will keep a *Book of Shadows* that contains rituals and spell lore. This is passed on to new initiates who must copy the material by hand. Each Witch then adds their own material as they learn and discover more. The *Book of Shadows* is not a straitjacket of belief and practice. The seasonal rituals, for instance, are in skeletal form. This allows each group to incorporate the basic material into its own rituals and from this to develop rituals that meet the needs of its members. Much of the newer ritual material used in Wicca has been channelled through dream, reverie and vision. This has fleshed out the bare bones of our Craft inheritance. The rituals are constantly reinterpreted as our understanding evolves, but on the basis of a shared core of information that preserves a common thread that is recognizably Wicca. There are common themes which are celebrated at the festival of Lammas, but whether the emphasis is on the sacrifice of the Corn King, the beneficence of the harvest Goddess, or both, will vary according to the group's needs. These will grow and change over time, as the needs of individuals grow and change. New parts will be added to the ritual and other parts taken away.

Each Witch keeps the core material that is handed down through initiation, but new Witches are encouraged to write a second volume, which is their personal *Book of Shadows*. This consists of rituals, invocations and spells, many of which they will have devised themselves. This material will grow and develop as they progress through their spiritual journey.

Since Wicca has little dogma, we are not burdened with convincing ourselves of vast doctrinal details and impossibilities against which our intellects rebel. The intellect is one of humanity's greatest assets and also one of its greatest handicaps. Its development has allowed us to master the environment around us (not always with very desirable results) at the expense of losing touch with our inner worlds. Often when people become interested in Wicca, their thinking side protests that it cannot believe in Elementals and magic and that mighty Gods and Goddesses stalk the Earth. This does not matter. Blind willingness to see everything as literal is as foolish as people who persist in believing that the Earth is flat.

Wicca operates in two realms of truth – metaphysical truth and psychological truth. Our ancestors operated in the realm of metaphysical truth. They believed that if they did not perform the correct rites at the Winter Solstice, then the Sun would die. Scientific observation shows that this is not case but if, together with literal interpretation, we reject the concept, we miss the point entirely: the Sun really will not rise. It is not however the Sun of our physical world that dies, but the inner Sun of our spiritual world.

What is required in Wicca is a simple belief that our consciousness is not dependent on the body, but can extend beyond the limits of the sensory world, and that the life force should be reverenced. Other than these simple beliefs in the life force and the powers of the human psyche, all we need accept is that the framework of ritual and symbolism in which Wicca operates contains age-old truths. These are not literal truths but meanings that are hidden and the truth of which will unfold over the years as we integrate them into our own lives.

Wicca sees itself as only one of the many religions and spiritual paths open to the spiritual seeker of today. We do not see ourselves as having a unique monopoly on truth. Indeed Wiccans believe that for a group of human beings to say that they do is ludicrous. Wicca sees the human race as evolving. As our understanding grows, so too will the picture we are able to produce of ultimate religious truths. In Wicca there can be no once and for all revelation of the right way to approach the Divine and the right way to live. In *The Gospel of Sri Ramakrishna*, the Hindu mystic and worshipper of the Goddess

7

expressed this most beautifully:

> God has made different religions to suit different aspi-
> rants, times and countries. All doctrines are only so many
> paths; but a path is by no means God Himself. Indeed one
> can reach God if one follows any of the paths with whole
> hearted devotion... One may eat a cake with icing either
> straight or sidewise. It will taste sweet either way.[2]

To Witches, deities manifest in different ways and can be worshipped and contacted through any form suitable to local conditions and personal needs. Wicca does not believe, as do the
patriarchal monotheisms, that there is only one correct version
of God and that all other God forms are false: the Gods of Wicca
are not jealous Gods. We worship Goddess and God, recognis-
ing that all Gods are aspects of the one God and all Goddesses
are aspects of the one Goddess, and that ultimately these two
are reconciled in the one Divine essence. There are many flowers in the garden of the Divine and therein lies its beauty.

This is Wicca today, but where did it begin?

Notes

1. Margaret A Murray, *The Witch-Cult in Western Europe: A Study in Anthropology*, p97, Clarendon Press, Oxford, 1921.
2. Ramakrishna, *The Gospel of Sri Ramakrishna*, p559, New York, 1971.

2

The Roots of Wicca

Early religion

The Gods of Wicca are those of our earliest ancestors. In Europe, from the Palaeolithic or Old Stone Age around 12,000 years ago onwards, we find paintings on the walls of secret caves that are difficult to access and many of which have been only recently discovered. These are paintings in glowing colours of the Horned Lord of the animals, God of the hunt and God of the hunted, who controlled the movements and fertility of the herds of deer, wild bison and larger, fiercer game, on which our ancestors depended. We also find crude images with the bulging bellies of pregnancy, great breasts and vaginas. These are images of the Great Mother Goddess, She who brings fertility to the people. This is no prettified Virgin Goddess, but the Earth Mother, strong and raw in her power.

With the Neolithic or New Stone Age, there were changes in our ideas about Goddess and God. With the development of agriculture, a settled way of life, and the recording of time, our ancestors noticed the effect of the Moon on women's menstrual cycles, on the gestation of seeds and on plant growth. The Moon, agriculture, the Earth in which the crops were planted, womanhood and motherhood became associated with the Goddess who was depicted now not just as Earth Mother, but also as the Moon. The phases of the Moon were notched in deer antlers in Europe from as early as 7500 BCE.[1]

The Moon has three major aspects – waxing, full and waning. Woman's life could also be seen as having three major aspects – pre-fertile, fertile, and post-fertile or menopausal. The Goddess too was perceived as having three stages – Virgin, Mother and Wise One or Crone, representing the three main phases of the life cycle, youth, marriage and death. The Gods too evolved. As well as being the Lord of the Animals, the God became associated with all that sprung from the Mother Goddess – the green vegetation which waxed and waned in the Spring and Autumn of the year, and with agricultural crops sown by the people themselves. The recording of time brought people a new realization, the link between sexuality and birth. They came to understand the male role in procreation. Women were not impregnated by the Moon as had been thought by earlier generations, but by man. The God was now seen as the Father God, Lover of the Great Goddess. The God of the Hunt became a phallic God.

These early ideas of the Gods evolved throughout the millennia. Tribes merged with others through conquest and marriage. New Gods were adopted and rationalization occurred. The principal Gods and Goddesses were married to one another. Other Gods were thought of as their children. Human societies discovered new and not always desirable needs. As societies became more complex, they needed more resources.

Organized warfare emerged which called for different Goddesses and Gods from those of field and hunt.

The Celts

Wicca is greatly influenced by the religion and culture of the Celts who, by 500 BCE, had become one of the dominant races of Europe. Unfortunately, much of what we know about the Celts is from the writings of their enemy, the Roman Emperor Julius Caesar, who was not an unbiased source. However, we know that although the Celtic priesthood, the Druids, had an alphabet called *Ogham*, they favoured an oral tradition. The Druids believed in reincarnation and the Celts had little fear of death. There were few monsters and demons in their mythology and they were not preoccupied with the idea of evil. They had no concept of sin and punishment and believed that when they died they went to the Summerland, where they were renewed and made ready for rebirth.

The four major festivals of Wicca are derived from Celtic festivals. Since the Celts were a pastoral herding people, their festivals revolved around necessary events in the herder's year. At *Samhain* (pronounced Sow'in) or Hallowe'en on the last evening of October, those animals that could not be kept through the winter were slaughtered and their meat salted to keep the tribe. This festival was therefore a feast of death. *Imbolc* or *Oimelc*, which is also known as Candlemas, took place on the first day of February. It celebrated the first lambing; for as the Celts became a more settled people and began to inhabit the mountainous areas of Scotland and Wales, they became dependent on sheep as well as cattle for their livelihood. Imbolc was also in Scotland and Ireland the festival of the Goddess Bride or Brigid. At Imbolc, she returned to Earth from her winter's rest and blessed and made fertile the land for the coming year. The early spring flowers – snowdrops, crocuses – were signs that the Goddess had walked the land. At *Beltane* or Bright Fire on May Eve, fires were lit on hills all over the land to symbolize the waxing power of the Sun. Cattle were blessed and driven through the fire to clean their hides of ticks and the people would dance deosil round the fire. *Lughnasadh*, the

festival of Lugh, God of Light, was held on the last evening of
July and first day of August. Lugh is a brilliant and many-skilled
God whose weapon is the spear. Amongst other things, he is a
harper, hero, poet, healer and magician. His festival was a great
summer celebration with games and feasting. In the modern
Wiccan calendar, this festival is also known as *Lammas*, originally *Loaf Mass*, a festival of the corn harvest.

The Celts had two other religious concepts which Wicca
retains – outdoor worship (modified for reasons of climate
and privacy) and Goddess worship. Goddesses and women
were very important in Celtic society. Goddesses presided over
poetry and the arts, the important trade of smithcraft, and in the
case of the Morrigan, over war. Women were warriors and
queens and from Julius Caesar's writings we know that dis-
putes of law were settled by the Celtic women.

After contact with the Romans, the Celts began to build temples, but the early Celts believed that the Gods were best worshipped in their natural environment; outside beneath the Sun
and stars, at sacred wells and springs, and on hilltops beneath
the sky. Altars were erected in sacred groves where none might
fell a tree. All over Europe, groves were protected in this way
until Christian missionaries wanting to destroy the ancient
Pagan temples began to fell the groves.

Mediterranean Paganism

Other strands of Paganism that have been absorbed by Wicca
were developed not in Northern and Western Europe, but
around the Mediterranean and Near East where, around the
time of Christ, there was a desire to unify the many Gods and
Goddesses into a trinity of Mother, Father and Child. Over a
thousand years later, Egypt saw another religious reform.
Alexander the Great had conquered Egypt during his great
sweep eastwards and on to India. When one of his generals
inherited Egypt after Alexander's death in 305 BCE and became
Pharaoh Ptolemy I, he was keen to establish a faith which
would be acceptable both to the Egyptians and to the Greek
newcomers. A triad of Egyptian Gods and Goddesses was to be
established who could be equated with a matching triad of

Greek Gods and Goddesses. Two priests were commissioned with the task. Manetho, the Egyptian priest, was a specialist in Egyptian history. Timotheus, the Greek priest, was descended from an Athenian family who had emigrated to Egypt and was familiar with the Greek Eleusian Mysteries of Demeter and Kore.

Ptolemy's new system was that the chief Deities of Egypt would be the Goddess Isis, her husband *Sarapis* and their child Horus. Isis' nephew Anubis, son of her sister Nephthys, became Guardian of the Dead. Isis' original husband and brother, the more well-known Osiris, was dropped. His attributions were too complex to fit into the new scheme and the incestuous nature of Isis and Osiris' relationship was unlikely to find favour with Greeks raised on the Oedipus myth. In theory, Sarapis was to be chief God, but Osiris retained his hold on the Egyptian population. He also retained his place in the Initiation Mysteries of Isis. Presumably, the initiates could understand the symbolic meaning of a brother/sister marriage.

Isis and Sarapis became both immanent and transcendent. They were rulers in the Underworld, Earth and Heaven. The reformed religion also made Isis not just one of many Egyptian Goddesses, but *The Goddess*:

> Queen of the stars,
> Mother of the seasons,
> and Mistress of the universe.[2]

On a statue to the Egyptian Goddess Neith, who in the reformed religion was also identified with Isis, was the inscription:

> I am all that has been, and is, and shall be
> and my robe has never yet been uncovered by mortal man.[3]

This is the Goddess as worshipped in Wicca; immanent, transcendent and mysterious.

The religion of Isis spread rapidly across the Mediterranean capturing the imagination not only of the Greeks, but also of the Romans. Evidence of Isis worship has been found as far away from Egypt as Britain, with London and York being principal centres. The religion of Isis contained many of the features of

Wicca today. The Isis religion was a Mystery religion which promised the initiate inner transformation and expansion of consciousness. As in Wicca, there were three levels of initiation. The Goddess Isis was also a patron of magic. Often, she was paired not with her original husband Osiris, or the newer Sarapis, but with Asclepius, the Greek God of healing. Her temples, rites and initiatory system therefore combined religion, magic, the processes of spiritual growth and healing.

Another important development in Mediterranean Paganism at this time came from Greek Neoplatonist philosophers whose ideas have influenced the Western Mystery Tradition to the present day. The Neoplatonists too were moving away from the idea of Gods and Goddesses as separate entities towards a more unified concept. The different Deities were seen as different personifications of the One, the ultimate Divine force that is beyond male and female.

The aim of the Neoplatonists was spiritual development either through the study of philosophy, or by awakening the higher intuitive faculties through theurgy. Theurgy was a system of ritual magic involving invocations to the Gods. The Neoplatonists had great respect for all the ancient Pagan traditions. Care was taken to reconcile their more sophisticated religious thinking with traditional practices. Like the followers of Isis, many Neoplatonists were vegetarians, but they did not condemn those who continued to perform the traditional animal sacrifices.

While the Neoplatonists saw the Divine as being outside the created world or *transcendent*, the Stoics believed that the universe was itself Divine and that human beings were part of this Divinity. In other words, the Divine was *immanent* or indwelling in the universe. The Stoics had high moral principles and believed that:

> For mortal to aid mortal – this is God,
> and this is the road to eternal glory.[4]

The Stoics' view that the universe is Divine and that the Gods are in-dwelling in Nature is very important within Wicca.

Paganism and Witchcraft

The stately world of the priests and priestesses of Isis and the thoughts of Greek philosophers poring over the mysteries of the Universe seem far removed from the traditional image of Witchcraft – the Witch with her cauldron and broomstick. What is the connection between the Goddess worshippers of the New Stone Age, the priesthood of Isis in their beautiful temples by the banks of the Nile, and the wizened crone of a Witch stirring her cauldron in the rural villages of Medieval England?

Long before Christianity, there was a division in the most urban part of Europe, Greece and Rome, between the Paganism of the temples and the Paganism of the woods and groves. Indoor temple Paganism took an *Apollonian* approach; the Greek God Apollo being a God of music and intellectual pursuits. This was a Paganism of stately ceremonies in clean white robes. It was religion which focused on the conscious rational mind and symbols of Light and Sun; of this Neoplatonism was a part. The Dionysian approach, named after the Greek God of wine Dionysus, was a Paganism of ecstatic vision, of trance, of the loss of individual consciousness and its merging into Nature. The rites of Dionysus were the rites of drumming and darkness, the rites of the Moon. They celebrated individual freedom rather than control by the state and a return to Nature, rather than seeking to evolve beyond it.

In Roman times, many of the practices of earlier Dionysian Paganism were thrust out of the mainstream of religion and became associated with Witchcraft. Witches were described as *drawing down the Moon*, or in other words Moon worship, and as going out in the darkness to collect herbs with bare feet, loose hair, their robes pulled up around their waists and armed with bronze sickles. On the dates of the larger festivals they went out on the hills to dance and chant and to tear apart a sacrificial victim, a black lamb. On the feast of *Lupercalia* on February 15, young men also took part, covering their bodies with goat skins and their faces with masks. Goats were sacrificed and people whipped with straps made from their hides to raise magical power. These practices were not favoured by the state, but were incorporated into Mystery Traditions such as that of Bacchus, God of Wine.

The devotees of Bacchus soon fell foul of the law. They were accused of plotting against the state in much the same way as medieval Witches were later seen as plotting the downfall of James I of England. In Rome decrees were made against the Bacchanalia and the God's adherents were imprisoned or executed.

The stately and controlled approach to religion favoured by the urban cultures of Greece and Rome was a necessary stage in the development of our human intellect. However, while this type of religion appeals to the conscious mind, it does not satisfy the larger part of the human psyche that is not intellectual. For some the gap between the solar and lunar oriented aspects of religion was bridged by the Mysteries of Isis and of Eleusis. These rites, like those of Dionysus, took place by night, but their aim was not to lose the sense of individuality and to enter ecstasies, but to awaken higher consciousness. The Mysteries were a middle way which combined the best of Apollonian and Dionysian Paganism; for we must have both Sun and Moon, light and dark, conscious and unconscious, if we are to find our spiritual destiny. The Mysteries were very beneficial, but in many cases they were not available to the majority of people. Only those rich enough to pay the fees and buy the necessary ritual clothing, and well-educated enough to understand the complex rites, could take part. The Mediterranean world was in a spiritual void and the time was ripe for the new religion of Christianity to step in to fill the gap.

The rise of Christianity

Initially, the growth of Christianity was slow. By the beginning of the third century CE, it was so torn by schisms that it seemed unlikely to survive as one religious entity. All this changed with the conversion of the Roman Emperor Constantine. In 324 CE, he declared Christianity to be the official religion of the Empire. Paganism was not immediately suppressed but now that Christianity had harnessed the powerful political force of the Roman Empire behind it, Paganism's days were numbered.

Unlike the religious tolerance which had marked the Pagan

religions around the Mediterranean, Christianity was true to its Judaic parent. It was an intolerant masculine monotheism. There could be no question of co-existence alongside the older religions. Christianity took the uncompromising view that it was right and all other interpretations of the Divine were wrong. Satan was the ruler of all those who had not espoused the Christian religion. Other Gods were not Gods, but demons and servants of the arch-demon, Satan. The fate of some Gods and Goddesses was kinder than others. In the Mediterranean, the local deities tended to become absorbed into Christianity as saints. However, many Gods, including the Goddess Diana and, in most areas, the Horned God, were relegated to the status of demons. Christianity succeeded, for a time, in making the *Gods of the old religion the Devil of the new.*

The European Pagan religions already condemned the practice of magic for evil social intent; but beneficial magic was widely accepted. Christianity condemned all magic – spells, incantations, herbalism, divination, weather lore – the whole gamut of activities by which human beings sought to control their environment. The Christian attitude was that these activities were not the prerogative of ordinary men and women, but the prerogative of the Church with its monopoly on the line to God.

Christianity was a missionary religion and over a period of a thousand years it became the dominant religion of Europe. Far to the north-east in the Baltic States, Paganism remained the predominant religion, but various political manoeuvres meant that by the fifteenth century, the last Pagan country in Europe, Lithuania, had succumbed to Christianity. The conversion of kings and nobles to the new faith did not, however, mean an instant conversion of their peoples. Enforcement of Christianity was difficult and frequently followed the pattern of its younger brother in masculine monotheism, Islam, of conversion by the sword. The Scandinavian king St Olaf made his subjects choose between baptism or death. Such forced allegiance can have been nothing but nominal. In Germany, the Emperor Charlemagne conducted mass baptisms of Saxons by driving them at sword point through rivers blessed further upstream by his bishops. Others such as Redwald, King of the East Saxons, whilst adhering to Christianity, had not quite grasped the principles of monotheism. Redwald kept two altars, one for the new God and one for the Gods of his fathers. Many felt that in such tricky matters as Gods, it was best to play safe.

What the Church later lumped together as *Witchcraft* had two elements – Pagan worship and magic. Pagan worship included *man-worshipping* (i.e. invoking the Gods into a priest or priestess) and the worship of the Divine in Nature, especially in evocative objects such as wells, trees and standing stones. Magic involved spell-making, divination, and healing. The concept of there being two types of religion: intellectual, solar-oriented, Apollonian religion which appeals to the conscious mind, and lunar, intuitive, ecstatic Dionysian religion which appeals to the unconscious, is important for understanding why Paganism continued to appeal. While Christianity could accommodate the Apollonian side of religion, a religion which emphasized the control of the unconscious by the conscious mind and the suppression of sexuality could not accommodate the joy to be gained through the celebration of Dionysian-type rites.

In Britain, the old Pagan ways died hard. Following the conversion of the Saxon kings, bishops produced a steady flow of books of penances condemning those who practised Paganism. In the middle of the eighth century, Archbishop Ecgbert of York[5] wrote condemning making offerings to *devils*, i.e. the Old Gods; Witchcraft; divination; swearing vows at wells, trees and stones; and gathering herbs using non-Christian incantations. The penances imposed for disobeying were not very severe and do not seem to have discouraged the errant Pagans. Little had changed by the eleventh century when King Canute issued laws against Heathenism or Paganism.

> We earnestly forbid every Heathenism: Heathenism is, that men worship idols; that is, that they worship Heathen Gods, and the Sun or the Moon, fire or rivers, water-wells or stones, or forest trees of any kind; or love Witchcraft.[6]

In other parts of Europe, it was the Goddess who proved hard to suppress. To satisfy those who leaned towards the female aspect of the Divine, in the fifth century the Christian Church authorized the veneration of the Virgin Mary. She was neither

Goddess nor entirely human, but something in between, the *Panagia Theotokus* or *Mother of God*. This did not satisfy those of a more Pagan outlook. Bishops complained that the Goddess continued to be worshipped under the names of Diana and Herodias. In the tenth century the Bishop of Verona in Italy complained that many people were claiming Herodias as their Queen or Goddess and declaring that a third of the world worshipped her.[7]

Church and Devil

Initially, the penalties for Witchcraft were relatively mild. The picture began to change in the thirteenth century when the Church formally declared Witchcraft to be a heresy. As all good Christians knew, the heretics were worshippers of the Devil. All the religious and magical practices on which the Catholic Church did not bestow its blessings – other Christian sects, Paganism and magic – were now lumped together. Whatever their aims and virtues, they were declared to be Devil worship. The Christian Church was Devil-obsessed. Despite some setbacks, the first 1,000 years of the Church's history had been a story of success and increasing power. Now, with the rise of Islam in the East and growing intellectual scepticism in the West, the Christian Church was losing its grip. If the Church's power was being challenged, there could only be one challenger, for the Church was the Church of God.

All rural communities had their wise women and cunning men who would act as doctors and midwives, who would cure a sick cow, solve the love problems of young men and women, advise those in distress and perform weather magic. Until officialdom espoused the cause of Witch-hunting, any actions against Witches tended to be local activities of the spontaneous, lynch-mob sort which occur when times are hard or when things go wrong in people's lives and they want someone to blame. Psychologists talk about *locus of control. Locus* is Latin for place. People with an external locus of control will tend to attribute the causes of their good and bad fortune to people or things outside themselves. Those with an internal locus of control tend to think that they make their own destiny. If things go

19

wrong, it is their own fault and if things go well, it is because they have talent or have worked hard.

Simple peoples tend to have an external locus of control. They ascribe the good and bad things that happen to them, not to their own actions, but to the actions of outside forces – spirits, angels, saints, Gods, demons, ghosts. Medieval Christians tended to ascribe good events in their lives to the work of God and bad events to the work of the Devil. The Devil was believed to need human servants to effect his unscrupulous desires. When something went wrong in people's life, they looked for someone who could be acting as the Devil's agent – a practitioner of *maleficium*, a Witch.

In the main, the accusations made against Witches are those which express the fears of a largely agricultural society – blighting crops; causing animals to die or miscarry; causing illness, miscarriage and death in human beings; and raising storms. These are the negative uses of the powers of the Witch that on the other hand could be used beneficially to produce good harvests, cure sick animals and people, increase fertility of animals and humans, and produce rain in drought. From the fifteenth century on, however, there were also political accusations. Witches were accused of undermining Church and state.

Despite fierce attempts to persecute those Christians whose views did not accord with Catholicism, the heretical sects which later transmuted into the Protestant movement flourished and grew strong. Nowhere was Protestantism stronger than in Germany. In the sixteenth century Martin Luther, an ex-monk, nailed to his church door a list of accusations against the corruption of a Church which took money from people to buy time off from Hell in a form of after-death insurance. It was in strife-ridden Germany that the evil madness of the Witch-hunts began. In 1484, eight years before Christopher Columbus sailed westward to find America, Pope Innocent III issued a Papal Bull[8] denouncing Witchcraft and declaring that Witches were blighting fertility by associating with demons. The Bull authorised the Dominican priests Heinrich Kramer and James Sprengler to prosecute Witches throughout Northern Germany. This was followed in 1486 by the publication by Kramer and Sprengler of what became the bible of the inquisitors, the infamous *Malleus Maleficarum* or *Hammer of Witchcraft*. This was an evil-mind-ed diatribe against women, who were seen as more likely to be Witches, and was full of the sadistic pornographic fantasies of two celibates. It ends with recommendations on how to conduct judicial proceedings against Witches which are nothing less than an official blueprint for torture and murder. These were the opening moves which led to the insanity of the persecutions which swept Europe and later America. The *Malleus Maleficarum* was translated from Latin into a number of European languages and was an immediate best-seller across Europe. There were nine reprints before 1500, a further five by 1520, and a further 16 editions by 1669.

Church approval made Witch denouncement and Witch persecutions a worthy activity. The fact that the property of condemned Witches was confiscated and distributed to the accusers and persecutors was another incentive. In England, Witch-hunting was a less popular pastime than in mainland Europe. English Witch persecutions, although bad, never reached the severity of their Continental or Scottish counterparts. In most European countries, the penalty for Witchcraft was burning at the stake and confessions were extracted by horrendous torture. In England, death was by hanging. Officially, physical torture was illegal, although the English magistrates did permit more sophisticated forms of psychological torture such as sleep-deprivation. Another saving factor was that the English Protestant Church had broken away from the Catholic Church in the mid-sixteenth century and was less affected by Papal pronouncements. The English attitude to Witches was also influenced by rationalists who did not subscribe to the devil-mongering theories of the Continent. No English edition of *Malleus Maleficarum* appeared until 1584 and, in the same year, an altogether more psychologically healthy work was published by the Englishman Reginald Scot – *The Discoverie of Witchcraft*.[9] This was an unusual book for the time, written from the point of view of a sceptic. Scot's book made explicit the connection between ritual magic and Witchcraft and included both Witchcraft practices and magical rites. It also includes some amusing accounts of conjuring tricks.

Overall in Europe, between 150,000 and 200,000 people were executed as Witches; of these around 100,000 came from

Germany. The extent to which those accused in the Witch trials were practising ancient forms of Paganism or were village wise women or cunning men is impossible to estimate. It is likely that the majority of those tortured and killed were the victims of the fears and fantasies of a superstitious age – the unusual, the eccentric, those with enemies wanting to settle old scores, and those whose names were blurted out by pitiful torture victims in their desperation to bring an end to their pain.

Fortunately, the New World largely escaped this madness. It was not until the end of the seventeenth century that the evil of the Witch-hunts crossed the Atlantic to America. It was in the Puritan settlement of Salem, Massachusetts, that the greatest outbreak of Witch hunting began. Most of those accused were the victims of maliciousness and hysteria. Altogether 141 people were arrested, of whom 19 were hanged. One, 81-year-old Giles Corey, who refused to confess to Witchcraft, was crushed to death beneath a wooden plank piled with rocks.

Giles Corey died a martyr, not for Wicca, for this does not seem to have been his faith; but to the powers of irrationality and hate. These powers are still all too alive in the world today.

The Return of the Pagan

Although Pagan religion had been suppressed by the Christian Church, Pagan culture had not. This was preserved in the culture of the country people. Their shrines had been made over to another God, but folk customs of Pagan origin such as May Day celebrations, the bringing of an evergreen tree into the house at Yule, the making of Bride's bed by Scottish Highland cottagers at Imbolc, customs for corn. harvest, well-dressing and others meant that Paganism was embedded in the life of the land.

Paganism was also embedded in the life of the mind. The ancient Greek scholar Euhemerus, whose book was one of the first to be translated from Greek to Latin, had argued that originally the ancient Pagan Gods were worthy men and women who had been made Gods by their grateful communities. *Euhemerism*, as it came to be known, enjoyed a revival in the Christian period. Isis was accredited with teaching the ancient Egyptians the letters of the alphabet, Minerva, the Roman

Goddess of wisdom, with inventing the art of working in wool, and Mercury was seen as the first musician.[10] Euhemerism provided a cover under which mythology could be preserved. Rather than demonizing the Gods as earlier Christians had wished, their qualities were venerated and set up as models for human behaviour.

The influence of Paganism became more active from the fifteenth century on. In the fifteenth century a Renaissance began, a rebirth of knowledge and scholarship that had been suppressed by Christianity. Developments in intellectual thought made people question Christian dogmas, a process hastened by the corruption into which the Church had fallen. For some of the disaffected, the solution was to adopt one of the new brands of Christianity. For others who were looking for something which orthodox Christianity could not offer, there were other avenues to explore.

In the eleventh and twelfth centuries, adventurous European nobles had ridden to the Popes' summons to the Crusades. Ostensibly worthy enterprises to defend Christian shrines in the Near East from the onslaught of Islam, the Crusades proved to be a rallying call for hundreds of thousands of European nobles and not-so-noble. Those whose forefathers had leapt from longboats shouting the name of Odin were now happy to don the Crusader's cross and perform rape, pillage and plunder in the name of Christ.

The Crusaders' armies marched eastwards and met their match. Their attempts to stop Islam were a failure. Instead, they brought back to Europe plunder, disease, heretical ideas and, most precious of all, ancient Pagan manuscripts which had been forgotten or destroyed in the West. The next 300 years saw a Renaissance in Pagan thought.

One of the most influential of the rediscovered books was the *Corpus Hermeticum*[11] or *Works of Hermes*. The *Corpus Hermeticum* was mistakenly believed to be of very ancient origin, the work of a mythical magician *Hermes Trismegistus*, thrice-greatest Hermes. However, in reality the writings dated from the first to third centuries CE and were primarily Neoplatonist in outlook. One of the most well-known of the works is the *Emerald Tablet* which contains the words familiar to many Witches and Pagans:

> That which is above is like that which is below,
> and that which is below is like that which is above,
> to achieve the wonders of the one thing.[12]

In other words, the microcosm is a reflection of the macrocosm. This is the basis of all astrology and divination: the patterning of the heavens, the runes, the tarot, is a reflection of what is or will come to be.

In 1450, the Italian nobleman Cosimo de' Medici purchased the *Corpus Hermeticum*, installed the priest and philosopher Marsilio Ficino in the Villa Carregi in Florence and commissioned him to begin the work of translation. The translation overthrew Ficino's Catholic ideas and he found himself more and more convinced of the truth of the Pagan religious vision. The universe was a visible manifestation of the Divine and the same Divine force lay behind all religions. Each religion was but a manifestation of a higher truth. Marsilio Ficino had the natal chart of a dedicated occultist: Sun and Mercury in Scorpio, with Aquarius rising and a practical streak of Moon in Capricorn. He was interested in practice as well as theory and did not stop at translation, but started to experiment with magic. Ficino was interested in magic as theurgy or spiritual development. His magic involved the use of chanting and music in order to achieve higher states of consciousness. Ficino was careful to try and keep on the right side of the Church by emphasising that his magic was natural magic dealing with the powers of the planetary spheres upon earthly things, rather than more dubious dealings with angels and demons.

Marsilio Ficino's religious and magical ideas were taken up by others, many of whom were less cautious in their approach. A notable successor was Pico della Mirandola. Where Ficino had gone no farther than trying to use natural (i.e. non-Divine and non-angelic) forces, Pico della Mirandola favoured the use of magical ceremonies to contact aspects of Deity or angelic forces. Pico della Mirandola also had the advantage of knowing Hebrew and he was able to introduce concepts from the Jewish mystical and magical system known as the *Qabalah* into the framework of the *Corpus Hermeticum*. The Church reacted: anyone found reading Pico della Mirandola's works would be excommunicated.

Magical ideas continued to evolve throughout the sixteenth and seventeenth centuries. In 1531, Cornelius Agrippa, a native of Cologne in Germany, published his *De Occulta Philosophia, On Occult Philosophy*, which contained more lists of magical correspondences between the planets, earthly activities and objects such as precious stones. Agrippa's ideas about magic are near to those of modern Witches. Agrippa maintained that magic depended not on dealing with demons, but on natural psychic gifts. Agrippa led an adventurous life travelling around Europe in frequent conflict with the Church. One of the highlights of his career was in Metz in Germany when he successfully defended a woman accused of Witchcraft and got her acquitted. Later in life, he was banned from his native Cologne and eventually from all of Germany. He had a number of spells in prison when his writings were judged as heretical and offensive.

The study of the *Corpus Hermeticum* and of the Qabalah, with its ten emanations of the Divine to which all Deities could be related, encouraged a new line of thought amongst some of Europe's intellectuals: belief that behind the cloak of different religious traditions lay common truths. Thus by the turn of the fifteenth and sixteenth centuries the German humanist Conrad Ruth[13] could declare that:

> There is but one God and one Goddess,
> but many are their powers and names:
> Jupiter, Sol, Apollo, Moses, Christus,
> Luna, Ceres, Proserpina, Tellus, Maria.
> But have a care in speaking these things.
> They should be hidden in silence
> as are the Eleusinian Mysteries;
> sacred things must needs be wrapped in fable and enigma.[14]

The Church was fighting a losing battle in trying to hold back those developments in human thought which led on the one hand to that empirical study of the world around us which is modern science and on the other to the empirical study of the human mind and spirit which gave rise first to the study of magic and later to the development of the science of psychology. Scientific revolutions are both caused by and in their turn precipitate breakthroughs in thought. One of the most radical discoveries or rediscoveries of the sixteenth century was that the Sun did not revolve around the Earth; something which was known by the ancient Greeks. The Earth and human beings were not the centre of the universe. In fact, the Earth revolved around the Sun. This discovery was made by the Polish physician and astronomer Copernicus. It is hard for us today to understand the impact it made. The whole world-view of Christian Europe – that we lived in a static unevolving universe created by an anthropomorphic male God in seven days – was totally undermined. Once the nature of the cosmos was questioned, the floodgates were opened. A new vision of the universe began to come into being, a vision which was Pagan and pantheistic.

Although few magicians were burned at the stake and there was no systematic persecution, some, such as Giordano Bruno, did die for their faith. As a child, he had mystical experiences and saw spirits on the hills beneath the beech and laurel trees of his native Italy. He found himself agreeing with the Pagan view: the Divine was to be found in Nature. Bruno became a Dominican but his ideas did not find favour with his superiors. He fled his monastery, hiding a heretical book he had been reading down the lavatory. The book was discovered and the Inquisition ordered his arrest. Bruno fled to Switzerland, France and finally to England where he lectured at Oxford University and was received by Queen Elizabeth I. He also visited the great English magician Dr John Dee, who shared his religious ideas. Bruno was an adventurous or a foolhardy man, depending on one's perspective. He was not content to pay lip service to Christianity and believed that a new religion should be formed which would overthrow the corruption into which Christianity had fallen. His excursions into magic led him to develop a religious and magical system based on the religion of ancient Egypt. With a naiveté verging on lunacy, he attempted to convince the Pope of the merits of his new ideas. On February 17 1600, he paid the price for his impetuosity and was burned at the stake, having declared to his judges:

Perhaps you who bring this sentence against me are more afraid than I who receive it.[15]

Solo magicians and Pagan thinkers were many, but the more liberal and open intellectual climate of the eighteenth century saw a new phenomenon: magicians banding together in magical societies, such as the Martinists, the Illuminati, the Rosicrucians and the Freemasons. Their members were some of the most advanced thinkers of their age and it is rumoured that American statesman Benjamin Franklin was a member of the Illuminati. The formation of the magical societies marked a new openness. While the practices of the societies were secret, their existence was not. For the first time in many centuries the magical arts were being taught in an organized fashion. An important magical book which appeared at turn of the eighteenth and nineteenth centuries was *The Magus* by Francis Barrett. This consisted of a magical compendium of correspondences, talismans, various aspects of natural magic, astrology, alchemy and Qabalah, but its most unusual aspect was what was in effect a coven advertisement.

> The Author of this work respectfully informs those who are curious ... that, having been indefatigable in his researches into those sublime Sciences, of which he has treated at large in this Book, that he gives private instructions and lectures upon any of the above-mentioned Sciences ... Those who become Students will be initiated into the choicest operations of Natural Philosophy, Natural Magic, the Cabala, Chemistry, the Talismanic Art, Hermetic operations of Natural Philosophy, Astrology, Physiognomy, & co, & co. Likewise they will acquire the knowledge of the Rites, Mysteries, Ceremonies, and Principles of the ancient Philosophers, Magi, Cabalists, Adepts, & co. – The purpose of this school (which will consist of no greater number than Twelve Students) [*i.e. thirteen including Barrett*] being to investigate the discovery of whatever may conduce to the perfection of Man; to bring the Mind to a contemplation of the Eternal Wisdom; to promote the discovery of both in respect of ourselves and others; the study of religion here, in order to secure to ourselves felicity hereafter; and finally, the promulgation of whatever may conduce to the general happiness and welfare of mankind.[16]

These were worthy aims indeed and, although couched in language of an earlier age, they are not dissimilar to those of us who teach the Mysteries today. The tide was turning.

Notes

1. BCE = Before Common Era. In modern usage by non-Christians, this replaces the BC (before Christ) of the Christian-based calendar. In non-English speaking Europe, e.v., *era vulgaris* is also used.
2. Lucius Apuleius, *The Golden Ass*, p231, based on the Robert Graves trans, Penguin Classics, Harmondsworth, 1985 ed.
3. RE Witt, *Isis in the Graeco-Roman World*, p67, Thames and Hudson, 1971.
4. Pliny, *Historia naturalis*, II, u, 18: probably a translation from Posidonius.
5. *Confessionale and Poenitentiale* of Ecgbert Archbishop of York, quoted in Margaret A Murray, The Witch-Cult in Western Europe: A Study in Anthropology, p22.
6. *Laws of King Cnut* quoted in Margaret A Murray, *The Witch-Cult in Western Europe: A Study in Anthropology*, p23.
7. Rutherius, *Praeloquiorum libri*, I, 10, in Migne, Latin Series, vol 136, col 157.
8. *Summis Desiderates Affectibus.*
9. Reginald Scot, *The Discoverie of Witchcraft*, 1972 ed, originally published 1584.
10. See Jean Seznec, *The Survival of the Pagan Gods: The Mythological Tradition and its Place in Renaissance Humanism and Art*, p22, Barbara F Sessions trans, Bollingen Series XXXVIII, Princeton University Press, 1972.
11. Scott, Walter, *Hermetica: The Ancient Greek and Latin Writings which contain Religious or Philosophic Teachings ascribed to Hermes Trismegistus*, Vol I, Shambala, Boston, 1985 ed.
12. The *Emerald Tablet* of Hermes Trismegistus.
13. Also known as Mutianus Rufus.
14. Jean Seznec, *The Survival of the Pagan Gods*, p99.
15. Vincent Cronin, *The Flowering of the Renaissance*, p258, Pimlico, London, 1969.
16. Francis Barret, *The Magus*, p1, The Citadel Press, NJ, 1967, (originally published 1801).

3

Witchcraft Revisited

History speaks

Until the eighteenth century, the Paganism which had excited
the imaginations of those seeking a return to the Elder Faiths
was the Paganism familiar to people educated in the Classics –
the Gods of Greece and Rome. From the eighteenth century
onwards, western and northern Europeans began to look not
only to the Mediterranean for their Pagan revival, but to their
own roots – to the Celtic and Norse-German Gods of their
ancestors.

In Britain, Stonehenge and other Neolithic monuments were
thought to be the work of the Druids and much speculation
began in England about Celtic practices. Many of the ideas
were romantic and historically doubtful. Just as Geoffrey of
Monmouth in the twelfth century had decided that Britons were
descended from the Trojans, so people began to speculate that
they were descended from lost Atlantis. However, what these
visions represented was a yearning for a genuine Pagan spirituality. A positive outcome of people's interest in their native
Paganism was a growing interest in folklore and folk custom.

The folklore revival also awakened a new interest in the
Witch persecutions of a few hundred years earlier. There were
three major stances: the Christian religious approach – Witches
existed and were in league with the Devil; the psychological –
there were no Witches and the whole thing was a crazed
fantasy dreamed up by churchmen with psychopathological
tendencies; and the sociological – the persecutions were a way

of consolidating the Church's power and oppressing the peasants. However, from the nineteenth century onwards a number of European researchers challenged these views. Another theory was put forward: that Witchcraft was a religion, the remnants of the *Old Religion* of Europe, the indigenous Paganism that Christianity had suppressed.

The first modern scholar to put forward the theory that Witches were Pagans was Karl Ernst Jarcke,[1] a professor of criminal law at the University of Berlin. From studying the records of a seventeenth-century German Witch trial Professor Jarcke argued that Witchcraft was a Nature religion and a survival of pre-Christian Pagan beliefs. Another slightly more complex theory was put forward a little later in 1839 by an historian, Franz Josef Mone.[2] Mone, who was director of the archives of Baden in Germany, also believed that Witchcraft was an underground Pagan religion. Mone believed that the German tribes who had once populated the north coast of the Black Sea came into contact with the cults of Hecate and Dionysus. They had absorbed the ecstatic religious practices of Hecate and Dionysus into a cult which worshipped the Horned God. Mone believed that this religion had survived into Medieval times until its adherents were persecuted as Witches. A more romantic view of the Pagan cult is portrayed by a French historian, Jules Michelet, in his book *La Sorcière*[3] published in 1862. Michelet's speculations are based on earlier accounts of Goddess worship in France such as those of John of Salisbury[4] who, writing between 1156 and 1159, said:

> ... they assert that a certain woman who shines by night, or Herodias, ... summons gatherings and assemblies, which attend various banquets. The figure receives all kinds of homage from her servants ...

While many harked back to the ways of Paganism, those European scholars who had re-appraised the Witch trials generally believed that the Craft had died with the fires of the Inquisition. Towards the end of the nineteenth century, a book emerged which suggested that Goddess worship had not been completely suppressed in Europe. In 1886, the American folklorist Charles Leland met an Italian fortune-teller and Witch from Florence called Maddalena. Leland claimed that as his friendship with Maddalena grew, she gradually imparted to him secrets that had remained hidden for centuries. These were the beliefs of the Italian Witch tradition that the Witches called the *Old Religion*.

In 1899, these were published in a book called *Aradia or The Gospel of the Witches*.[5] Charles Leland claimed that not only were the Italian Witches practising magical arts and preserving interesting pieces of folklore, they were also practising a Pagan religion – a Goddess religion. The Italian Witches' beliefs owed much to the Gods of Classical Rome and the Etruscan civilization that preceded it. The chief Deities were Diana and her daughter, Aradia or Herodias. These two Deities were seen as being two aspects of the one Goddess and their names were used fairly interchangeably. It appeared that through all the centuries of persecution, the Goddess still lived.

The ideas of other European scholars about Witchcraft excited the interest of the English anthropologist, Egyptologist and folklorist Margaret Murray. Margaret Murray's contribution was important in the development of modern Wicca and we owe much to this fascinating woman who lived to the grand age of 100. In 1921, she published *The Witch-Cult in Western Europe: A Study in Anthropology*.[6] In this, she analyzed the sixteenth- and seventeenth-century Witch persecutions and concluded that the inquisitors were persecuting an underground Pagan religious movement that worshipped the Horned God. To Margaret Murray, the followers of the Old Religion were those who had secretly kept the older faith throughout centuries of Christian persecution. In remote villages, people met together in small groups – covens – and practised in secret the rites of their ancestors. They had also preserved the lore of herbs and plants, which was the traditional craft of the village wise woman and cunning man.

The new interest in the religious practices of European Witchcraft went hand in hand with a parallel development, a longing for a return to a Nature-based religion and also to a religion of the Goddess. Wicca was to fulfil this longing. From the nineteenth century onwards, many thinking and spiritual people had grown to believe that society was declining because of an over-emphasis on the masculine at the expense of the feminine. They saw this imbalance as encouraged by monotheistic, male-based religious thinking which distorted the worldview of Western society. From the late eighteenth century onwards, rapid industrialization and the rape of Europe's natural scenery and resources caused many people to feel that *the time was out of joint*; that common sense was being sacrificed to material progress with potentially disastrous results. This feeling increased after the horrors of the First World War.

Some found their religious answers in the East. An effect of the European countries' urge for colonies was to create a continual traffic of ideas to and fro between Europe and Asia. Just as the Crusaders had returned from the East infected with heretical thoughts, so too did Europeans return with new religious visions. At the end of the first World War, the colonial magistrate Sir John Woodroffe writing under the name of *Arthur Avalon* published his influential book on Tantra and Goddess energy, *Shakti and Shakta*.[7] In this, he called for a restoration of the equality of the sexes in outer society and a return to the worship of the Divine Mother and Divine Father. Sir John believed that all things were possible when the supreme personifications of the Divine were God and Goddess who:

> ... give and receive mutually, the feminine side being of equal importance with the masculine. *On the knees of the Mother*, as the author puts it: *All quarrels about duality and nonduality are settled. When the Mother seats herself in the heart, then everything, be it stained or stainless, becomes but an ornament for her lotus feet.*[8]

The call for a return to a Pagan religion was woven into literature for public consumption by writers such as Dion Fortune, whose novels described the religion of the Great Goddess and Horned God. Dion Fortune appealed to the Horned God:

> Shepherd of Goats, upon the wild hill's way,
> lead thy lost flock from darkness unto day.
> Forgotten are the ways of sleep and night –
> men seek for them, whose eyes have lost the light.
> Open the door, the door which hath no key,
> the door of dreams, whereby men come to thee.[9]

Although Leland's *Aradia* hinted that Witches in Italy were worshipping the Goddess and still practising the Old Religion at the end of the nineteenth century, it was not until the 1950s that there was any indication that the Craft was being practised by organized covens in England. The tide changed with the initiation into Wicca of Gerald Brousseau Gardner. Gerald Gardner was a former colonial administrator who had been practising ritual magic, but this was not what he sought. He had experienced mystical visions of the Goddess and male-oriented ritual magic did not fulfil his religious longings. In the late 1930s, Gerald met the Witch Dorothy Clutterbuck through the Rosicrucian Theatre. Despite her quaint English surname, Dorothy Clutterbuck, or *Old Dorothy* as she was known, was not a traditional village Witch. She was a wealthy lady who lived in the south-coast seaside town of Bournemouth, which is close to the New Forest, an area with long associations with the Craft. Dorothy Clutterbuck had been born in India in the days of the British Raj and it appeared that she never married, but returned at some point to England. Whether Dorothy Clutterbuck came from a Witch family herself or was able to join a coven as an outsider is not known, but in 1939 she was sufficiently senior to initiate Gerald Gardner. In Wicca, Gerald Gardner found what he sought – a Goddess-oriented religion which preserved the remnants of traditional village Wise-craft with the Pagan traditions of Europe's past. Wicca also offered more. Its members were familiar with the Classical Pagan Mysteries, ritual magic, the Paganism of Greece and Rome, and, from their days in the Raj, they had a knowledge of Eastern traditions of Goddess worship and the use of etheric energy. This produced a dynamic cross-fertilization of ideas that transformed Wicca from a religion of the past, into a religion for the future.

Gerald Gardner had very different ideas from other Witches practising the Craft at that time. While they harked back to the persecutions of the past, believing that the Craft would best endure by remaining a secret and closed movement, Gerald believed that the Craft had the potential to fill what he saw would be the religious and spiritual needs of many in the generations to come. However, the Craft could only fulfil this role if enough information was published for people to know about its existence and for the persistent to access it. Like all religious visionaries, Gerald found that his enthusiasm for new ideas did not always find favour with his elders. Dorothy Clutterbuck was not keen on publicity, but two years before her death Gerald managed to give out some information under the guise of a novel, *High Magic's Aid*.[10] This was published in 1949 under his Latin Witch name of *Scire, To Know*.

Old Dorothy's death in 1951 coincided with the repeal in Britain of the *Witchcraft Act*. Gerald now felt free to publish a non-fiction work and in 1954 *Witchcraft Today*[11] appeared, the first account of modern-day Wicca. Margaret Murray wrote the introduction. Within the Craft there has often been speculation that Margaret Murray was herself a Witch, but in any event she was keen to support Gerald Gardner's book and wrote that he had shown that Witchcraft was descended from ancient rituals and that it had nothing to do with evil practices. It was:

> ... the sincere expression of that feeling towards God which is expressed perhaps more decorously, though not more sincerely, by modern Christianity in church services. But the processional dances of the drunken Bacchantes, the wild prancings round the Holy Sepulchre as recorded by Maundrell at the end of the seventeenth century, the jumping dance of the medieval *Witches*, the solemn *zikr* of the Egyptian peasant, the whirling of the dancing dervishes, all have their origin in the desire to be 'Nearer, my God, to Thee', and to show by their actions that intense gratitude which the worshippers find themselves incapable of expressing in words.[12]

The religion of Wicca which emerged from Gerald Gardner's books is a religion based on initiation into a Mystery tradition which practised rites based on the seasonal cycle, out of doors, often *skyclad* or in naturist fashion, using the Wise-craft of our ancestors and giving honour to the female Divine – the Goddess. Three major strands of belief and practice had merged: the Dionysian ecstatic and shamanistic practices of the Paganism of the woods and groves; the more Apollonian temple religions of later Paganism; and magic. In the twentieth century the word *Witchcraft* had come to mean not just a particular form of magic using incantations and spells, but a whole system of religious philosophy and belief. Wicca worked within groups called covens with three degrees of entry, but the degrees were marked by initiation rites which had been elaborated using concepts from the magical societies such as the Rosicrucians and Freemasons, who had themselves harked back to the rites of Isis and the Eleusian Mysteries when devising their ceremonies. The ancient idea of dancing in a circle to raise power was as old as the Stone Age and was a known Witch practice, but Witches did not traditionally use a magic circle cast with a sword. This concept had however merged into the Witchcraft tradition and circle dancing now took place in cast and consecrated circles with guardians at each of the four cardinal points. The use of magic and spells was still part of the tradition, but now these were set into a religious framework that stood halfway between the Apollonian and Dionysian forms of Paganism. The orgies that had appealed to our ancestors were not needed in an age which was moving towards greater sexual freedom in everyday life and where population control rather than fertility was the problem that faced society.

Gerald Gardner's *Witchcraft Today* was followed in 1959 by *The Meaning of Witchcraft*.[15] On the premise that all publicity is good publicity, he decided to make himself available to the media. This resulted in the 1950s and 1960s in a spate of articles about Wicca that informed those whose religious and spiritual ideas were sympathetic of the continued existence of the Old Religion. Gradually people began to find their way to covens, not only those which Gerald was rapidly founding based on the New Forest tradition he had inherited, but also to other covens who were willing to accept outsiders.

Gardnerian Witches initiated by Gerald and his initiates have become one of the major branches of Wicca. Another major branch is the Alexandrian tradition whose members derive their initiation from Alex and Maxine Sanders via a Gardnerian initiatory line. After Gerald's death in 1964, Alex took over the role of *media Witch* and successfully publicized the existence of the Craft, not only in England, but also elsewhere in Europe. The two traditions use more or less the same ritual material and have been steadily converging in recent years. The differences are more in ritual style and outlook than anything else. Loosely speaking, the Gardnerians are more Low Church and

35

the Alexandrians more High Church. Alexandrian Witches tend to be more interested in ritual magic than in folk Paganism.

As well as Gardnerian and Alexandrian Craft, there are other traditions that have brought in outsiders. Gardnerian and Alexandrian Wicca are derived largely from one particular tradition, based in the New Forest area of the South of England; although this has been cross-fertilized by contact with other British traditions. Another important branch of the Craft springs from the Witch known as *Robert Cochrane* who claimed to have been initiated into a hereditary coven at the age of five and to have become a Magister at the age of 28. He traced his Witchblood back to 1734 and a Traditional coven in the Warwickshire area. In the 1960s he came to know a number of Gardnerian Witches and in the early 1960s he formed a coven with a number of leading occultists of the day. His ideas about the Craft featured in Justine Glass' book *Witchcraft, the Sixth Sense*.[14] The Cochrane tradition was more male-oriented than Gardnerian Craft and had a stronger emphasis on the agricultural cycle and links with the land.

Gardnerian and Alexandrian Craft have been taken to both the United States and to Canada. The Gardnerian Tradition was taken to the United States in 1964 by Rosemary and Raymond Buckland who founded a flourishing branch of the movement. Some of the ethos of the Gardnerian Tradition evolved differently in the United States than in its English birth-place, in that there has been stricter adherence to the *Book of Shadows* than is found in English covens. This *formalism* has had the effect of creating a strong and powerful Gardnerian Wiccan tradition in the United States, something that is not easy to do when transplanting from Europe a tradition rooted in the land. Gardnerian and Alexandrian Craft in Canada has had more contact with English covens and has evolved slightly differently from the United States.

Robert Cochrane died in June 1966, reputedly from an accidental overdose of the amanita mushroom, but covens in Britain and, in the United States, the *Roebuck* coven, have continued working in the Cochrane tradition. Evan John Jones and Doreen Valiente, authors of *Witchcraft: A Tradition Renewed*[15] and *The Rebirth of Witchcraft*[16] have published work derived from Robert Cochrane but this is rather different from the original and has evolved into a more Goddess-oriented tradition.

America has also developed its own Craft traditions. With its larger population and willingness to try anything new and different, Wicca, like other religious groups in the US, tends to have more sects than in the UK. As well as the Gardnerian, Alexandrian and other traditional groups, new groups appear all the time as people start their own covens and decide to call their particular interpretation of Gardnerian, Alexandrian or other Wicca by a new name. For those who are interested, Margot Adler, a Wiccan priestess and the grand-daughter of the founder of Adlerian psychology, has published a book entitled *Drawing Down the Moon*[17] which gives a comprehensive account of Wicca in the US.

One branch of Wicca that began in the United States is the Dianic Craft which was developed by Morgan McFarland and Hungarian Witch, Zsuzsanna Budapest. This was inspired by the Women's Movement. Dianic covens have a matriarchal focus. Many exclude men and see their tradition as a sisterhood, as *wimmin's religion*. Others work with men, but see their role as less important than that of women. Many Dianic groups worship only the Goddess and those that acknowledge the God see the male deity as a part of the mystery of the Goddess.

A related movement is the feminist Craft, one of whose principal exponents is the American Witch Starhawk. On Samhain (Hallowe'en) 1979 her book *The Spiral Dance: A Rebirth of the Ancient Religion of the Great Goddess*[18] was published in California. This stimulated the founding of thousands of covens, primarily though not exclusively of women, in the United States and other parts of the world. Starhawk approached the Craft from a different stance to British Wicca which was rooted in both natural magic and in the occult traditions. Starhawk had been initiated into the American Faery Tradition founded by poet Victor Anderson and the bard Gwydion Pedderwen. This borrowed much from Gardnerian Craft practice but favoured a spontaneous ritual approach.

From here, Starhawk's approach took another turn. Guardianship of the land was a philosophy that the Craft has always espoused. With its roots in an agricultural cycle, the Craft recognized that the survival of humanity depended on the continuing plenitude of the land. The relationship between the Earth and her inhabitants is one of mutual protection and love. This was a very different attitude from that of Christianity and other Near Eastern monotheisms. The Craft, with its emphasis on the Goddess, the Earth, empowerment of women, reverence for the reproductive process and honouring the body, had great appeal for many women, for whom masculine monotheisms seemed anti-feminine, narrow and unwelcoming. The feminist Craft looked outward to the political realm and in particular to two aspects of politics that had become very important in the 1970s onwards – the peace movement and the ecological crisis. The eco-feminist approach has drawn many women and men interested in Green politics to take up Wise-Craft and Goddess religion.

Both the Gardnerian and Alexandrian Traditions have been developed in Continental Europe by people who have sought initiation into the British traditions and have then transplanted them into their own countries, combining the Witch lore which has been preserved in Britain with their own local Wise-craft and Pagan traditions. To seek for esoteric knowledge in the misty isles of the Western seas has a long historical precedent in Europe. Britain, and Ireland beyond, have been considered sacred isles since ancient times and some of the major Druid training colleges in Celtic times were in the British Isles.

In Europe, Wicca spread first to Northern Europe. In Ireland, this was stimulated by the Wiccan authors Janet and Stewart Farrar who settled there some years ago. Gardnerian Wicca was taken to the Netherlands in the 1970s by the Silver Circle, followed by Alexandrian Wicca and the Wiccacentrum Aradia in the 1980s. From the Netherlands, groups have been set up in nearby Belgium. In Germany, although there were Witches before the 1970s, the Craft became more active from the 1970s on, stimulated by German Witches who had contact with Gardnerian covens in England and by American Witches in the US armed forces who were stationed in Germany. Later, in the 1980s, the German Craft movement received new impetus from a series of seminars and lectures given by Alex Sanders in the last years before his death. This resulted in Alex initiating a number of German Witches into the Alexandrian Tradition. Starhawk's book *The Spiral Dance* was published in German in

1983[19] and many eclectic feminist groups sprang from this. The German Craft development was also aided by the publication of *Das Hexenbuch*[20] by a group of Alexandrian initiates. There are now representatives of Alexandrian, Gardnerian, and most of the other large branches of Wicca in Germany. Across Scandinavia, there are flourishing combined Gardnerian and Alexandrian covens, and in France, there is now a small but growing Wiccan movement.

In the Southern hemisphere, there are covens in New Zealand and Australia. There are also Witches in Japan. Australia has the wider selection of groups, with Gardnerian and Alexandrian covens and some covens with other traditional origins. Practising Wicca in New Zealand seems to be relatively straightforward in that the seasonal cycle is not unlike that of Europe. The Australian climate, however, particularly in the Tropical zone, makes following a sabbat cycle developed in Northern Europe rather difficult. Other problems arise in the Southern Hemisphere. Do you celebrate Yule when everyone else in the country is celebrating Christmas or do you celebrate on the shortest day in June? Considerable thought has to be put into making a sensible interpretation of the Sabbat round. An additional problem in both Australia and New Zealand is that Wiccan circles are cast sun-wise or deosil. In the Northern hemisphere, the sun appears to move clockwise, but in the Southern hemisphere it appears to move anti-clockwise. Magical groups in Australia and New Zealand tend to follow the Northern hemisphere practice and to work clockwise, but in Wicca where attuning ourselves to the forces of nature is more important, then the issue is more problematic. Different groups have come to different solutions, but I found it impossible to cast a clockwise Wiccan circle in Australia and to me the flow of the power seemed to be definitely anti-clockwise, the Australian direction of the sun.

Since 1939 when Gerald Gardner was initiated and the early 1960s when Alex Sanders launched the Alexandrian branch of the Craft, thousands of people have been initiated into Wicca all over the world. People often ask me how large Wicca is and I have to reply that I have no idea! Wicca has no central organization which can do a headcount, but it is certainly large and growing. So how is this religion practised today?

Wicca

Notes

1. Karl Ernst Jarcke, *Ein Hexenprozess in Annalen der deutchen und auslandischen Criminal-Rechts-Pflege*, p450.
2. Franz Josef Mone, *Über das Hexenwesen in Anzeiger für Kundeder deutschen Vorzeit*, pp271–5 and 444–5.
3. Jules Michelet, *La Sorcière*, 1966 ed., pp127–8, 138.
4. Policraticus, *Sive de nugis curialium et vestigiis philosophorum*, lib, II cap 17, C Webb ed., pp100–1.
5. Charles G. Leland, *Aradia: The Gospel of the Witches*, C W Daniel Company, 1974 ed.
6. Margaret Murray, *The Witch-Cult in Western Europe: A Study in Anthropology*, Clarendon Press, Oxford 1921.
7. Arthur Avalon (Sir John Woodroffe), *Shakti and Shakta*, Dover, NY, 1978 ed. (originally published 1918).
8. Arthur Avalon, *Shakti and Shakta* pp731–2.
9. From an invocation to Pan in Dion Fortune, *Moon Magic*, Aquarian Press, Wellingborough, 1978.
10. Gerald B Gardner, *High Magick's Aid*, Atlantis Book Shop, 1949.
11. Gerald B Gardner, *Witchcraft Today*, Rider & Co, London, 1954.
12. Margaret Murray in Gardner, Gerald B, *Witchcraft Today*, p16.
13. Gerald B Gardner, *The Meaning of Witchcraft*, Aquarian Press, Wellingborough, 1959.
14. Justine Glass, *Witchcraft, the Sixth Sense*, Wiltshire Book Company, North Hollywood, California, 1970.
15. Evan John Jones with Doreen Valiente, *Witchcraft: A Tradition Renewed*, Hale, 1990.
16. Doreen Valiente, *The Rebirth of Witchcraft*, Hale, 1989.
17. Margot Adler, *Drawing Down the Moon*, Beacon Press, Boston, 1986.
18. Starhawk, *The Spiral Dance: A Rebirth of the Ancient Religion of the Great Goddess*, Harper and Row, San Francisco, 1979.
19. Starhawk, *Der Hexencult als Ur-Religion der Grossen Göttin*, Verlag Hermann Bauer, Freiburg im Breisgau, 1983.
20. Anon, *Das Hexenbuch: Authentische Texte moderner Hexen zu Geschichte, Magie und Mythos des alten Weges*, Goldmann Verlag, 1987.

4

The Circle of Being

The rites of Wicca

In Wicca, we contact the Divine through ritual and through the enactment of ancient myths which express eternal truths about human beings and the universe we inhabit. Some Witches worship alone, but those who belong to a coven will generally meet for the eight sabbats, the major seasonal festivals, and also at the 13 Full Moon esbats. Some covens, and particularly those which emphasize training, will meet more frequently.

Where possible, Witches like to perform their rites outside, close to the world of Nature; for it is in the Goddess and God's creation that it is easiest to feel their presence. Outside working is not always practical. Climate and the fact that not all covens have access to private land mean that often Witches will create a temple in their houses in which to honour the Gods. For those who do not have the luxury of spare space, then a room will be cleared for each rite.

What takes place in a Wiccan rite? The main function of the rites is to worship the Gods. A second function is to perform magic. Divination and spells for healing and to help people with their life problems are an integral part of the work of a Witch. Magical working takes place principally at esbats. These are seen as the most appropriate time to ask the Gods for their help. The sabbats emphasize not so much receiving, but giving back. They are acts of thanksgiving to the Gods who give us life and being. The sabbats take place at eight roughly-equidistant points around what is often called the *Wheel of the Year*.

41

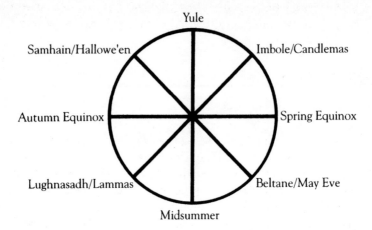

The wheel of the year

The rites, and in particular the sabbats, are also celebrations. Sabbats frequently end with a feast which takes place in the sacred circle which has been made for the rite. This is not considered to be separate from the rite, but an integral part of it. We eat and drink of the bounty of the Goddess and God to celebrate and honour what they have provided for us. In Wicca, this is considered pleasing to the Gods; for we are taught that our Gods love us and are pleased when we are happy.

The idea of worshipping Gods through ritual can seem strange to us in the modern world. For our ancestors, ritual functioned to mark the transitions between different life stages. Birth, sexual maturation, marriage, giving birth, kingship, war and death were all marked by rites of passage. These rites contained powerful symbols which helped us to understand the meaning of each part of life's journey. We were taught that each stage of the life cycle was but part of the Spiral Dance of life and death, of which we and all Nature are a part. Our griefs, pains and sorrows were transient. Like the ever-changing wheel of the seasons, they would pass, transmute; death would become life once more. Thus we were taught courage, endurance, and to look with objectivity on our own individual concerns, which were part of the greater whole. Myth and ritual touch on our deeper inherited levels of consciousness. This is why so many people entering Wicca feel that they have been Witches before.

Somehow, they know instinctively the form of the rites and, in entering the Wiccan circle, they feel that they have *come home*.

The world of the circle

Whether indoors or outdoors, the rites of Wicca always take place within a sacred and consecrated space called *the circle*. However, a Wiccan circle is not necessarily exactly circular. Outside, natural wooded clearings do not grow to such convenient shapes and, when working Wiccan rites indoors, the priestess will often cast the circle around the perimeter of the whole room so that the physical barriers of the walls and the psychic barrier of the circle coincide. Traditionally, the circle was nine feet in radius and one of the uses of the nine-foot cord in Wicca is to mark out the circumference of the circle. The nine-foot radius is a comfortable size for a coven of thirteen, but a circle can be made to any size that is appropriate for the group.

The Wiccan circle differs from that of ritual magic. Readers of occult novels will be familiar with the preparations of the white magician. Considerable effort is expended in marking out a chalk circle on the floor of a room from which every speck of dust has been removed. The magician draws strange symbols around the circle and sometimes a barrier of salt is poured along the edge. Some Witches do create a physical barrier when they cast their circles. Alex Sanders had a portable wooden circle painted with esoteric symbols that could be neatly folded into quarters for easy transportation, but this was not used for the majority of rites. Sometimes Witches who cannot keep a separate room for a temple will paint a ritual circle on their floorboards and then cover this with a carpet when not in use. When working ritual outside, some Witches will draw a physical circle in the earth, but the usual custom is to draw the circle not upon the ground, but in the air. The circle is not a physical one, but a mental one.

Why do Witches work within a circle? The circle is an archetypal symbol of wholeness that has been used for millennia as a sacred place of healing and refuge. In Wicca, the circle is said to exist *between the worlds*. It is poised between *the world of* men and the realms *of the Mighty Ones*, between humankind and the Gods, between the astral world and the physical, between the psychological and the spiritual, in a space where those who are in the physical body can meet with non-physical forces in a safe and harmonious way. It is like a clearing in the jungle of everyday life where we can rest from its clamour and demands. The circle is a place of peace where our sometimes warring conscious and unconscious minds can meet and work in harmony. By entering the sacred precincts of the circle, we are not only clearing a physical space (if we have to clear the living room of furniture), we are also clearing a space in our own minds. This is a space where something can happen and the disorganization of our psyches can be made whole.

The altar

Within the circle will be an altar. This is placed either in the north of the circle or at the centre facing north. Certain directions have always been considered more sacred than others. In Islam, which functions without an altar, this is not a set direction, but instead prayer is oriented to a sacred place, Mecca, the birthplace of the Prophet. In Christianity, the sacred direction is east, the direction of the rising sun.

In Wicca, the north is traditionally considered to be the home of the Gods and the most sacred direction. This is a reflection of the influence on Wicca of our European ancestors. The Pole Star in the north was considered particularly sacred in the mythology of Norse and German peoples. It was also the direction of the Spiral Castle of the Celtic Goddess Arianrhod, *Caer Arianrhod*, where the dead heroes of the Celts went to dwell. The north is also the direction through which the Sun passes at night and the point at which the Moon's influence is strongest in relation to the Sun. The north therefore represents the deepest part of the unconscious mind. The differences in altar orientation between Wicca and Christianity reflect their Dionysian and Apollonian leanings: the religion of the night versus the religion of the day, of unconscious versus conscious.[1] The north is not necessarily used in the Southern hemisphere. In the Southern hemisphere, the Sun is in the north at Noon and in the south at midnight. A good case can therefore be made for placing the altar to the south, oriented towards the Southern pole.

Regardless of whether we use north or south, having the altar on the north/south axis is significant in that it aligns the circle with the Earth's magnetic currents. Traditionally, this has been considered important both in magic and in another important human activity – sleep! In the Northern hemisphere, in order to align the electro-magnetic field of the body with that of the Earth, traditionally we are told to always sleep with our heads to the north and our feet to the south. Mediums often used to sit with their backs to the north when giving clairvoyance in much the same way that a Wiccan Priestess will stand with her back to the north when the power of the Goddess is invoked upon her.

The quarters and the Elements

The four cardinal directions of the circle – East, South, West and North – are associated with the four Elements of Air, Fire, Water and Earth. In the Northern hemisphere Air is placed to the East, Fire to the South, Water to the West, and Earth to the North. In addition, there is a fifth Element which cannot be perceived by the physical senses. This is called Ether (sometimes spelt Aether or Aethyr), Akasha or Spirit. Ether is associated with the centre of the circle.

The Wiccan circle

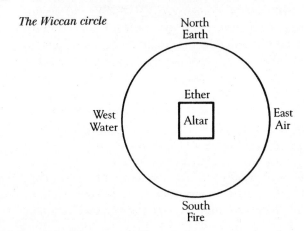

North
Earth

Ether

West
Water

Altar

East
Air

South
Fire

The Elements can be thought of as energy in different states which has molecules vibrating at different speeds. In esoteric teaching, the physical universe is seen as being composed of energy in four different forms. Energy at its densest and slowest, where molecules are locked together to form solid shapes, is Earth. Water is less dense. It is fluid and can form solid shapes only when held by a container. Energy that has sufficient form to be seen, but not form enough to be grasped or held in a fixed shape, is Fire. Air is energy that is formless; where the molecules move so quickly that they cannot be seen by the eyes except through Air's effects on other objects, such as the wind blowing through the trees. In the world around us, Air corresponds to the sky and wind, Fire to the Sun, Water to the sea, and Earth to the land.

The fifth Element, Ether, verges on the physical and forms force fields around physical objects. Although Ether is so fast-moving that it cannot be seen by the physical eye, we begin to perceive these force fields or etheric counterparts of physical objects when we develop etheric sensitivity through Wicca, magic and other forms of psychic development. What people perceive as the aura is part of the force field of the human body that permeates the physical body and extends a little beyond it. This force field as a whole is called the etheric body.

Life can exist on many levels other than the physical. The Elements are not physically alive. They do not have the attributes of physical life – bodies that metabolise and reproduce. Like all things in physical existence, however, the Elements have etheric counterparts. These are Elementals, which are alive and conscious on the etheric plane. The Elementals can be thought of as non-physical beings on a different path of evolution from that of humanity. They are more specialized in their functions and are thus in some ways more limited, but they are also immensely powerful. Elementals will allow us to communicate with them, but they must be treated with respect.

Elementals congregate around their naturally occurring element on the physical plane. Human beings have always been aware of these naturally occurring Elementals. In deep caves, we feel that unseen eyes watch us. When we touch standing stones and certain rocks, we sense that they are tingling with some kind of life force. Sometimes the wind appears to be a living thing with a will of its own. Different languages have given them different names, but pools, wells, rivers and the sea have always been thought of as inhabited by water nymphs, mermaids and undines. The magical tradition names the four groups of Elementals:

Air   Sylphs
Fire   Salamanders
Water Undines
Earth Gnomes

People tend to think of the Elementals as humanoid. A glance at art will show women with long flowing hair like strands of waterweed inhabiting rivers and small men with gnarled features inhabiting the Earth. Elementals were endowed with forms appropriate to their nature. These images are not formed in an arbitrary way. Human consciousness works in a similar way in all times and cultures and the forms in which the Elementals have been depicted over the ages are very similar. These symbols can be very helpful. Contact with Elementals causes an appropriate symbol to be stimulated in the psyche. We then perceive the force as the symbol. This is an act of passive clairvoyance. Stimulating the symbol by deliberately visualizing it will cause the process to happen in the opposite direction and will bring us into contact with the force behind it. This is an act of active magic and it is in this way that in ritual we invoke the Elements at the quarters. It is important, however, to make a distinction between the entity and the image with which the human mind clothes it. Elementals are not really lovely ladies with fishes' tails. However, these are useful symbols that express to our minds the essence of the Elementals' nature.

Preparing the circle

Humans have always believed in the *Otherworld*, the Land of Faery, a spiritual realm that is neither of Heaven nor Earth, but lies somewhere between. This is the world of the traveller who falls asleep and find himself lured by a beautiful maiden to a land where the years pass like days and no one ever grows old; a land beyond the bounds of time. This is the realm of the Wiccan circle; a sacred space not ruled by clock time or by linear thought, but by the timeless truths of the myths and dreams of the human psyche. No watch or clock may be brought into the circle and a distinctive feature of Wiccan rites is a strange acceleration of time: what seems like one hour is really three or four or five.

Really?

When people first enter Wicca, they may find it difficult to create this sacred space. There is no border crossing through which we can pass and find ourselves automatically in the Land of Faery. To enter, we must make an inner journey via the actions of casting the circle. How can we make this journey?

If we are performing ritual outside, this is relatively easy. The process of journeying to the working site; of preparing it; gathering wood for the fire; watching the sunset disappear behind the trees; listening to the evening song of the birds; all these turn our minds away from the concerns of the mundane world to remind us of more important things – the world of Nature, the ever-burgeoning life force of which we are a part.

Indoors, this *switching off* can be more difficult, but one of the skills Wicca teaches us is concentration. It is the ability to focus on one idea and to exclude all others that enables us to prepare ourselves for the circle. As the symbols of the circle become integrated into our psyche, they precipitate a change of consciousness without any conscious intervention on our part. As one priestess said to me, 'As soon as I hear the swishing of the broom, stillness ripples through my mind. The outside world just fades away.'

Preparing ourselves – the chakras

The simple preparation of sweeping the circle is traditionally our only preparation for entering the rite. However, for working our own rites indoors, we have adopted a technique that originated far away from the misty hills of Herne's Britain. This is the Eastern technique of opening the chakras. To some, the idea of using the chakra system may seem alien, but to borrow from the East is not a new development in Wicca. Wicca owes much to the ancient Mystery schools of the Mediterranean and Near East, which themselves were cross-fertilized by ideas from the East. Nor is the idea of energy centres in the body an exclusively Eastern concept. The Celtic God Cernunnos is depicted on the Gundestrup Cauldron sitting in a meditative position reminiscent of the Buddha while holding a snake, an image often used to depict energy rising up the spinal column from the base of the spine chakra. Witches have always worked with these energy centres or chakras, but it was in the East that the terminology and mapping of the energy systems was most developed. It is to the East, therefore, that we turn when we want to explain what Witches are doing with their bodily energies. We readily use the chakra system to help people understand and gain the control over these energies that is necessary in Wicca.

There are seven major chakras in the body which are known by their traditional Sanskrit names and also by more mundane names. The first, the *muladhara* (root support) chakra, is at the base of the spine; the second is the sacral or *svadisthana* (sweetness) chakra which rules the belly area below the navel; the third is the *manipura* (lustrous jewel) chakra at the solar plexus below the breast bone; the fourth is the chakra at the centre of the breast bone which is known as the heart chakra, the *anahata* (unstruck); the fifth is the throat chakra, the *visuddi* (purify); the sixth is the third eye, the *ajna* (knowing) chakra at the centre of the forehead; and the seventh is the crown chakra, the *sahasrara* (thousandfold), at the top of the head.

Clairvoyantly the chakras are seen as pulsating or spinning circles of light that follow the colours of the spectrum. The base of the spine chakra is seen as a pulsating circle of red light; the sacral chakra is orange; the solar plexus is yellow; the heart chakra is emerald green; the throat chakra is bright blue; the third eye is violet; and the crown chakra is seen as a pulsating circle of brilliant white light.[2]

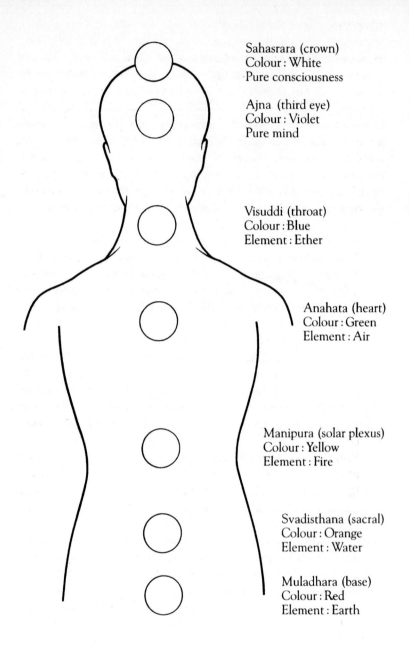

Sahasrara (crown)
Colour: White
Pure consciousness

Ajna (third eye)
Colour: Violet
Pure mind

Visuddi (throat)
Colour: Blue
Element: Ether

Anahata (heart)
Colour: Green
Element: Air

Manipura (solar plexus)
Colour: Yellow
Element: Fire

Svadisthana (sacral)
Colour: Orange
Element: Water

Muladhara (base)
Colour: Red
Element: Earth

The chakras

Opening the chakras

In a group, the technique of opening the chakras can be carried out by each person individually, or one person can talk the rest of the group through the process. In the beginning, it is best if someone whose clairvoyance is developed acts as group leader. She or he can then talk the group through the exercise while checking that everyone has opened each chakra before moving on. Chakras can be opened either from the crown chakra down or from the base of the spine chakra up. Initially, most people find it easier to work from the base up and it is this upward-flowing energy that is needed for circle casting and spells.

1. To open the chakras, first visualize a round circle of pulsating red light at the base of the spine. Visualize this getting larger and larger until it covers the whole of the lower spine. Now imagine that you are drawing a current of energy into the chakra so that it grows warm and begins to glow and pulsate with red energy and light.

2. Draw more and more energy into your base of spine chakra as though it is a tank being filled with red light. Then, as the flow of energy comes into your body, allow it to coil round and round inside you like a snake. Allow the snake of energy to rise, still spiralling until it reaches the level of your belly.

3. Visualize the snake spiralling round and round at the level of your belly. As it does so, visualize your sacral chakra in the centre of your belly beginning to glow with spinning orange light. Allow the orange circle to grow larger and larger, spinning with energy.

4. Draw more energy in from the base of the spine. Bring it up, past your sacral to the level of the solar plexus chakra. Concentrate now on the base of the spine again. Renew the energy in your base of spine chakra by drawing in more energy from outside, until the red glow at the base of the spine begins to spin faster and faster and to grow wider and wider.

5. Draw more energy up the spine and into the sacral chakra so that this too spins faster and grows wider, glowing with

a bright orange light. Then allow the snake of energy to rise up through the centre of your body to the level of the solar plexus. Here it begins to activate the solar plexus chakra that starts to glow with a golden yellow light.

6. Go back down to the base of the spine and draw more energy up the centre of the body and into the solar plexus chakra. Allow it to open wider and wider. Allow the chakra to spin faster and faster until there is a golden spinning sun at the solar plexus.

7. Go back to the base of the spine again. Draw more energy in and up the spine, past the sacral chakra, past the solar plexus, up to the centre of the breast bone, where there is a small green fiery glow which is the heart chakra. Let the energy you have drawn up feed the fiery glow, so that it begins to spin faster and faster, and grow wider and wider, until it covers the whole of your chest with a green glowing light.

8. Go back to the base of the spine again and draw energy up through the spine, past the heart chakra to the throat, where there is a small blue glow. Allow the energy to stream into the throat and to spin the chakra faster and faster until there is a pulsating blue centre at the throat.

9. Go back to the base of the spine again to renew your energy. Draw energy in through the base of spine chakra, up through the sacral chakra, through the solar plexus, through the heart chakra, to the throat. Then go back to the base of the spine again. Draw a current of energy right up through the body, up past the throat and into the third eye at the centre of the forehead. Allow this energy to merge with the violet spot at the third eye and to spin the third eye energy faster and faster until there is a spiralling violet centre in the middle of the forehead.

10. Go back to the base of the spine. Draw more energy into the body and up past the sacral chakra, past the solar plexus, past the heart, past the throat and into the third eye. Allow the violet glow to spin faster and faster. Then allow the current of energy to shoot up through the head and out of the crown. Allow the energy to cascade down the body, bathing it in light, and flowing down to the feet in a white stream.

11. Go back to the base of the spine. Draw up more energy right

up through the body, past the sacral chakra, past the solar plexus, past the heart, past the throat, past the third eye and out again through the crown chakra and down the body to the feet. Repeat this for as long as you wish.

When we first do the exercise, most people have some chakras that are difficult to open. These vary between individuals, but often the throat and sacral chakras present problems. For those who have problems with the sacral chakra, try opening the chakras in the reverse order – from the crown chakra down. There will then be a build up of energy before the sacral chakra is reached which will make it easier to open. For those who have problems with the throat chakra, singing a few notes or sounds just before starting can be a help.

Closing the chakras

If we have opened the chakras, we must also close them. If we are doing this in preparation for a ritual, then the chakras will be closed at the end of the rite. Closing the chakras can be done much more quickly than opening them. One of the easiest ways is to imagine each chakra as a stained glass window of the appropriate colour.

---

1. Starting at the top, the crown chakra, draw a fountain of white light down the outside of your whole body. Let it flow over the third eye, completing closing the violet light as though a white shutter is being drawn over it.
2. Then draw more white light down from the crown past the third eye to the throat chakra, and then over the throat, shutting the chakra.
3. Draw more light from the crown down and over the heart chakra.
4. Now draw more white light down over the top of the head, over the third eye, over the throat, over the heart chakra and down over the solar plexus chakra.
5. Then from the crown of the head draw more white light

down right past the solar plexus, past the sacral and down to the base of the spine.

6. Do not however attempt to close the base of spine chakra or crown chakras. These are left open to absorb energy.

Preparing sacred space

The Wiccan circle is cast deosil or sunwise. This is the direction of the Sun's journey and is the direction associated with the build up of energy and power. In the northern hemisphere, sunwise is clockwise. In the southern hemisphere, it is anti-clockwise. It is customary to speak of the series of actions involved in creating the circle as casting or drawing the circle. The process is also called building the circle or, even more graphically, building the Spiral Castle, that Otherworldly dwelling glimpsed by the Celtic heroes and heroines of the past. Casting the circle involves symbolic gestures and words. These outer acts are pleasing things of great beauty that act as triggers for the unconscious and focus the minds of the group. The important part is not, however, the outer activity, but the inner activity of the mind.

It is easy with ritual to become so preoccupied with the outer form that we forget the inner process. Once they have mastered the outer form of the rites, one of the most important things we teach our initiates is on occasion to dispense with the outer form and to create the circle with the inner mind only. This is to train the mind in concentration and visualization. It does not make outer ritual redundant. Most Witches prefer to physically perform ritual, but the psyche is lazy. It is easy to allow ourselves to slip from the level of concentration and visualization necessary to truly make magic into a ritual of beautiful and meaningless gestures. To make the mind do all the work on occasion is a useful antidote.

There are two ways to cast a circle. One is for the circle to be cast with the whole coven inside. The other is for a priestess and priest to cast the circle while the rest of the coven wait outside. In this case, once the circle has been cast, the coven members are brought in through a gateway in the north-east made by lying a broomstick or besom on the ground crossed by a sword. To enter the circle, we leap over the besom and sword. For some sabbats there are ritual questions that are asked which help to focus our minds on the purpose of the rite. Once these have been answered, men are greeted in their Craft name by a kiss from a priestess and women by a kiss from a priest.

There are practical reasons why one method of opening the circle may be favoured over another. When working in an indoor temple, it is useful to be able to use the whole of the available space. If the coven is to wait outside the circle, either some of the room will have to be excluded, or they will have to wait outside the room altogether, which means they cannot participate in the processes of casting the circle which prepare the psyche for magic.

When working outdoors this is less of a problem. However, indoors we feel there are psychological advantages in commencing the rite by having the sacred space gradually created around us and assisting either physically or mentally in its creation. A useful compromise is to bring people into the sacred space formally over the besom and sword and then to cast the circle around them. As with all such matters, however, groups must find what works best for them. Some groups prefer to use one method for sabbats and another for esbats. It is important to try out different methods and to see what works best on different occasions.

When casting a circle, we prepare the place where the sacred space is to be made by sweeping it with that popular symbol of Witchcraft, the Witch's broom or *besom*. The broom handle may be decorated with ribbons – green and red are usual. It may also be carved. In outdoor rituals, sweeping the circle with a besom can have practical uses, but the main purpose is to symbolically sweep clear our minds. As the circle is swept, we put aside all thoughts of the outside world; all the frustrations and worries of everyday life and, most importantly, any negative thoughts and emotions that have no place in the circle.

Once we have swept the circle, we usually say an introductory invocation which focuses our minds on the purpose of the rite. Covens tend to have favourite invocations which they use for esbats; but at sabbats they may use special invocations appropriate to the season. This is an esbat invocation which we often use.

Esbat Invocation

Let us worship the power,
the power which moves the universe;
for behold the Lords of Light have set their stars upon the
    heavens,
the Earth spins and the Moon holds her course.
Let us walk proudly and hold our heads high;
for the Sky is our Father and the Earth our Mother,
and we are the children of the Gods.

With the sweeping, we have cleared the space which is to be used for the circle from of all unwanted influences. With the invocation, we have turned our minds to the Gods. What we do next is to seal off the space to create a vacuum that can be filled with spiritual forces and magical energies. The order in which the remaining actions are carried out will vary slightly according to the preferences of different covens, but the essential components are the same.

Casting the circle

The circle is cast using the four traditional Elements of the Wise – Earth, Air, Fire and Water – and what are known as the magical tools. On a Wiccan altar, there will be symbols of the Elements: a smoking censer of incense for Air, lighted candles for Fire, a bowl of water for Water and salt for Earth. There will also be the magical tools or weapons which are used by Witches to direct their magical energies. The tools may be very elaborate and beautiful or very simple and plain. When Witches were persecuted, their tools had to be well hidden, or so innocuous as to be mistaken for household implements. However plain they might appear, the tools are always set aside for magical purposes by ceremonies of consecration. Consecration of tools can be a simple matter, or something to which a complete ceremony can be devoted. For tools that carry power – the sword, athame or ritual knife, and wand – more elaborate consecrations may be desired.

The world of the circle is a mirror image of the outer world which is still largely male-dominated. Although she will be assisted by a priest, the first actions of casting the circle are usually carried out by a priestess; for while both High Priest and High Priestess are in charge of the circle, it is the High Priestess who has ultimate authority. The reasons for this are many. It is not because the Goddess is superior to the God, or the female superior to the male; but because it is feminine energy which is considered to be the impregnator on the magical and spiritual planes, just as male energy is on the material plane. Whilst both male and female are necessary for any act of procreation, whether physical or magical, in the magical realm the flow of energy is not from the male to the female, but from the female to the male.

In Gardnerian Wicca, less importance is placed on this symbolic gesture, but in Alexandrian Wicca when casting the circle, the magical tools which are symbols of power, and in particular the magic sword, are taken from the altar by the priest, who hands them with a kiss to the priestess who uses them. She returns the tools to the altar via the priest in a similar way. This does not apply to the besom or broomstick, which is not considered a magical tool.

When we talk of the actions of God and Goddess, of male and female, we are not referring to the two physical sexes. When we say female energy, we mean not only the female energy which is in women, but also the female energy in men. One of the reasons Witchcraft has been popularly associated with women is because women tend to find it easier to generate etheric energy which is produced by the lower chakras of the body and which is necessary to produce acts of sympathetic magic. Women tend to be more instinctively in touch with this etheric energy, the power of which will wax and wane with the hormonal processes of their menstrual cycles, pregnancy and menopause. Men have to learn to make use of this power by gaining access to their own inner feminine.

Another reason why women take a more active role in casting the circle is that one of Wicca's important myths says that out of love for the Goddess, the God *knelt and laid his sword and crown at her feet*. The sword and crown are symbols of the God's power. The meaning of this symbolic gesture is that although the God could overcome the Goddess with his physical strength, he chose not to do so. Instead he lays himself open to her spiritual power.

This gesture also symbolizes the relationship between what are often called the four worlds. These are the physical world, the world of Earth; the emotional world, the world of Water; the intellectual world, the world of Air; and the spiritual world, the world of Fire. The crown and the sword are symbols of the world of Air. This is the intellectual world, the world of the head, which in recent millennia has been dominated by men. In the circle between the worlds, the God subordinates his intellectual world to the spiritual and intuitive world of the Goddess. In Wicca, both sexes must learn to use not the world of the intellect, the world of the conscious mind, but the world of the unconscious, the world of intuition.

The first part of circle casting is to sterilize the circle edge with water that has been purified by mixing it with salt. First, the water must itself be prepared by consecrating it. Ordinary tap water can be used, but in these days of chemical treatment of water, many people prefer to collect water from a pure source such as spring or, if this is not possible, to buy bottled water for circle casting. Water is usually consecrated by a priestess; for Water, like Earth, is traditionally seen in magic as a feminine Element. The words for casting a Wiccan circle vary between traditions. The words used here are those generally used in the Gardnerian and Alexandrian traditions. Placing the blade of her athame into the water, the priestess says:

> We exorcise thee, O Creature of Water,
> that thou cast out from thee
> all the impurities and uncleanlinesses
> of the spirits of the world of phantasm.
> In the names of (the God) and (the Goddess).

What are these *impurities*, *uncleanlinesses* and *spirits of the world of phantasm*? Traditionally, Water is regarded as an Element that can absorb outside influences. This is due partly to the physical nature of water: it can be contaminated. There is not only the visible contamination of mud, but also the invisible contamination of disease, bacteria and, in modern society, fluoride and chlorine! The *world of phantasm* refers to a different type of contamination. Water can also absorb etheric or emotional energies. To prepare Water for use in the circle, we want to clear it of any influences that it has absorbed. To drive these out, the priestess draws power from her base of spine chakra into her solar plexus. She then projects this through her arms and hands into the blade of the athame and thence into the water.

To Witches unfamiliar with chakras, these concepts may seem an additional complication. However, if our magic is effective, we will have been using the chakras without being aware of it. The power which Witches were traditionally taught originates from within themselves is etheric energy drawn in through the chakras. Most of us learn to use this energy instinctively without consciously thinking about its origin at all. However, for those who, before initiation, were not natural Witches, it is much easier to use this power if we understand its source and can activate our chakras to produce it. When we have worked in Wicca for a while, our athame or sword will have become impregnated with our own etheric energy. As soon as we pick it up, we will begin to project power down the blade automatically. When we first become involved in Wicca, however, most of us must think consciously about producing power. This is easier if we understand the chakra mechanisms which produce it.

As the priestess projects the power, she visualizes it as violet or golden coloured light entering the water and giving it a coloured tinge. The colour of the Element of Ether is traditionally violet, but Ether can be manipulated by the mind to take on any colour of the spectrum. Many people prefer to visualize the power that flows from the athame or sword via the solar plexus as golden yellow, the colour of the chakra.

The visualization is very important; so too is the role of the coven. Whilst one priestess alone can make a Wiccan circle, her actions will be infinitely more powerful if the coven assists her by performing the visualizations with her. A useful way of reminding the coven of its role is, where appropriate, to use the pronoun *we* rather than *I* when we are casting a circle with others.

The actions of the priestess and the coven have the effect of cleansing the water but, in order to retain its psychic purity, salt is added. Salt is a sterilizer and in a magic circle it is used to prevent cleansed water from absorbing any new influences.

First, the priestess blesses the salt with her athame. Again the priestess and coven visualize the power as golden or violet light as it enters the salt.

Blessings be upon this Creature of Salt.
Let all malignity and hindrance be cast forth hencefrom,
and let all good enter herein.

With salt, the priestess performs a blessing rather than an exorcism. Unlike water, salt is already pure. The priestess is not driving malignity and hindrance from the salt. Instead, she is asking the salt itself to drive malignity and hindrance from the circle. The priestess adds the salt to the water and draws an Earth-invoking pentagram over it.

But remember and ever mind,
as water purifies the body,
so the scourge purifies the soul.
Wherefore do I bless thee
that thou mayest aid me.
In the names of (the God) and (the Goddess).

The Element of Earth is activated by the pentagram and the positive force of the blessing is added to the water.

If we are casting the circle with the coven members inside, the priestess will now consecrate the priests with the salted water and her priest will then consecrate the priestesses. If the coven is outside the circle, this consecration, together with the purification with incense which follows, will be done to the circle at this point and to the people after the coven has been brought into the circle.

The consecration consists of making on each Witch the symbol of his or her initiatory degree with the water. Traditionally, the degree symbol used was that of the most junior member present, since the higher degree rites were not to be seen by those who had not undergone the initiation. Now that so much has been written about Wicca and the degree symbols are more generally known, many covens use each Witch's appropriate degree symbol at all times.

The priestess now uses the salted water to consecrate the

place of working. Starting in the north, she sprinkles the ground with the salted water. As she does so, she and the coven concentrate on the consecrated water forming a barrier that seals the circle and prevents other minds and etheric entities from entering in.

Having consecrated the circle, the next stage is to purify the coven and the place of working with incense. While Water and Earth are traditionally feminine Elements, Air and Fire are considered masculine. In some covens, the priestess will purify the circle with the censer. We prefer the priest rather than the priestess to cense the coven members in the appropriate degree symbol and then the circle. The censer of incense symbolizes both Fire (the burning charcoal) and Air (the incense smoke). The priest commences in the north. He and the coven concentrate on the censing making the circle a place of purity.

A psychic vacuum has been created and a barrier can now be drawn around it to make the circle as a sacred place, a safe space. For the consecration and purification, it is more convenient for the coven to stand, but at this point, particularly in Alexandrian Wicca, it is customary to kneel in honour of the Goddess, as the God knelt when he first gave her the sword.

The priest hands the priestess her athame or sword and, commencing in the north, she begins to cast the circle. Outdoors the athame is usually used. Indoors, the sword, which is a symbol of the coven will rather than the individual will, is frequently used. Although the sacred direction is north, the priestess does not begin the words of the casting until she reaches the east. The north is the home of the unconscious world of images, not the conscious world of words. It is at the east that we enter the domain of the spoken word.

We conjure thee, O Circle of Power,
that thou beist a boundary
between the world of men and the realms of the Mighty Ones;
a Guardian and a Protection
that shall preserve and contain
the power which we shall raise within thee;
wherefore do we bless thee and consecrate thee
in the most sacred and powerful names
of (the God) and (the Goddess).

As she casts the circle, the priestess projects power from her solar plexus through the blade. Meanwhile, she and the coven visualize violet or golden yellow light flowing down the blade and making a barrier around the circle.

After the casting, in the Alexandrian rite the priest will often purify the circle with a candle or lamp. Here the light symbolizes not the Element of Fire, but the light of the divine force that will be drawn into the circle with the invocation of the Goddess and God.

The circle has now been cast and one of what Carl Jung called the organising archetypes has been put into action. The second stage is for the Four Quarters, or Watchtowers, to be invoked at the four cardinal points of the circle.

The quarters

The circle is a place of safety, but to strengthen it guardians are called upon to protect it. The guardians of the quarters are referred to as either the *Mighty Ones* or the *Lords of the Elements*. This is a result of a fusion between two different ideas; that of the *Mighty Ones* as powerful, ancestral guardians of the Witch's clan, and the idea which originated in ritual magic of the Elementals. In some traditions, the *Elemental Lords* are thought of as inhabiting guard towers called *Watchtowers*.

Invoking the quarters involves making contact with Elemental forces in the outer world and also Elemental forces within ourselves. In the outer world, although the Elementals are most often found around their physical Element, they can move quite freely about the astral plane. They can be drawn to any place by magic; just as human beings can travel to any place on the planet. Some environments are much more hospitable to us than others. In some environments, we can only survive in special circumstances and only for short periods. However, because of our skills and flexibility, we are able to survive in a much wider range of environments than can Elementals. If Elementals are to be contacted away from their natural home, a suitable artificial environment must be created; just as one would prepare a tank of water for a fish or a warm cage for a tropical bird. In a magic circle, this is done by having the physical Elements present in the circle to act as a home for the Elementals. Their symbols are always present on the altar throughout the rite.

Invoking the quarters

Covens will usually have specific visualizations which they use for each of the quarters. In Gardnerian Wicca, the names of the Lords of the Elements are rarely mentioned. In Alexandrian Wicca, the Elemental Lords are invoked and visualized, using the Greek names of the four winds. Traditions and covens that are more oriented towards the Celtic or other mythologies may use other names. Some covens visualize Celtic totem animals at the quarters rather than the Elemental Lords. One system uses a black bull in the North; an eagle in the East; a white mare for the South, and a salmon for the West.

Generally the circle itself is thought of as feminine. The quarters are seen to protect the circle and are usually visualized as predominantly masculine. However, it can be an interesting exercise to experiment with female quarter guardians, especially for a women's ritual. Covens vary as to what they find appropriate. The important thing is that the coven agrees appropriate visualizations for the particular rite and that the group works with the visualizations over a long period of time.

Correspondences

Element	Air	Fire	Water	Earth
Qualities	Hot and moist	Hot and dry	Cold and moist	Cold and dry
In Nature	Sky Wind	Flames Sun	Sea Rivers	Earth Mountains Standing stones
Colour	Blue	Red	Blue-green (like the sea)	Brown

Season	Spring	Summer	Autumn	Winter
Weapon	Sword	Wand Candle Spear Arrow	Cup	Shield Pentacle
Elemental	Sylphs	Salamanders	Undines	Gnomes
Elemental Lord	Eurus	Notus	Zephyrus	Boreas
Ages	Youth	Young man	Mature man	Older man

The images for the Elemental Lords are derived from sets of magical correspondences between the Elements and other phenomena, such as the seasons and magical weapons. These have been built up over the centuries and some draw on the *Corpus Hermeticum.*

For those who wish to use the Lords of the Winds as Guardians of the Quarters, Eurus can be visualized as a pale youth with light-coloured hair, dressed in blue garments, wearing a sword and standing against a background of blue sky on a windy spring day. Notus can be visualized as a man in his twenties or thirties dressed in red garments and armour and bearing a spear. His hair is the gold of summer sun. Behind him a great fire blazes. Zephyrus can be visualized as a mature man in sea-green garments, emerging from the waves bearing a cup. His hair is russet red, the colour of autumn. Boreas can be visualized as an older man with dark grey hair streaked with black. He wears brown or black robes. He bears a pentacle or shield. Beside him is a standing stone.

To invoke the quarters, a priest or priestess will hold the appropriate Elemental symbol at the quarter and concentrate on drawing the Elementals to it, while his or her partner draws the Elemental pentagram with an athame. The symbols used are usually the smoking censer at the East, a lamp or candle in the South, Water in the West and the pentacle in the North. Sometimes the priestess will take the more active role and will draw the invoking pentagrams. At other times the coven may prefer the priest to draw the pentagrams. Sometimes four of the coven will be appointed Guardians of an Element for the duration of the rite. They will tend the fire if there is one, keep the censer stoked, and will invoke the quarter for their Element. This can be a useful way to improve our understanding of and relationship to particular Elements. In some covens, all the coven members will draw the pentagram with their athames. From a practical point of view, this is usually more appropriate for outdoor working. A coven full of athame-waving Witches is not necessarily a good idea in a confined indoor space.

Before the pentagram is drawn, the person who is invoking will draw power through his or her base of spine chakra to activate the solar plexus. He or she will then send a current of etheric energy through the athame to make the pentagram. The coven will then visualise light of the appropriate Elemental colour flowing out of the blade and forming a pentagram, as the priestess or priest says the words of invocation.

Invoking pentagrams

Each point of a pentagram is associated with a particular Element and has different invoking and banishing pentagrams which are visualized in the appropriate Elemental colour.

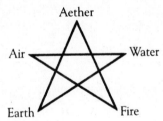

The Elemental pentagram

To make invoking pentagrams, we commence at the opposite end of a line to the Element in question. For Air we start at the top right hand point of the pentagram, the point of its opposite Element, Water.

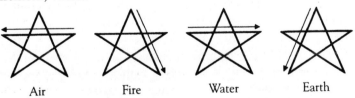

Elemental-invoking pentagrams

To draw the pentagram, follow the direction of the arrow. For instance, with Air, start at the right hand point and trace along the horizontal line to the left hand point and then down to the bottom right hand corner. Continue until you have completed the pentagram so you are back at your starting point. Then draw the first line again to seal the pentagram by making a sixth and final stroke. This will end the pentagram at the appropriate Elemental point. The other pentagrams are made using the same principle.

In this example, the name of the Elemental Lord is used. The first quarter that is invoked is the East.

> Ye Mighty Ones of the East,
> Eurus, Lord of Air,
> we summon, stir and call ye up,
> to guard our circle and to witness our rites.
> Hail and welcome!
>
> Coven: Hail and Welcome!

While the invoking pentagram is drawn, the coven visualizes the Element and then an image of the Elemental Lord appearing behind the pentagram. When the presence of the Element has entered the circle and the Elemental Lord has been successfully visualized, the priestess or priest will bid him welcome.

The priest and priestess will then invoke the Watchtowers of the South, West and North.

Banishing the circle

The circumference has been drawn and the four quarters invoked. The cross within the circle is complete. What happens within the circle, I will leave to later chapters, but first I will explain how we dismantle that which we have created.

If we have opened our chakras at the beginning of the rite, it is important before banishing to ensure that we close them. It is then customary to close the circle with a blessing prayer to thank the Gods for their assistance and to send out positive thoughts to those who have been unable to attend the meeting.

Banishing the quarters

The final action is to banish the quarters. This is done by going to each of the quarters and performing a banishing pentagram. With banishing pentagrams, we start at the point where the invoking pentagram finished, the point of the Element. We then retrace our steps. The quarters are banished deosil starting from the East.

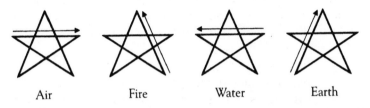

Air	Fire	Water	Earth

Banishing pentagrams

The coven visualizes a pentagram of the appropriate colour suspended in the Air at the quarter. At the East, a priest or priestess will say:

> Ye Mighty Ones of the East,
> Eurus Lord of Air,
> we thank you for attending
> and ere ye depart to your fair and lovely realms,
> we bid you: Hail and farewell!

> Coven: Hail and Welcome!

At the same time, we draw the banishing pentagram. When we draw invoking pentagrams, we visualize light flowing out of the athame. To banish, we must visualize the lines of light that form the pentagram being drawn back into the blade of the athame. As the movements of the banishing pentagram are made, one by one, the lines of the pentagram disappear. By drawing the energy back in this way we are drawing back the energy we have invoked out of our own psyches and replenishing it. Banishing is very important because we do not wish to leave our etheric energy hanging about around the circle.

Having banished the East, we proceed to the South, the West and the North in the same way. Thus is our journey finished.

The Rite is ended.

Notes

1. In Near- and Middle-Eastern magical systems, where the Deity is seen as a force of light ever at war with a Deity or other powerful being of the dark, then the north which is the point at which the force of the Sun is at its weakest is associated with evil. Hence in Qabalah, the north is seen as the province of qlipothic magic. This is not the case in Wicca.
2. Some people see the third eye as indigo and the crown chakra as violet. If you have already been taught this system, you might find it easier to stick to it.

5

Making Magic

The popular image of the Witch is not as a worshipper of the ancient Gods, but as a worker of spells and magic. What part does magic play in Wicca today and what is its rationale in this scientific age?

Magic can be defined as the art of causing change in ways not yet fully explicable to science. Traditionally, Witches were people set apart. They were seen as having special powers beyond the range of the 'normal' person. Some people do come to Wicca as natural Witches who are already in touch with their own inner power, possibly from childhood. Others learn to develop their magical and psychic abilities after training. Most people can learn to do magic to some extent but, like all skills, some people are better at it than others. However, our basic abilities can be improved with practice. In the future, much that is inexplicable today may be part of a *psycho-technology* which can be taught to us all.

People often ask if magic works and the answer is that it does, but not all the time. Each piece of magic we do is rather like a different game. Our success will depend on the strength of the opposing team. By *opposing team* I do not mean *the forces of darkness* or other horror movie notions, but the other trends, energies and psyches that are being brought to bear on the situation. Magic is also influenced by cosmic tides. Some astrological configurations are more favourable for certain types of magic than others. Magic is also influenced by the wills of other human beings in the situation, including the person for whom the work is being done.

In Wicca, we believe that each of us has free will. We cannot have other than free will because each of us in our innermost centre is Divine. It is possible therefore for people to refuse help and to set up barriers against our magic and this is a choice which must be respected. This can be a conscious refusal, but hidden unconscious motives of people involved in the situation are also very important. Sometimes, for instance, we may have worked very hard to help someone to sell their house, only for completion of the sale to be continually thwarted by a whole series of extremely unlikely mischances. Here Witches have to be good psychologists and try to find the source of the blockage. Is the person secretly afraid of change and unwilling to leave the familiarity of their old town? Is it perhaps their partner who is unwilling: do they want different things?

If magic works, how does it work? Traditionally, this is not something that Witches have worried about much. In my first circle after initiation I was told we were going to clear someone's new house of an oppressive atmosphere. Everyone sat in a circle, joined hands, closed their eyes and seemed to slip into trance. My problem was that they hadn't told me what to do. Doing what seemed logical, I visualized a house full of grey mist. I went into each room, gathered all the mist by the window, opened the window and fanned it all out, shutting the window behind it. I finished and opened my eyes to find one of the priests smiling at me. 'Very good,' he said encouragingly, and the rite moved on.

Some covens have a lot of post-initiation training. In others new initiates are left to work out for themselves how to make magic. For the *natural* Witches and the very intuitive, this is the best way: explanations would only confuse them! For those burdened with a more thinking psyche, explanations are useful; but I am conscious that as yet we understand only part of the truth. There is much that we have still to learn and we must await the input of generations to come, but here I offer some of the points which to me are important.

The group mind

For a coven to make group magic involves breaking down the barriers between the psyches of the individuals in the coven and a fusion of a part, though not all, of their consciousness into a *group mind*. There is a level of awareness at which human psyches can communicate directly with one another without the intervention of the usual modes of communication. In that receptive state, symbols can come from the sum total of the group mind that are not the product of any one individual in the circle, but are the products of the group itself. Through the workings of the ritual, the group becomes a separate entity, the sum, but more than the sum, of the parts.

Jung thought that there were two levels of the unconscious. The first he called the *personal unconscious* and the second, the deeper layer, he called the *collective unconscious*. Beyond the personal unconscious, that part of ourselves which may eventually become conscious, along the lines of land reclaimed from the sea, there lies the collective unconscious. The collective unconscious is a common and inherited collective psyche. The *group mind* of the coven exists on the borders of the personal and collective unconscious. When our minds have learned to access a group mind, they can, as it were, travel via this route to come into contact with other psyches.

Group magic involves creating links between the personal unconscious of one person and another. These links are initially made only within the circle but, over months and years, the group remains linked outside the circle, so that coven members are in semi-permanent psychic contact with one another. This does not mean that we spy on each other's thoughts! However, when we create a group mind, we open up part of our psyches to one another. This creates strong bonds between people. A lot of telepathic communication occurs, some of which comes into consciousness and some of which does not. People who work together in a Wiccan group will however be aware when someone in the group has problems. They will often have clairvoyant dreams about one another and, as one of our group complained, it is very annoying to write letters to people who immediately ring you up as soon as you put the pen down!

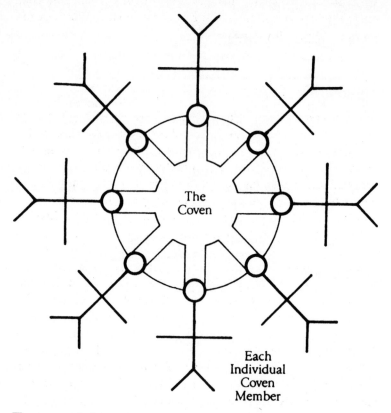

The
Coven

Each
Individual
Coven
Member

The group mind

The group mind consists of branches from the personal unconscious of each member that join together. The group mind is
then the centre of a star whose rays are a projection of the psyches of individual members of the coven. A group mind is not
made overnight. It is built up as we create links of love and trust
with one another. In his book *The Science of the Paranormal*[1]
the experimental psychologist Dr Lawrence Le Shan set out the
conditions which he considers necessary for psychic events, to
occur. These are more likely to happen between individuals
who interact together in a group which is co-operative rather
than competitive; where the group is non-authoritarian; and
where people like each other. All this gives us some useful
pointers to the atmosphere we must foster in our covens if they

are to be successful. It also means that we must be careful when we bring new members into the group to ensure that they are compatible with the rest.

The rationale of magic

Our understanding of how magic works has been greatly improved in recent years by some of the more forward-thinking researchers. One to whom we owe a particular debt is the late Maxwell Cade who was a pioneer in biofeedback research. Maxwell Cade and his co-workers[2] used biofeedback instruments to plot the changes in brain patterns that occur with a number of activities relevant to Wicca, such as meditation, healing, and psychokinetic activity.

To explain how we achieve the altered states of consciousness in which we can perform magic, it is necessary to explain something about the activity and structure of the brain. The brain produces electrical activity at different frequencies which appear as distinct brain rhythms. In terms of cycles per second, the slowest rhythm is *delta rhythm*, which in most people is found only in deep dreamless sleep. However, it also appears when people are performing magical activities such as healing. *Theta rhythm* is a slightly faster rhythm which in most people appears only when dreaming. However, it also appears in the brain rhythms of people who are experienced meditators and in healers. *Alpha rhythm* is faster again. Alpha rhythm appears when we close our eyes and is associated with the first stages of relaxation. It appears in conjunction with other rhythms in when we enter the meditative state. The fastest rhythm, beta, is the normal waking rhythm of the brain.

The brain consists of a base, the brain stem, which is an extension of the spinal cord; above this is the limbic system together with the cerebellum. Above the cerebellum is the cortex. Both the limbic system and the cortex are divided into two hemispheres, the left and the right. The nerves that control our hand and foot movements enter the spinal column and rise to the brain. At a point in the base of the skull, they cross over so that the activities of the right hand side of the body are controlled by the left hemisphere of the brain, and the activities of the left side by the right hemisphere of the brain. In about two thirds of people, usually the right-handed, the left hemisphere is dominant. The remainder, some of whom will be left-handed and some ambidextrous, will have the right hemisphere dominant.

In most people, the left hemisphere of the brain is associated with logical thought – discriminating one thing from another, putting things into categories and speech. The right hemisphere is more holistic and is responsible for recognizing shapes such as faces, interpreting maps, appreciating art and music, seeing the whole picture rather than the parts, and seeing the similarities between things rather than the differences. For simplicity's sake, I will call the logical linear side the left brain and the holistic side the right brain; although for some people these positions will be reversed. The right brain, which controls the left hand, is very important in magic, hence the traditional association between left-handedness and Witchcraft.

There are four major states of consciousness which are important in a Wiccan circle. The first is the state of *everyday waking consciousness* during which our brains function mainly at beta rhythm. The right brain can be considered the seat of the unconscious and the left brain of the conscious mind. In most people there is an imbalance in brain activity, with the dominant left brain being the most active. People who have practised meditation or other spiritual disciplines, however, show a synchronized pattern of activity with both hemispheres of the brain acting in co-ordination.

When we enter a Wiccan circle, there is an initial change of consciousness from our usually lop-sided, everyday brain state with its beta rhythm, to a second state which we can call *synchronized consciousness*. This is associated with balanced left- and right-brain activity and beta and alpha rhythms. It can be thought of as a higher or deeper state of consciousness and, to the extent that these spatial concepts are meaningful, it is both. As we practise visualization exercises and concentrate totally on, for instance, the point of the sword as we cast the circle, we learn to use our right brains until the two halves of the brain work equally well and we can use either as appropriate. The first stage of spiritual development can be seen as the awakening of the right brain, i.e. gaining access to our unconscious minds.

In learning new levels of consciousness, this first stage can be the most difficult and it is easy to give up. Most of us have a voice in our heads that constantly monitors our behaviour and comments on our performance in everyday life. This is the voice which harangues us for making idiots of ourselves as we argue incoherently with our boss who has given us the fifth conflicting instruction that day; the voice that hums the latest song on the radio until it drives us crazy; which agonizes with guilt about drinking too much at that party last night; and which tell us what a weak-willed, worthless person we are for eating all those cream cakes when we are supposed to be on a diet!

In order to achieve deeper states of consciousness, we have to stop this inner parent, this *noise in the system*. We must learn in the circle to concentrate totally on what we are doing. Unless we are in a profession that requires total sensory concentration, for instance racing drivers, ballet dancers or tightrope walkers, how often in everyday life do we exclude everything else and concentrate totally on one thing – say eating, driving or watching television – to the exclusion of all else?

We are not only subject to inner distracters; we also look outward. Normally this outward-looking part of our attention is needed for survival. In Nature, if you watch deer grazing, you will see that they are constantly looking up, alert for any predators who might approach. Birds' eyes give almost 360 degree vision so that they can take flight against marauding cats. In our own lives, we may not face predators, but we must practise the same outer scanning as we walk down the street, so that we do not fall down holes and step in front of passing cars. In order to achieve deeper states of consciousness we have to let go of the *inner watcher*. In the circle, our whole attention must be focused on our intent. This can only be achieved with practice.

As we learn to concentrate our minds and get the two halves of the brain working in harmony, we can enter a third state of consciousness – the *meditative* state. In this state there will be some everyday beta activity. We will still be aware of the world around us; but the most prominent rhythm will be alpha rhythm. There will also be a lesser but significant amount of theta activity. Usually, theta rhythm is only present when we are dreaming. In this deeper meditative state, we are able to access the world of images in a way that is usually only possible when

75

we are asleep. It is in this state that clairvoyance occurs and images of the future emerge which would normally remain unconscious. This theta activity is essential for magic.

The fourth brain state is the *contemplative* state which in Eastern systems is called *samadhi*. This is associated with the presence of beta, alpha and theta rhythms as before, but in addition a strong delta rhythm appears. Normally, delta rhythm appears only in deep sleep and it is associated with physical healing. This is the state which we aim to achieve when we have the Divine force of the Gods invoked into us. When we are first invoked on, we may reach only the third meditative state, but with time, we can enter the state of samadhi, a state that is associated with a vast expansion of consciousness. There is then no sense of subject and object, you and I, self and other, but only a sense of being at one with the universe.

The magical realities

Changing our levels of consciousness, and the changes in brain rhythm associated with them, involve moving into different levels of reality. Lawrence Le Shan's classifies reality into four different levels. These are very helpful in explaining Wicca.

The everyday world which we see with our senses, Le Shan calls *sensory reality*. This is the reality which we perceive with what Jung calls the *sensation function*. It is the world of bricks and mortar, of smell, taste, sight, sound and touch: the world where we believe in what we can see. The *sensory reality* is the world of the Element of Earth. In Buddhism, the outer material world which we perceive with the senses is treated as *Maya*, illusion. Christianity has always sought escape from the material through asceticism and the *denial of the flesh*. In Wicca, we believe we should enjoy the material world and, in particular, the beauties of Nature. However, the material is only one level of reality and to achieve our full potential as human beings we must learn to move in other realms.

Another of Lawrence Le Shan's realities is the *mythic reality*. This is the reality of sympathetic magic where *anything can be identical with anything else*. A person and a wax image can be connected by making the image look like the person, by incorporating part of the person's body such as hair or nail clippings, or by a naming ceremony which includes a verbal spell to give the image the same name as the person. In the mythic reality:

> The part is identical with the whole, the name with the thing, and the symbol with its object. Each can be treated as if it were the other.[4]

Some of the methodology of sympathetic magic, such as *poppets* or doll-type images made of wax or other materials, has been used by Witches for millennia. Poppets tend to get rather a bad press and figured frequently in Witch trials. Studies of Witchcraft in Anglo-Saxon England[5] abound with cases such as that of a widow who in 970 was accused of trying to murder a man by driving nails into a poppet. Later in history, the famous case of the Berwickshire Witches, who supposedly plotted against the life of King James I of England and VI of Scotland, revolved around the use of a wax image. Such images can be used to do harm, but the image itself is entirely neutral. It is the intent with which it is used that is important. The most common use of images today is as a vehicle for distant healing.

Cord magic, which is very popular with Alexandrian Witches, also has a long history. It was used by our Neolithic ancestors, as well as in more recent Medieval times. At the beginning of the eleventh century, Bishop Burchard of Worms[6] in Germany describes how women who had been deserted by faithless lovers would render the offending man impotent by making three knots in a cord. Knotted cords were also placed in trees or at road forks as a combined form of psychic lightning conductor and astral insurance policy. The cords would direct harm and injury away from the users' lands and towards those of their neighbours. Amongst sailors, winds would be bound into knotted cords and released when needed. Today, cord magic can be done by one Witch alone using a knotted cord with nine knots called the *Witches' Ladder*. It can also be used by a group to make a cord wheel. In a cord wheel, each person concentrates on the intent and then releases a slip knot in order to seal it.

The *mythic reality* functions on the principle of *as above, so below*, derived from the famous emerald tablet of Hermes Trismegistus.

> That which is above is like that which is below,
> and that which is below is like that which is above,
> to achieve the wonders of the one thing.[7]

In the mythic reality and in sympathetic magic, the symbol and the object, the macrocosm and the microcosm, are subject to the same laws, structure and activity. By bringing them together through ritual, trance, etc, the microcosm can be made to affect the macrocosm. Sympathetic magic is more difficult for contemporary Westerners than for earlier cultures. It is the reality of pre-literate cultures, the realm of *dreamtime*, where dream and reality are indistinguishable. To access the mythic reality, we must let go of the hold that the conscious mind has on the psyche.

Sympathetic magic operates in a symbolic world, but symbols alone will not produce magical effects. The objects that we use must be *brought to life* and given a consciousness of their own. To do this, we must use the trained will to *break off* part of our psyche and despatch it to perform our intent. The psyche has always had the potential to split off parts of itself so that they can function autonomously as separate personalities. These *sub-personalities* can appear good or bad, as the guides of spiritualist mediums who often have superior intellectual and spiritual gifts to the medium, or as bad sub-personalities such as the poltergeists which are sometimes manifested by sexually-awakening adolescents. In these cases, the split occurs outside the control of the conscious mind, but the processes required to produce sympathetic magic are similar to these and similar also to those required in *evocation*. Evocation differs from invocation. When we *invoke* we bring into our everyday psyche something hidden in the deeper levels of ourselves which then expands our consciousness. To *evoke* means to *call forth* or to *call up*. Here we break off part of our psyche and separate it from ourselves, in the same way that some scientists think the Moon was broken off from the Earth. This broken-off part will still be under our control to some extent, in the same way that the Moon is subject to the Earth's gravitational pull;

but it will move into its own independent orbit. Evoked consciousness is similarly broken off and *flung out* of the circle by the will of the group and *sent* to do its work.

For a material object to hold evoked consciousness, it must have a form or body. This is supplied by an etheric force field formed from the etheric energy released by the coven. Etheric energy can be manipulated by the mind and can be formed into shapes by visualization. The chakras that release etheric energy are the emotional centres and to do sympathetic magic we must feel personally and emotionally involved with the individual for whom we are practising our art.

If we are to be responsible practitioners of magic, this must go hand in hand with spiritual development and the growth of self-knowledge and inner wisdom. In making magic we must examine scrupulously our motives for each piece of work we do. If we are asked for magical help, we must use our wisdom to decide whether it is truly beneficial for the person concerned. Does it harm none? Is it in accordance with the tenets of the perfect love that must be the aim of all magic? Does it serve the greater good?

Making magic in a Wiccan circle is frequently described as *work*. The term is appropriate because magic is hard work. Perhaps I should also make explicit that it is not paid work. Witches work magic on behalf of people who have asked for help and also for people who have not asked but who are thought to be in need. Wicca does not however take payment for magic and a glowing sense of altruism has to be the Witch's only reward!

The mythic reality is not just the realm of active psychism, magic. It is also the realm of the passive psychism that is used in divination. The phrase *as above, so below* has been largely replaced by a more modern term used by Carl Jung, that of *synchronicity*.[8] *Synchronicity* is a *meaningful coincidence*. Such coincidences often occur via dreams. For instance, the night before we visit a strange town, we dream that we will bump into an old friend. The next day we make the visit and bump into this old friend. Someone who is bound to the world of sensory reality would describe this as a coincidence, a random coming together of events, but when we experience numerous such *coincidences*, we begin to question their randomness. Jung believed that we begin to experience synchronistic events when we come into contact with the archetypes. These archetypes are activated by Wiccan initiations. When we first enter Wicca, we are likely to find ourselves surrounded by synchronistic events; so much so that we cease to notice them and start to take it for granted that helpful meaningful coincidences will occur.

The principle of synchronicity is the principle by which divinatory symbol systems such as the tarot, runes and I Ching work. They operate by *taking the temperature of the macrocosm*. Events that are happening in the *macrocosm*, the greater world, are interpreted by looking at the *microcosm*, the snapshot picture of symbol patterns that appears in reading the tarot cards, rune stones or yarrow stalks. Astrology works in the opposite way. We gain understanding of the life patterning of the individual, the microcosm, by examining the macrocosm of the patterns in the stars at the time of the individual's birth.

Jung's concept of synchronicity has elements of the mythic reality, but also of the next level of reality, the *transpsychic reality*. These may be a continuum rather than discrete levels. The *transpsychic reality* is the reality where the individual has not ceased to exist as a separate entity; but at the same time he or she is beginning to touch on the greater reality of the Whole. Lawrence Le Shan uses the analogy of the wave and the ocean. We are each of us waves that are distinct from the ocean as a whole; but without the ocean the wave cannot exist, and without the waves the ocean does not exist. (This is incidentally a very useful starting point for a meditation exercise.) The individual can have wishes and desires that are different from those of the wider whole. It is therefore possible to try and contact by ritual or prayer the forces of the wider whole and seek their influence to achieve the individual's ends.

The transpsychic reality is the realm of the *collective unconscious*, that sub-stratum of the human psyche which we hold in common. This is the reality in which ritual magic and much magic that is done in Wiccan circles works. Often when we are working magic we may be trying to influence someone else. By changing our own mode of consciousness so that we open ourselves up to the transpsychic reality, we open our channels into the collective unconscious. In this way, we can reach the same psychic space as the person we are trying to influence.

Much understanding of what happens when we do magic can be gained from Maxwell Cade's experiments with healers. These showed that, when healing, healers experienced consciousness change and advanced healers entered *samadhi*. What is perhaps more interesting is that healers' patients would also enter the same state of consciousness. No physical contact between healer and patient was necessary and the patient need not be able to enter this state of consciousness ordinarily. Healing could take place over a distance and without the patient being aware that he or she was receiving healing. This is the type of healing which is frequently carried out in Witches' circles and it is not seen by Witches as involving any different processes from other forms of magic which similarly aim to achieve change at a distance and without physical intervention.

We may through magic leave the transpsychic realm altogether and enter the next level of consciousness where we become totally at one with the other person whom we are trying to help. If we go into even deeper levels of consciousness, we lose all sense of our individuality and melt into the last reality which I shall call the *unitive reality*. Here things are not discrete and separate; all objects merge into one another and all are part of a greater whole that is the cosmos. This is what mystics call the *Way of the One* and it is the experience which is associated with the fourth state which we have described: samadhi, the state we enter when the Gods are invoked upon us.

Initially, as we learn to practise Wicca, we experience changes of consciousness only within the circle. Gradually, there will then be a change in our everyday waking state, until we find that we maintain higher levels of consciousness permanently. We are then able to go about our everyday activities while open to higher levels of awareness. As the Flemish mystic John of Ruysbrock said:

Then only is our life a whole,
when work and contemplation dwell in us side by side,
and we are perfectly both of them at once.[9]

Raising the power

Magic involves the use of energy and a change in consciousness. In a Wiccan circle, the first step is usually for the group to perform a circle dance and chant in order to release etheric energy or *raise the power*. The dance and chant can take place after we have invoked the Gods into the circle, but sometimes we do this earlier. After all the concentration, visualization and stillness of the circle casting, it is good to do something active.

Dance is one of the eight ways of raising magical power which in Wicca are known as the *eight-fold paths*. The origins of such power dances are ancient, dating back at least as far as the Palaeolithic or Old Stone Age. In Palaeolithic religious practice, the dance was a means by which the members of the tribe achieved emotional and rhythmic unity between themselves and between themselves and their totem animal. The dances were led by a shaman priest who adopted the guise of an animal by wearing its skin, horns and tail. The purpose was to obtain food. In a state of changed consciousness, the tribe could communicate with the animals they wished to kill; leading the animals to where they lay in wait and persuading them as it were to sacrifice their lives for human survival. This is a practice still carried out today by native peoples who have not lost contact with this older way of life.

The dance is a feature of Dionysian religion which, with its ecstatic practices, seeks to release us from our individuality, so that we can merge with others and with the outer universe itself. This letting go of our individuality releases us from the strait-jacket of our persona and our Ego, so that we can touch the true centre of our being. This lies not in the rational world of the conscious mind, but in the depths of our unconscious. This state is enjoyable in itself, but in Wicca the dance also has a more specific purpose as a means of performing magic. There are two ways in which the dance can be used. Both involve a change of consciousness, but the second also involves the release of etheric energy.

Traditional Witch belief has always held that the human body has within it latent power which can be released through dance and chant. This power used by European Witches is the same as the etheric energy which is used in various forms of

Yoga, including Tantric Yoga. Etheric energy is absorbed by clothing and for this reason ritual magicians wear special robes rather than ordinary clothes, so that the energy is not carried into everyday life. However, ritual clothing, as well as other clothing, inhibits the release of this energy into a central cone of power. Many Witches perform their rites naked, unless it is an outdoor ritual where it is too cold.

The ease with which this power can be released is partly a matter of practice. Rather like driving a car, it is something which after a while we can do without thinking about it at all. It is also a matter of mood and quite possibly a matter of the strengths of certain celestial influences. Traditionally, Witch gatherings are held at the full Moon. In the *Great Mother Charge*, we are told that *better it be when the Moon is full.* This is partly for practical reasons. As those who live in rural areas will know, prior to the days of cars, it was not feasible to travel about the countryside in the pitch darkness. However, the major reason why, in these days of artificial lighting, Wiccan meetings usually take place near the full Moon is the long-held belief that the Moon affects our physical and etheric bodies and that our psychic and magical abilities are greater at the full Moon.

In recent years, the influence of the Moon on the human mind and body has been borne out by scientific research. Scientists have discovered that, as well as having its well-known effects on the mentally unstable, lunar energies also influence physiological events such as bleeding and the incidence of the outbreak of certain diseases.[10] The effect of the Moon may be indirect rather than direct, in that the phases of the Moon cause fluctuations in the Earth's magnetic and electrical fields. The human body can detect very subtle changes in the Earth's magnetism caused by the lunar cycle and it is this ability to detect magnetic changes which is used by dowsers and some healers.

The full nature of the connections between lunar and other celestial energies and events in our physical and etheric bodies and our psyches are yet to be fully explored. However, as those who have tried it will know, working magic at times other than the full Moon is more tiring and requires greater effort than full Moon magic. The powers of the full Moon can be used to energize the etheric body in ways which are not possible when its influence is weaker. However, despite these disadvantages, the waning moon is a good time for magical work of a *winding-down* nature. This is magic that causes things which are happening to cease to happen. Cancer is something which responds well to a combination of waning Moon and waxing or full Moon magic.

In magic, the direction of movement has special significance. Since deosil or clockwise is the direction of the sun, it is associated with the direction of evolution and has been seen traditionally as the direction of *good, white* or *right-hand path* magic. Conversely widdershins or anti-clockwise is often seen as being against evolution and the direction of *bad, black* or *left-hand path* magic. This is over-simplification. Usually in the circle the dance is performed deosil, but on occasion we find widdershins magic useful. Not everything that grows and evolves is good. When we are working magic for someone with cancer, we find it more successful if we operate on two levels and perform deosil magic in order to give the person's auto-immune system the strength with which to fight the cancer and widdershins magic to stop the progress of the cancerous cells. Homeopathic medicine can be seen as *deosil* medicine which stimulates the auto-immune system versus conventional and conventional allopathic *widdershins* medicine which attacks the disease.

The dance, like other movements in the circle, works well with a balance of male and female energies and, if possible, the ring should consist of alternating members of each sex. If the coven does not have an equal balance of male and female members, then some members can sit in the centre of the circle to direct the power. Alternatively, four members can be chosen as Elemental Guardians to direct power from the cardinal points of the circle to the dancers. The easiest way to direct it is through an athame.

When dancing to raise power, the effect is enhanced if the coven is linked together on an etheric level. Depending on the level of experience of the group, this can be done by the whole group or by one of its more experienced members. I will assume the latter and that this person is a priestess, but it can be done by either sex.

At the beginning, the priestess raises energy in her base of spine chakra. When it has built up sufficiently, she allows the energy or power to flow out of the chakra and to spiral around her body in a deosil direction like a snake. When a strong spiral of energy has built up, she then visualizes the energy shooting out to the priest in front of her and entering his base of spine chakra. As the priestess' energy enters the priest, it will merge with his own energy. The merged energy stream should then be directed out of his body and spiralled deosil around him until it is sufficiently strong to direct to the next person along.

When the spiral of energy returns to the priestess, she will absorb it, not into her base of spine chakra, but into the next level up, her sacral chakra. The snake of energy is again directed round the circle. As it returns to her, she will absorb it into her solar plexus chakra. Meantime, the other dancers will be constantly drawing more energy into their base of spine chakras and allowing the energy to rise up their bodies so that as the main spiral passes through them it is made stronger and stronger. This goes on until the power has reached the level of the third eye.

To the clairvoyant eye, the cone of power rising through the chakras of the dancers looks like a rainbow which is red at the level of the base of spine chakra and then passes through the spectrum until it reaches the level of the third eye where it will appear violet. Many books on Wicca described the cone of power as violet because this is the point when Witches will look at the power to make sure it is there! As the spiral reaches the topmost chakras, the crown chakra is stimulated and in its final form the power looks more ultra-violet/silver-white, a mixture of the colours of the energies of the crown and third eye chakras.

As the power reaches the top of the head, it is projected towards the centre of the circle, so that all the energy is joined into one column of light above the ground. This projecting of the energy is done by the third eye and crown chakras. Working together, they push the power out in spiralling lines of energy which twist around one another and join at the tip. This is the making of the alicorn, the unicorn's horn, and as myths and legends tell us, it is a powerful magical tool.

Using the power

What happens next will depend on the purpose of the dance. The dance can serve as an introduction to the magical working by linking the group's consciousness into a group mind and creating a reservoir of energy which can be drawn upon later in the rite.

The dance is also used to perform specific pieces of magic, for instance healing or getting someone a job. Through dance and chant, we not only release etheric energy, we are also using the hypnotic rhythms of dancing and chanting to enter into a deeper state of consciousness. This level is associated with a very relaxed state of mind where visual imagery becomes vivid and powerful. Here we do not actively will something to happen, we create an image of it having happened.

When the power reaches the third eye, the chakra of clairvoyance and *seeing*, we visualize the *intent* – what we want to manifest. Magic works much better with pictures than words because in order to do magic we must use the older and deeper levels of the psyche. If we want someone to get well, we could picture them being bathed in golden healing light and their body absorbing it and beginning to glow with vitality. If someone has broken their leg, we might visualize them walking at first very tentatively, then more and more surely, until they are running and jumping. As the power joins above the centre of the circle, it is as though an astral negative has been developed into a picture which is brought into being in the material world. Holding for the last time to the image of what is desired, the cone of power is now sent, i.e. the dancers let go of the energy and allow it to fly out of the circle and towards its destination.

The dance is usually accompanied by a chant. These can be chants from the *Book of Shadows* or chants specially constructed for a particular magical intent. One of the best known chants for raising power is the *Witches' Rune*. When we dance the *Witches' Rune* as a dance of power, we evoke the magical energies of the Witches' tools.

The Witches' Rune

Darksome night and shining moon,
East then South then West then North,
Harken to the Witches' Rune,
Here we come to call thee forth.

Earth and Water, Air and Fire,
Wand and pentacle and sword,
Work ye unto our desire,
And hearken ye unto our word.

Cords and censer, scourge and knife,
Powers of the Witches' blade,
Waken all ye unto life,
And come ye as the charm is made.

Queen of heaven, Queen of hell,
Hornèd Hunter of the night,
Lend your power unto our spell,
And work our will by magic rite.

By all the powers of land and sea,
By all the might of moon and sun,
As we do will so mote it be,
Chant the spell and be it done.

Eko, eko Azarak!
Eko, eko Zamilak!
Eko, eko Cernunnos!
Eko, eko Aradia!

The last verse of this chant is also used on its own. In chanting, the way in which the voice is used is all important. We can say the words of a chant in two ways. With a meaningless chant such as 'Eko, eko Azarak', we can use it solely to occupy the conscious mind and keep it out of the way! In this case, the words of the chant are fairly unimportant. Such chants are similar to the playground chants and skipping rhymes which children use, many of which are themselves corruptions of old magical chants. The *Witches' Rune* is a very long chant and can be long because Witches use it so often that they can say it in their sleep. Usually, however, chants will only be four or six lines. Below is a healing chant. This is based on an Anglo-Saxon chant and has been used for centuries.

The Healing Rune

This is the spell that we intone,
Flesh to flesh and bone to bone,
Sinew to sinew and vein to vein,
And each one shall be whole again.

If the words of the chant are not meaningless but are an expression of the intent, then we can stimulate the throat chakra to inject each word we speak with energy. This is easier if at the same time we use the words to create a picture in our minds. If we say the *Witches' Rune*, we can visualize the *darksome night* and the *shining moon*, etc. This type of spell chanting is called a *making*. We use the energized words and visualization to call into being what we say.

The dance itself is emblematic of the transpsychic reality where we are both separate and joined, individual yet one. In the circle dance, the rhythmical movement of the dance has the effect on the dancers of releasing hold of the Ego and allowing individual personalities to merge into one group entity. This sense of unity is not a collective illusion, but a reality. Below the level of consciousness, in the deeper levels of the unconscious, individual psyches can merge as one. What is felt by one is then felt by all and telepathy in the form of shared emotions and shared images and visions occurs. Our psyches and the psyche of the person we wish to help may also blur and merge. Here, rather than breaking off part of our own energized psyche and sending it to do something, we enter into the psychic space of the individual we wish to help, so that our state of consciousness and the intent that we are visualizing is implanted in their psyche.

We share emotions and images rather than thoughts because at this level we have passed beyond the realm of words and language, the symbol system of the conscious mind. We have descended into the unconscious, the source of two levels of our nature which are not human but are our highest and our lowest, the animal and the Divine. It is this paradox – that in becoming close to our animal selves we also find the source of our Divinity – which was the great insight of Dionysian Paganism. The dance that unites our animal energy and our inner Divinity breaks the hold of the normal everyday conscious mind which deludes us that we are separate and alone. It allows us to reunite once more the world within and the world without. This is the world of Wiccan magic. How do we find entry to that world?

Notes

1. Lawrence Le Shan, *The Science of the Paranormal*, pp136–7, Aquarian Press, Wellingborough, 1987.
2. See Maxwell Cade and Nona Coxhead, *The Awakened Mind*, Element Books, Shaftesbury, 1987.
3. Lawrence Le Shan, *The Science of the Paranormal*, p165.
4. Lawrence Le Shan, *The Science of the Paranormal*, p165.
5. B Thorpe, *Diplomatrium Anglicum aevi Saxonici*, pp229–30.
6. Nineteenth book of the *Collectarium* of Burchard, Bishop of Worms. See P Fournier, *Etudes Critiques sur le Decret de Burchard de Worms*, pp217–21.
7. The *Emerald Tablet* of Hermes Trismegistus.
8. Carl Jung, *Synchronicity: An Acausal Connecting Principle*, in *Collected Works*, vol 8.
9. John of Ruysbrock, *Adornment of the Spiritual Marriage, etc.*, Wynschenk Dom, P, London 1916.
10. Michel Gauquelin, *The Cosmic Clocks*, pp130–47, Granda Publishing Ltd, St Albans, Herts, 1973.

6

The First Initiation: Opening the Door

> Know that each man has it within himself, by virtue of his manhood, to be a priest; and each woman, by virtue of her womanhood, to be a priestess ...[1]

Initiatory traditions

Most traditions of Wicca are entered via a rite of initiation. In some hereditary and traditional groups, this is termed *adoption into the family* or *adoption into the clan*. The purpose of the initiation rite is to cause a spiritual awakening in the initiate that will link him or her to the group mind of the coven and also to the coven's *greater family*, the tradition. Each coven has its own group mind which is separate from any other. For this reason, if Witches who have already been initiated are joining a new coven, perhaps because they have moved to a different area, they may be asked to undergo a coven initiation ceremony. Initiation is a word with many meanings. There are four main types of initiation.

The first is initiation as a *rite of passage* into adulthood. This marks the transition from adolescence and helps us to understand and take on our responsibilities as adults. In tribal societies this is usually carried out by older men for men and by older women for women.

The second type of initiation is *inner initiation*. This occurs as the result of the interaction between the Self and the personality, and later between the Self and the Divine spark within. This inner initiatory process may happen without any ceremony, with the Self and later the Divine spark as the only initiators. The initiation ceremonies and teachings of religious, spiritual and magical groups may precipitate or speed up this initiatory process, but they are not essential to it. In this sense, initiation is that process which awakens within us the Divinity hidden at our innermost core. This type of initiation is performed within the Self and by the Gods.

The third type of initiation is *initiation into a spiritual, magical or religious tradition*; for example, initiation into Gardnerian Wicca, the catholic priesthood, the Freemasons, Druidry or initiation into a particular occupational craft, each of which held its own lore and secrets. Most of these occupational craft traditions have been lost to us, though there are some remnants in Freemasonry and also amongst Gypsy horse traders. The initiatory processes of the priesthood are practised by some Pagan paths including Wicca.

The fourth type of initiation – *initiation into a particular order, lodge or coven* – is closely related to the third, but may be separate from it. Some Wiccan covens will be members of a particular tradition such as the Gardnerian or Alexandrian traditions. In these groups, the initiation into the coven will be an initiation into that coven's group mind. It will also be an initiation into the group mind of a *greater family*, that of the tradition of which that coven is a part. This creates an inner kinship with what is in effect a widespread family or tribe. Other covens may be stand-alone groups. The group may be a closed family tradition. Other stand-alone groups are established as the result of a particular leader or leaders drawing students to them, or because a group of friends decided to form their own coven. The quality of stand-alone groups will vary according to the spiritual and magical development of those who establish them.

In Wicca and the Western Mystery Tradition generally, we speak of *properly contacted* groups. These are groups whose group minds have strong inner contacts to the Gods and whose leaders are advanced in their own initiatory processes. In Wicca, groups in *properly contacted* initiatory traditions will have the accumulated initiatory power of many generations of initiates. Coming into contact with such groups can speed up our inner development; not only because of the amount and level of teaching they can offer, but also because they contain a *power-house* of spiritual energy. Initiation into a properly-contacted tradition can precipitate or speed up the second type of initiation – the inner growth process which returns us to the Godhead.

In recent years, some Wiccan writers have suggested that people who are unable to contact a Wiccan group should practise self-initiation. There are many types of self-initiation. One is a ceremony that we devise and perform ourselves in order to tell the Gods that we are theirs and are willing to serve them. This type of rite can best be called *self-dedication*. Many followers of Wicca perform self-dedication ceremonies, sometimes many years before they think of seeking to join a coven. Some are content to practise the Craft alone and do not seek to join a group, but this is not easy. The Craft has been written about in many books, including this one, but most writers see their texts as introductions only. Wicca is essentially an oral tradition, taught by practice and example rather than by words. It cannot be learned solely from books.

Working alone does not mean solely learning from books. Spiritual growth and the ability to perform magic are gained through hard work and persistence. There is much that we can learn from our own inspiration. Revelation comes to us from opening ourselves to the true Self in that second aspect of initiation which I have described – the inner process of growth. However, in opening ourselves to that process of growth, we enter upon a difficult path. Practising Wicca causes spiritual and psychological changes in the practitioner. Self-initiation can be rather like removing one's own appendix, a last resort that may be necessary if stranded alone in the wilderness hundreds of miles from the nearest doctor, but somewhat fraught with complications. The analogy is appropriate in that it is difficult to operate on ourselves because we cannot see properly what we are doing. Similarly, it is difficult to guide ourselves through the initial stages of spiritual and magical development without anyone who is more advanced on that path to turn to for objective advice and encouragement. In exploring any new territory it is better to have a guide, or at least a map drawn by someone who has been there before. It is important to have realistic ideas of our own attainments and abilities, and guidance as to when and how to use them.

Unfortunately, self-initiated Queens of all Witchery and Thrice-Greatest Maguses abound, who have read a few books, worked a few rituals on themselves, and then set up groups to initiate others, claiming all sorts of initiatory lineage that they do not possess. Beware of those claiming to be the Divine Mother Witch of England and other such titles. If self-dedication is good enough for us, it is good enough for others. Setting up groups to initiate others into traditions to which we do not belong is foolish and wrong. While we can dedicate ourselves to the Gods, we cannot link ourselves to the group mind of a particular tradition, unless those on the inside of that group mind open the door to us. We cannot storm the gateway unaided. Fortunately, greater communication between groups and more openness means that it is more difficult for these abuses to flourish.

Traditionally, initiation has always been difficult to achieve. If there are barriers placed in our way it may be that part of the test is to work to overcome them and to patiently persist until time and circumstances allow contact to be made with a coven. For those who cannot work regularly with a group, it may be possible to contact a coven which will train people who can attend group meetings only infrequently and will supervise their development through regular training sessions and correspondence.

Many people come to their first degree initiation having already opened themselves up to the Divine and Elemental forces. They may have developed their magical abilities and have strong inner contacts with the Gods. These people are considered naturals and are already initiates in the occult sense, although not yet initiates of Wicca. Some naturals have been initiated into Witchcraft and the Pagan mysteries in former lives and the effect of these initiations carries over into this one. Others have succeeded in this life in making inner planes contacts themselves by virtue of their own understanding and spiritual gifts. For these people, the initiation ceremony serves the two latter purposes of initiating them into a Wiccan tradition and into a particular coven. Others will have been initiated into other magical groups or traditions practising various forms of the Mysteries.

Those wishing to join covens who have already performed a self-dedication ceremony or who have practised another form of magic or Witchcraft for many years may feel resentful when they are asked to undergo another initiation. This is not to denigrate what they have already achieved. The purpose of the second initiation is to open them up to what they have been unable to access on their own – the group mind of the coven they wish to join and the wider family of the coven's Wiccan tradition.

Rites of initiation open us to an expansion of consciousness, but they do not automatically bestow *powers* and great spiritual insights. What is provided is a gateway to a path up a mountain which we must climb; a door into other levels of consciousness, the levels from which psychic and magical powers spring. Initiation is the means of opening the gateway. In some traditions, Witches wear the symbol of the Egyptian ankh, the *crux ansata*, which to the Egyptians was a symbol of eternal life. However, the ankh was also a key; in this case the key of initiation that opens the gateway into everlasting life.

Most Wiccan traditions have three levels of initiation. In Gardnerian and Alexandrian Craft, the first degree initiate is known as a *Witch and Priest* or *Witch and Priestess*, and the second and third degree initiate as *High Priest* or *High Priestess*. The first initiation confers initiation into the Craft. The second initiation, which confers the rank of High Priest or High Priestess, is given when someone is competent to conduct rituals and to instruct first degree Witches. In many traditions, at second degree, people may *hive off* to form their own covens and to initiate at first degree. The third degree is usually given to couples who have attained a level of seniority in the Craft. In some traditions, the third degree is only given to those who have successfully initiated and trained Witches at first degree level. In other traditions, the third degree initiation is given prior to a couple *hiving off* to form their own coven. Third degree Witches can initiate others to the first, second and third degree.

Some traditions do not have a system of three degrees. Instead, there are two senior people, usually an older couple, who run the coven, the *Master* and the *Lady*. They are assisted by the *Maiden*, a younger woman who is deputy to the Lady, and a *Summoner*, a male Witch who does much of the administrative work of the coven. These positions are gained by election either on the part of the coven or by the individuals themselves who decide they are ready to run a coven. Some Gardnerian and Alexandrian covens will also have a Summoner and a Maiden. In these covens, the positions are usually held by second degree initiates.

To some, the concept of three levels of initiation into Wicca is alien, but this system is very old and was a feature of many of the ancient Mysteries. The Mysteries of Isis and Eleusis had three levels of initiation and the Mysteries of Mithras considerably more. Reginald Scot, in *The Discoverie of Witchcraft*, published in 1584, describes three levels of admission into the Witchcraft. The first admission ceremony was public when the candidate was admitted as a novice. For a woman, the second and third ceremonies took place with the High Priest alone and were encounters with the Horned God. In modern Wicca, this encounter with the Horned God is celebrated in the second degree initiation. Scot tells us that the third female initiation was when the High Priest:

... requireth homage at hir hands: yea he also telleth hir, that she must grant him both hir bodie and hir soul.[2]

This probably refers to a sexual union with the God incarnate in the High Priest. What happened to male initiates is not described. Scot records that after the earlier ceremonies, the initiate was responsible for performing magic, but after the third ceremony she had an additional responsibility of recruiting others to the Craft. Margaret Murray in *The God of the Witches*[3] describes only those who have received the second and third stages of initiation as the priesthood.

Margaret Murray also quotes de Lancre, a seventeenth-century French magistrate involved in Witch trials. He made a distinction between Witches who practised natural and sympathetic magic, but who were not necessarily Pagans, and those who were Pagans who adhered to the religion of the Horned God. The latter were considered more powerful. In modern Wicca, all Witches fall into the latter category. They are priests and priestesses of the Old Religion as well as Witches.

Wicca is an esoteric religion with an initiatory religious and magical system. In this, Wicca differs from forms of Paganism that have open rituals and meetings and do not involve a formal ceremony of commitment. Followers of Wicca are also different from Witches who practise sympathetic magic purely as a magical art and may also practise a religion such as Christianity or no religion at all. Just as not all Egyptians were initiates of Isis, so all Wiccans are Pagans, but not all Pagans are Wiccans. Some Pagans belong to other initiatory traditions such as Druidry. Many people wish to worship the Pagan Gods without the more formal commitment to a tradition which initiatory paths demand. Both types of Paganism have an important role to play.

In addition to the usual three degree system some covens have an *outer court* whose members can attend some coven ceremonies and possibly seasonal celebrations. Some covens also have a preliminary neophyte initiation before the first degree. This allows the neophyte to learn more and to explore further before making a full commitment. After a year and a day, neophytes will either proceed further or decide that this is not their path. The neophyte stage is akin to the postulant in religious orders. A postulant is a Latin-based word for one who knocks upon the door. In the *Book of Shadows*, the candidate for initiation is referred to as a *postulant*. Most covens, however, do not operate a neophyting system, believing that the willingness to take a step into the unknown is an essential feature of initiation. These groups follow the practice of not allowing anyone into their circles until they undergo the first degree initiation.

There is no set time limit before a would-be Witch is initiated. There is a tradition that the candidate should wait at least a year and a day. This provides time for the candidate to get to know the coven and undertake preliminary instruction. However, if the candidate can be prepared more quickly the period may be reduced. Conversely, if the coven feels that the individual's motives are confused, a longer period of training and soul-searching may be required before things are clarified. The period before initiation is a time for the group and candidate to get to know one another to find out if they are compatible. While a long waiting period can be frustrating for the initiate, this is better than making a mistake.

An important aspect of joining a coven both for the coven and the candidate, is compatibility and trust. While people may be very dedicated and suitable for the Wiccan path, it may take some time before they find a coven with whom they 'hit it off'. One of the aims of a system of spiritual development such as Wicca is to open us to others and to help us become more accepting of and loving towards other people. However, it is important to be realistic about human nature. Introducing someone into a group who will not relate well to the other members will be disruptive and will weaken the group's magical links with one another. It will also not be a good training ground for the initiate. People will often travel hundreds of miles to work with a coven of people with whom they can build true bonds of love and friendship and who can provide the right teachers for them.

Initiation as rebirth

Initiation is a rebirth and a spiritual awakening. Carl Jung[4] describes five types of rebirth. Three of these reflect the major different belief systems about what happens to people after they die.

There are also two kinds of rebirth which can take place within our lifetime. Both are important in Wicca. *Renovatio* or *renewal*, is what happens at initiation. A second type of rebirth, *indirect rebirth*, is what we experience when we take part in group mystery rites. In Wicca, these include the sabbats or seasonal rituals, which celebrate the inner transformation processes within humanity and Nature.

Initiation involves the rebirth of *renovatio* or *renewal*. The first initiation can be considered a gateway to a partial renewal. The essential nature of the personality is not changed, but the personality develops new directions and weak or damaged parts are healed, strengthened or improved. The third initiation is a gateway to a complete renewal, whereby the essential nature of the personality is changed through a process of transmutation.

The rebirth of the first degree is a rebirth into the community of Wicca. The initiation ceremony is similar to Qabalistic

97

and Masonic initiations, and owes its origins to the ancient Mystery religions. A key difference between Wicca and other forms of magical initiation is that women are initiated by men and men by women. An exception is that a woman can initiate her daughter. She who gave the first birth can give the second.

The initiation ceremony

In some traditions of Wicca, initiation rites are generally performed skyclad or naked. In other traditions, ritual robes of a particular design and colour may be used. These serve a similar purpose to ritual nudity, which is to separate us from our normal everyday persona. Ritual nudity can seem strange in a religious context. This is because, under the influence of Christianity, we in the West have been taught to see the body as a sexual object. In Paganism, however, ritual nudity is a very ancient tradition. By the Celts, nudity was considered to offer supernatural protection and although we have no record how it was used in religious rites, we know that the Celts frequently went into battle naked, their bodies covered in warpaint and tattoos. In the Mystery rites of Isis and Osiris, the initiate also commenced the rite naked; although by the end of the rite he or she was reclothed in ritual garments. In initiation the removal of clothes has a symbolic meaning. To pass through the gateway of initiation, we have to be willing to cast aside our persona and to enter the circle as we first entered the world, naked, vulnerable and free of all pretence. It is as a child seeking entry into the world that we come to the edge of the circle for initiation.

Preliminaries

People are usually nervous before an initiation. In itself, this is no bad thing; but once the candidate or postulant enters the circle, it is important that he or she is sufficiently relaxed to follow what is happening. Before the initiation begins, it is our practice to give candidates some time to meditate on rebirth and what they wish to achieve from it. We also ask people to meditate on the four Elements which are a major theme of the work of the first degree initiation. When the date for the initiation is fixed, candidates are asked to examine their personality – which aspects they would wish to lose and which to improve and strengthen – and to relate these to the Elements. In the meditation time before the rite, the postulant can then ask the assistance of the Lords of the Elements in achieving these goals.

The Element meditation can be done in a number of ways. If the rite is outside, we may leave the initiate alone in a place apart with symbols of the four Elements on which to meditate. A fire can be lit both for meditational purposes and for the more practical purpose of keeping the initiate warm. It is also useful for helping to find the initiate again. Losing one's initiate in a large forest where by night all the clearings look exactly the same is somewhat embarrassing.

Indoors, we will provide meditation time, but we also take initiates blindfold, either into the temple or to another quiet place, to perform a ceremony known as the *Element Balancing*. This takes the initiate on an inner journey through the Elements and in a sense it is rather like invoking their own inner quarters. We find this especially useful because the candidate stands outside the circle when it is cast. The candidate will not therefore be balanced by the invocation of the four Elements at the quarters.

The rite for *Element Balancing* is given below. A priest or priestess waits silently while the blindfold candidate is brought in and then laid on the ground face up with his or her head to the north. Those who have brought the postulant then silently withdraw. We prefer the initiator not to take part at this point. The initiator's words will have maximum impact on the candidate if his or her voice is not heard until the start of the initiation itself.

Element Balancing

About you all is impenetrable darkness.
You float upon the waters of a black sea.
You float endlessly, directionlessly.
There is no direction;
for there is nothing but water.
Water stretches into the far corners of the universe.

Your body is light and floats upon the water.
The water becomes warmer and warmer.
You are floating upon the waters
of the womb of the universe,
and my voice is as the wind,
whispering in your ear.

You are becoming more and more sleepy.
Your past life is slipping away from you;
floating away on the darkness of the waters.
Let it float away;
be at peace.
All is warm and dark and still.

A great silence reigns over all the universe.
It awaits the moment of rebirth.
Your past life and thoughts are but a dream to you now.
You are becoming sleepier and sleepier.
You are at peace, at rest.

You are sinking,
sinking into the deepest sleep.
And as you fall into that sleep,
you dream.
You dream that you are sinking down,
down below the waters;
down, down to the great sea bed.
You lie there for a moment,
your back resting on the sand.

The currents stir the sand against your trunk and limbs.
The swirls of sand sink onto your body.
Softly the sand covers your eyes, face and hands.
The sand envelops you layer by layer;
gently and lovingly,
slowly over a million years.
The sand settles upon your body;
until you are buried deep beneath the sea,
deep beneath the earth.

Deep beneath the earth you lie,
unmoving, waiting;
whilst above you time and change march on.
Your limbs cannot move;
but you hear within you,
the steady beating of your own living heart.
Buried deep you lie in waiting,
and far above,
muffled by earth, you hear
the growing of seeds and the roots' spreading struggle;
for above you the sea has receded,
and a new world has been brought to birth.

The Earth is waking from a deep sleep.
All around you
you feel the quickening pulse of life.
Worms make their tunnels about you,
and far above,
you hear the scraping and scurrying of rabbits.

A warmth steals through you:
the sun is warming the ground above.
And you feel a stirring in your limbs,
an urgency not felt,
for many a thousand year.
The soil around you lightens and loosens:
your hands move,
and you thrust your hands upward.
The soft soil falls about your fingers.
The earth is crumbling,
crumbling all around you.
You struggle to your feet and climb upward,
the soil falling in cascades about you.
You clamber upwards and so emerge,
your eyes blinking and aching,
into the light.

Wind blows against you;
wind not felt since long ago.

The earth is blown away from your body.
Your heart rejoices and your eyes see
all about you is the Spring
of a new born world,
green and fresh,
and in ecstasy.

You spirit soars within you,
and your whole body and being,
feel light, so light,
that gravity cannot hold you.
You float into the air,
higher and higher,
leaving far behind,
the green and growing Earth.

You float higher and higher.
About you everything is blue.
Blue sky stretches out all around you,
as far as the eye can see.
Your body is becoming lighter and lighter,
and less and less dense.
It is becoming a body of light.
You are becoming transparent,
more and more transparent.
You are floating higher and higher,
on and on.

You float and feel the air about you.
You are floating like. a gossamer sail in the blue.
There is a great calm all around you.
No wind can buffet you,
as you float in the silent blue.

Little by little,
the air is growing warmer and warmer,
within you and without you,
and looking upward you see,
hovering far above,

the fiery disc of the golden sun.
Its rays reach out to caress you;
its golden light beckons you;
its warmth caresses your body;
falling in cascades about you.

You are drawing nearer and nearer,
closer to the sun.
Its light is becoming stronger and stronger,
brighter and brighter,
more and more intense.
Its orb is beginning to fill the whole expanse of your vision.
You have no fear and you float,
drawn irresistibly into the radiance of the sun.

You are swallowed by the sun's golden light;
wrapped in a golden glow which becomes a golden flame;
journeying nearer and ever nearer to the centre –
the source of its heat.
The flame is becoming hotter and redder.
Your body is beginning to burn;
but there is no pain.
Your whole being is aglow with flame.

Fire is within you and fire is without you;
fire that does not burn because you yourself are fire.
You are the flame of life,
and the flame of life is you.
Flames run their flickering tongues,
along your golden, fiery limbs;
flickering, licking tongues of fire;
purging and cleansing in a golden glow.
There is no pain for you yourself are fire;
only the flame of life,
around you and within you,
a glowing oneness with fire.

And now you are beginning to move.
Your body is beginning to travel through the flames.

You are moving away from the centre of the sun;
not back to Earth,
but further and further away.
The red flames are changing into many colours.
The flames are becoming the colours of the sunset:
amber and orange, pink and gold.
You are travelling through the sun
and emerging into night, the blackest night,
Where no star shines.

Far below you,
you can see
the flaming orb of the sun;
but leaving this behind,
you turn and float away,
leaving behind you all the Elements,
and reaching
Nothing.

Be at peace now in the silence
of the temple of the Gods.
Let all be still within you,
and without you.
Let all thoughts
slip away from you.
Forget all cares and be at peace.
Lie still in the great darkness
that is the womb of the Universe.

You are unborn;
your former life is but a dream to you now.
It is no more.
Its achievements, its hopes, its fears –
let all slip away from you;
be at peace, at rest.

You wait between the worlds
of the past and the future.
Empty out all thought,

and empty,
feel a great breeze blow through you,
cleansing and releasing you from the past.

Your body has dissolved into the darkness.
You are finite no longer.
You flow into the four corners of the universe.[5]

Once the *Element Balancing* has finished, we like to leave the candidate in silence for a while before one or two coven members of the opposite sex to the initiate who are called the *sponsors* come to perform the binding.

As candidates for initiation, we are blindfold and bound by ritual cords. The binding involves three cords. One cord is tied first around the candidate's wrists, which are placed upright behind his or her back. The cord is then taken up and round the candidate's neck, back round the wrists and then back up to the neck. In some traditions, a long loose end is left hanging from the front of the neck by which the initiator can lead the candidate around the circle. The second cord is tied above the candidate's left knee rather like a garter, and the third around the candidate's right ankle. In this way the candidate's feet are *Neither bond nor free.* The postulant is almost committed but not quite; for at the last moment he or she is free to draw back and to declare that he or she is not ready for initiation.

The binding symbolizes our spiritual state before initiation. The cords in Wicca are known as *the material basis.* This is a phrase of many meanings, one of which is that the postulant is bound to the world of matter, of materialism, the world of the Ego. Before the rite we are prisoners, but not completely. By seeking initiation, we have taken the first step on the path of our spiritual journey and to symbolize this, our feet are almost free. At the end of the initiation we are freed from the cords and can throw away the fetters that hold us back from our spiritual destiny. We are set free to seek and find ourselves.

The bound candidate is like the Hanged Man in the tarot. The Hanged Man hangs happily from one foot, with one foot bound and one foot free, he has his hands bound behind his back. The Hanged Man is not seeking to escape from this position. His strange position of suspension between the worlds, hanging between Heaven and Earth, is a chosen one. So too is that of the postulant, who bound now stands between the worlds, at the edge of the circle awaiting release.

To allow this binding and blindfolding, we must make an act of love and trust and be prepared to become vulnerable as a child. If we are to journey into ourselves, we must be prepared to let go of our defences, postures and disguises. Only then will our Egos let us avail ourselves of the secret powers of the Gods that lie buried deep within us. This is a very difficult and challenging thing to do. We like to pretend we are strong and dislike making ourselves vulnerable, but as Jung wrote:

> In the end one has to admit that there are problems which one simply cannot solve on one's own resources. Such an admission has the advantage of being honest, truthful, and in accord with reality, and this prepares the ground for a compensatory reaction from the collective unconscious: you are now inclined to give heed to a helpful idea or intuition, or to notice thoughts which had not been allowed to voice themselves before. Perhaps you will pay attention to the dreams that visit you at such moments, or will reflect on certain inner and outer occurrences that take place just at this time. If you have an attitude of this kind, then the helpful powers slumbering in the deeper strata of man's nature can come awake and intervene, for helplessness and weakness are the eternal experience and the eternal problem of mankind.[6]

The initiation therefore opens us to the influence of the beneficial forces in the universe. These are very willing to help, but only if asked; only if sought.

At this point, we are given two passwords. These are traditionally secret, but since they have already been published in many books, I will state them here so that their meaning can be discussed. They are *Perfect Love* and *Perfect Trust*. Perfect Love is something which few of us are capable of achieving at all times and with all people. However, in the world of the sacred circle, we seek to act in accordance with the principle of Perfect Love and to take that principle out with us into everyday life.

Perfect Love is a love that loves others because they carry a spark of the Divine within them; even though at times they may deviate far from it. We can *love perfectly* and love others only to the extent that we are able to love ourselves. Self-hatred and lack of self-esteem mean that we will be incapable of the unselfish outpouring of love that is implied by the words *Perfect Love*; an outpouring of a force that seeks nothing in return. The return is the joy which we receive from our own act of loving; for to love enriches the lover as much as the loved.

Perfect Love becomes possible in the circle because of the intimate contact between the Ego and the Divine. Our consciousness is opened to the qualities of the Goddess and God that are invoked into the priestess and priest and become manifest within the circle. If we invoke the Great Mother and the Horned God, epitome of female and male love, our Egos will absorb their qualities. It is then possible to manifest them in our own lives. This happiness is not just for the priest and priestess on whom the God or Goddess is invoked, but for all those who participate in the experience. The ritual and the group working will at that point have united the group on the level of the collective unconscious and what happens to one will happen to all.

The coven is the community of the Goddess and the God and must be made in their image. It is a home, a place of wholeness, truth and love in which we can grow to spiritual maturity. Entering a circle with someone is one of the most intimate things we can do with another. Along with the removal of clothes, go many other barriers to friendship and intimacy. The friendships formed within our new spiritual family, the coven, create very strong bonds between people that are one of the pleasures of coven life.

We cannot enter into Wicca at all unless we are prepared to give the group into which we are to be initiated *Perfect Trust*. Unless we allow ourselves to be bound and blindfold by them, we cannot undergo the initiation that brings us into Wicca. However, Perfect Trust does not just mean trust in others. It also means trust in ourselves and trust in the wider powers of the universe, trust in the Gods.

We are born full of fears, fears of the unknown and of the dark. There are fears both of what is within and what is without. We are afraid to look within ourselves because there is much about ourselves that we despise and of which we are ashamed. We do not wish to acknowledge this to ourselves, let alone to others. In Wicca, however, we must face these things. We must see our souls naked and unveiled. We are afraid of the dark, the things that go bump in the night, but we must enter into that darkness. We must discover the forces that surround us and which move the universe. We must look upon the face of the Goddess and the God.

With the removal of our clothes, we are like crabs removed from their shell; we feel exposed and endangered. We trust, but there is also an element of fear. This fear is appropriate, for initiation is not a step to be taken lightly. We are afraid of what we will meet with in the circle and so we should be; for what we will meet there is ourselves – good bits and bad bits, wise bits and foolish bits, spirit and flesh. We are blindfold because we are blind. Symbolically, this is the true state of our vision; for we have not yet seen ourselves in the mirror of truth. Until we have done so, the veils of our Egos come between us and the rest of creation. Like the child in the womb who has not yet been exposed to the day, we await in darkness our entry into the circle of light.

Once the candidate has been *properly prepared*, he or she will be taken to wait outside of the circle while it is cast. In some groups, the initiate will be placed near enough the circle to hear the words of casting. Alternatively, he or she may be left alone and brought to the circle edge when it is time to enter the circle. Both methods have advantages. To be left alone bound in the darkness is a very sobering experience. While it does not take very long to cast a circle, to the bound initiate it can seem a long time indeed. There is plenty of time for reflection and to question whether one really wants to do this after all! However, for the candidate, it can be a very beautiful experience to hear the casting of the circle for the first time at his or her initiation.

The rite

A circle is cast as described in 'The Circle of Being' chapter. The initiation then commences with the Bagahi Rune. The meaning and origin of the Rune are obscure. The first known version appears in a Medieval manuscript of the thirteenth-century troubadour Rutebeuf which is now in the Bibliothèque Nationale in Paris. This may be in a form of Basque and many Witches believe it is an invocation of Basque God names. There is only one other place in the Book of Shadows where the Bagahi Rune appears and this is in the Samhain sabbat. Samhain is the feast of the dead and the first degree initiation can be seen as a death to the old life and a birth into the new. This is a copy of the Medieval text.

Bagahi Rune

Bagahi laca bachahe
Lamac cahi achabahe
Karrelyos
Lamac lamec bachalyos
Cabahagi sabalyos
Baryolas
Lagozatha cabyolas
Samahac et famyolas
Harrahya!

Not surprisingly, the spelling of these words has been corrupted over the years and slight variations appear in different versions of the *Book of Shadows*.

Although in the Gardnerian and Alexandrian traditions the ceremony is performed by the High Priest in a woman's initiation, the role of the High Priestess is very important. The first degree initiation is considered an initiation of the Goddess, a birth into the community of the Great Mother. Thus reborn, the initiate becomes a child of the Goddess and will become a brother or sister of all those in the coven. The presence of the High Priestess is considered essential for the initiation to be valid. The Goddess can create without the God, but the God cannot create without the Goddess. Still in modern Wicca, in many traditional covens, the female initiate traces her line of initiation not from the initiating High Priest, but from the High Priestess of the rite.

In the original first degree initiation text in the *Book of Shadows*, although the God names are called upon in the Bagahi Rune, the God is not invoked into the High Priest. As with the Mysteries of Isis, the first initiation is that of the Goddess, the mother, and it is only in later Wiccan initiations that the God appears. The thinking behind the rebirth symbolism of the first initiation is that of the ancient past, when our ancestors had not learned to record time and were unaware of the male role in procreation. Woman was thought to become pregnant by the intervention of the Goddess, the Moon.

In our first degree initiations, we prefer to have both God and Goddess present and feel this is more appropriate in our current age where the role of the father is so important. In particular, when a woman is initiated, we invoke the God into the initiator, so that it is the God rather than the priest who performs the initiation. The aspects of the Goddess and God that are invoked will be those appropriate to initiation – the Mother aspect of the Goddess and the Father aspect of the God. The invocation of the Goddess is always followed by *The Great Mother Charge*. This conveys to the new initiate much about the importance of the Goddess in Wicca. She learns that the Goddess is *Queen of all Witcheries*, that from Her *all things proceed* and to Her *all things must return*. The emphasis on the feminine is in marked contrast to the religious liturgy that most Westerners will have heard if they have been practitioners of Christianity, Judaism or Islam.

The *Book of Shadows* mentions *reading* the Charge, but the rite and in fact the whole of the initiation work much better if the High Priestess and Priest know the whole ritual by heart. Learning the Charge sounds rather an awesome undertaking and some covens read from the text. Having been initiated by a High Priestess who appeared to know not just the Charge but the whole *Book of Shadows* by heart (a daunting but challenging revelation!), I was converted to the benefits of this approach. It is also more conducive to the smooth flow of ritual when the participants know what they are doing and do not have to fumble in the dark trying to read. Wicca is an oral tradition and, besides secrecy, there are sound and ancient occult reasons why rituals were never committed to paper. The Druids, for instance, had an alphabet but did not use this for sacred texts, which they learned by heart. Reading is an activity of the left brain, but magic is an activity of the right brain. Magic requires us to effect a change of consciousness that is much easier to maintain without the interference of the left brain's linear thought.

Once the Gods have been invoked, the initiation itself commences. A priestess makes a door in the circle. If the candidate has been left in a place apart, the sponsors will leave to fetch the initiate. The besom is then laid across the threshold of the doorway. The broomstick is a male and female symbol, *the rod which penetrates the bush*, and it is via this symbol of sexual union that the candidate enters the circle of rebirth.

Confronting ourselves as we really are is the first step on the journey into Wicca and, indeed, into all magical and initiatory systems. Across the gateway of the broom, the initiator places the point of a sword or athame on the postulant's heart and gives a challenge.

> O thou who standest on the threshold
> between the pleasant world of men
> and the Terrible Domains of the Lords of the Outer Spaces,
> hast thou the courage to make the assay?
> For it were better to rush upon my blade and perish
> than to make the attempt with fear in thy heart.

The Challenge is made in dramatic terms because it is important that the postulant understands that there are spiritual and psychological dangers in seeking inner growth. These are all the more dangerous because they are subtle and unobvious. One of the straightforward dangers is that having commenced the initiation, the postulant may panic; for as Jung explained:

> ... if we step through the door ... we discover with terror that we are the objects of unseen factors ... It can even give rise to primitive panic, because, instead of being believed in, the anxiously guarded supremacy of consciousness – which is in truth one of the secrets of human success – is questioned in the most dangerous way.[7]

The unconscious mind is extremely powerful. What each of us ordinarily thinks of as *me* is only a tiny part of us, rather like the tip of the iceberg. Beneath are untold strength and power, but we will have to learn to control this strength and power if they are not to overwhelm us. The words of the Challenge show us that physical death is a lesser thing than spiritual death. Many initiates have come to the Challenge with *fear in their hearts*, but the fear is not the true barrier. We may come to the circle afraid, but what we must be willing to do is to endure the fear.

The challenger stands in the role of what readers of H P Lovecraft novels will know as the *lurker on the threshold*, the Shadow who stands on the portal of the unconscious. In Jungian psychology, the *Shadow* personifies those parts of us which we dislike and reject. This is the figure we fear to face. The Shadow contains all within us that we do not wish to see; but Wicca is about seeing. The effect of first degree initiation is inevitably to raise the Shadow, and we must confront it. Jung writes:

> The meeting with oneself is, at first, the meeting with one's own shadow. The shadow is a tight passage, a narrow door, whose painful constriction no one is spared who goes down to the deep well ... For what comes after the door is ... the world of water, where all life floats in suspension; where the realm of the sympathetic system, the soul of everything living, begins; where I am indivisibly this and that; where I experience the other in myself and the other-than-myself experiences me.[8]

The symbol of the first degree, the downward pointing triangle, is the Element of Water. In order to be born we must enter the waters of the womb, the world of the magic circle. When the Guardian of the Portal challenges us and asks if we have the courage to *make the assay*, we must be ready to enter the circle, the world of Water, the stream of life, and to leap upstream with the salmon of knowledge to its spawning ground, the place of origin of our own being.

What we see when we negotiate the *tight passage*, the *narrow door*, when we undergo the spiritual birth of initiation over the broomstick and leap into the waters of the unconscious, is our own reflection mirrored in the water. This reflection is not the bright spectre of ourselves that we like to present to the world. It is the darkness that we have hidden and which awaits us on the other side of the veil – the *Shadow*. So long as we project everything negative in ourselves onto others, we avoid seeing where the true source of that negativity lies, which is within ourselves. Once we can face up to the Shadow, a great deal of the journey is already done.

Our persona has been removed with our everyday clothes, which were left outside the circle. It remains only to step forward with courage into that darkness. We must take that step blindfold; even as when we entered the physical world we entered into a world we had not seen. We do not know what we will meet there. We have yet to see our own faces reflected in the mirror of truth; but we have two passwords to sustain us.

> I have two perfect words,
> Perfect Love and Perfect Trust.

With love and trust we enter into the circle; trusting in the rightness of what we have decided; possibly trusting in the rightness of our own decision more than we have ever had to before, especially if we are young. We submit ourselves to the rite and whatever it will hold and so, in love and humility, we cross the boundary of the circle into the welcoming arms of the initiator:

> All who have are doubly welcome.
> And I give thee a third
> to pass thee through this dread door.

The initiator places the sword on the ground underneath, crossed with the broomstick, and gives *the third*. This is not a password but a kiss. In some covens the candidate is swung across the threshold by the initiator. If there are sponsors waiting with the initiate, then they may follow the older tradition of pushing him or her into the circle from behind. The initiator will then (hopefully) catch the initiate prior to giving him or her the kiss. For a man who is being initiated by a woman the symbolism of the new birth is very obvious. The sponsoring priestess is the mother who gives the final push that brings the initiate to birth in the world of the circle. It is the High Priestess who as Goddess/midwife receives him into her arms. Alternatively, the sponsors can lift the initiate over the threshold so he or she, as it were, flies in. This adds a certain element of surprise to the proceedings! Obviously the relative weights and sizes of the initiate and sponsors are a practical consideration here.

The world that the initiate has entered is the world of the circle.

> ... a boundless expanse full of unprecedented uncertainty, with apparently no inside and no outside, no above and no below, no here and no there, no mine and no thine, no good and no bad.[9]

Having entered the circle, the initiate is led to the four quarters and presented to each in turn.

> Take heed ye Mighty Ones of the East/South/West/North that ..... is properly prepared to be a Priest(ess) and Witch.

This is a very short and simple part of the rite, but an important one. A major purpose of the initiation ceremony is to introduce us to the Lords of the Elements so that they will recognise us and come when called upon. In inner terms this means that our psyche and four functions will henceforth be accessible while we are within the circle. Once the initiate has been presented to the quarters, the rite calls for the coven to:

> Circle three times with dance, step and chant.

It is usual here to chant the *Witches' Rune* which is given in the previous chapter. In addition, a nice practice adopted by many covens is to place initiates in the centre of the circle and joining hands to push them across the circle from one person to another. This is very disorientating but also exhilarating and very good for releasing tension. Talking about the inner symbolism of Wicca makes the rite sound very serious. However, to use the Goddess' words, Wicca is a religion of *mirth and reverence*, of seriousness and laughter, and this part of the rite usually leans towards the latter.

When we have all recovered from this energetic activity, the initiate is placed in the West of the circle. The West is the cardinal point that corresponds to the Element of the initiation, the Element of Water. Also the West, because of its association with the setting sun, is considered to be the quarter of death. In Wicca, where life and death are seen as an ever-turning wheel, the West is the point where we begin the return journey of rebirth.

The candidate is then given instruction on how Wicca views the relationship between humankind and the Gods. This explains that the Divine is immanent within us and can be united with the Gods, the Divine forces in the outer universe. The initiate is now taken from the Western quarter of the circle, the quarter of death, to the East, the quarter of the rising sun, the point of birth. The initiator then kneels before the initiate and kisses his or her feet.

> In other religions the postulant kneels
> while the priest towers above him,
> but in the Art Magical we are taught to be humble
> and so we kneel to welcome thee.

This is one of the most important and moving parts of the ritual. It is an act of humility on the part of those who are initiating and a reminder that to initiate is both a privilege and a great responsibility. For the initiate, the kiss is a symbol of the sacredness of the body that has been given to us by the Gods, so that we may experience the beauty and joy of the material world. For a woman, her body is considered a temple of the Goddess whose Divinity she carries in the centre of her soul. For a man, his body is the temple of the God. For both sexes, the body is a shrine to be reverenced and not despised, to be honoured and not treated with shame.

The initiate is next asked whether he or she is ready to swear the oath. If so, the cord around the initiate's ankle is tied loosely to the opposite ankle so that the initiate still has *Feet neither bond nor free*. The initiate's measure is then taken with a piece of cotton, wool or string. The measurements are those of a shroud: the length of the body, the distance around and the head and the heart. These measurements were considered by the ancients to be extremely powerful because they had strong sympathetic links with the individual. In the world of symbolism, where one symbol may have many meanings, the measure is not only the winding sheet, but also the umbilical cord that links the initiate with those who have given the initiation.

In the Alexandrian tradition, the measure is taken but returned to the initiate at the end of the rite as a sign of the initiator's trust in the initiate. Our own practice is to retain the measure. This is not in order to have power over our initiates, but to remind us and them of our responsibilities and links to one another. At the third degree, when the initiates become equal to their initiators, we return the measure. This symbolizes that they now have no higher authority than themselves and must take full responsibility for their own development.

Once the measure has been taken, the initiate is symbolically scourged. This is not designed to cause pain. This is not because of Western squeamishness. Most people are prepared to suffer in order to be worthy of initiation. The initiation ceremonies of our ancestors and of tribal peoples included physical ordeals. For these peoples physical endurance was very valuable. Our ancestors' lives were hard. They had to endure physical pain which modern medicine has done much to alleviate and had a difficult existence battling with animals in hunting, with the elements against which they had little shelter, and against other humans for scarce food resources. Resistance to pain and willingness to persist in the face of difficulties were essential for the survival of the tribe. Only those prepared to prove their worth could be admitted to full adulthood. Primitive societies could not afford passengers. Today such physical endurance is a minor part of our lives and the gifts of initiation are not won by undergoing a small amount of physical discomfort. It is an effort of the mind, soul and spirit which is required to achieve the goal of initiation – higher consciousness.

In most traditions, the initiate at this point takes a new name, by which he or she will be known in the Craft. This is then used in the oath. The wording of the oath reflects a climate of persecution, promising to protect our brothers and sisters even unto death and never to reveal the *secrets of the Art* except in an appropriate fashion. These words present problems to writers of books such as this. How do we speak about Wicca while retaining the element of secrecy that must always be part of a

Mystery religion? This requires delicacy of judgement in steering a course that is acceptable to the majority of Wicca. However, this exercise of judgement does not just apply to writers. We are all responsible for ensuring that we teach the Mysteries only to those who are worthy and responsible people.

After the oath, the initiate is consecrated three times with the symbol of the first degree, the downward pointing triangle of Water. The blindfold is now removed and the initiate enters the light of the sacred circle. He or she has negotiated the narrow passage that leads from the darkness of the womb to the light of the magical world. The initiate is reborn.

In seeking to enter Wicca, we admit to ourselves our helplessness and weakness and, in that paradoxical way of the unconscious, the source of our being is filled with strength. Now that the initiate has entered the circle in weakness and humility, he or she is greeted with a kiss and presented with the magical weapons, the Witch's *working tools*. These are eight in number and are symbols not of weakness, but of power. Initiates are now given the *First Instruction*. This tells us that our Witch power comes from within us and that there is no part of us which is not Divine. We are also told that the *Wiccan Rede* or *Law* is:

> Eight words the Wiccan Rede fulfil:
> an (if) it harm none do what you will.

In other words, we must decide for ourselves what is right and what is wrong, always bearing in mind that we should not cause harm to others. The initiation is now almost at an end. The initiator, taking an athame, salutes the new Witch with an invoking pentagram:

> I now salute you in the name of (the Goddess) and (the God) newly made priest(ess) and Witch.

The initiate is presented to each of the Watchtowers. The initiation proper is now complete and the initiate can be introduced into that finest of Wiccan arts, feasting.

Notes

1. Adapted from Dion Fortune, *The Sea Priestess*, p158, Aquarian, Wellingborough, 1989.
2. Reginald Scot, *The Discoverie of Witchcraft*, p23.
3. Margaret Murray, *The God of the Witches*, p66.
4. Carl Jung, *Archetypes and the Collective Unconscious*, pp113–5, paras 200–5, Routledge & Kegan Paul, London, Second edition 1968.
5. Vivianne and Chris Crowley, 1981.
6. Carl Jung, *Archetypes and the Collective Unconscious*, p21, para 44.
7. Carl Jung, *Archetypes and the Collective Unconscious*, p23, para 49.
8. Carl Jung, *Archetypes and the Collective Unconscious*, pp21–2, para 45.
9. Carl Jung, *Archetypes and the Collective Unconscious*, pp122–3, paras 220–1.

7

The Journey Onwards

We have been initiated. We have undergone a ceremony and been proclaimed a priest or a priestess and a Witch. What happens next? Initiation does not suddenly imbue us with magical and mystical powers that we did not possess before. These are developed gradually as the result of effort. In the first degree we must work on and learn about our craft and begin what is a lifetime course of learning and training. Many covens have specific courses of training for new initiates. Others prefer to work with each individual in the way best suited to him or her. Regardless, however, of the outer skills we need to learn as first degree Witches, initiation is likely to precipitate changes in our inner world and to lead us on a journey of growth. While each of us is different, the human psyche has certain patterns of growth and change that are universal. These have been the starting point of the Pagan Mysteries throughout the millennia.

The circle cross

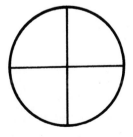

The circle cross

The symbol of the circle cross is very important in the work of the Wiccan first degree. This symbol has many meanings. Very importantly, it represents the four Elements of the Wise surrounded by the fifth Element of Spirit or Ether. One of the major tasks of the first degree is to achieve control over the world of the four Elements. The four Elements are found on the material plane as solid matter, liquid, combusting energy and gas – Earth, Water, Fire and Air. They are also found on the inner planes as the Elementals and the Elemental Lords. Part of our work in the first degree will be to learn to work with the energies of the Elements in ritual and magic. The four Elements or energy types also exist in the realm of consciousness, the psychological realm. Carl Jung believed that there are four ways by which people experience the world and thus four basic personality types. These correspond to the four Elements of magic and to the ancient Greek idea of the four *humours*.

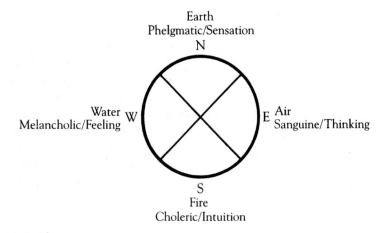

Earth
Phelgmatic/Sensation
N

Water W
Melancholic/Feeling

E Air
Sanguine/Thinking

S
Fire
Choleric/Intuition

The four functions

Jung divided the four functions into two groups – *perception* and *judgement*. *Perception* tells us what is happening. It is the process by which we receive information. The two perceptual functions are *sensation* and *intuition*. *Judgement* takes decisions about what to do with the information gleaned by perception. Our judgmental functions are *thinking* and *feeling*.

Sensation operates through the physical senses, our eyes, ears, etc, and is the means by which we discover facts. *Intuition* shows us meanings and relationships that are beyond the reach of the senses. Sensation is grounded in the present. It tells us what is happening now. Intuition tells us how situations are likely to develop in the future. Intuition is the function of the imagination – telling us how things might be. Sensation is the function of factual memory – telling us how things are and used to be.

Thinking tells us whether something is logical and rational. *Feeling* is equally important. It tells us what is valuable, worthy and good. Thinking without feeling is cold and cruel. It applies the letter of the law without taking account of individual circumstance. Feeling without thinking is partisan. People are seen as more important than rules. It will favour those it likes and ignore those it does not. It will adopt ideas because it admires the person who teaches them rather than because they seem meaningful and true.

By invoking the Elements at the quarters, we activate the four functions within the psyche. The circle and the four quarters are a pattern of perfection for the personality and provide a template for our psychological and spiritual growth. Our spiritual journey into the core of our being, to our own inner Godhead, is a journey to wholeness. The circle cross of the four Elements within the circle of the balanced personality is a symbol of this balance and wholeness. When we achieve balance, we stand in the centre of the circle, at the crossroads of the four functions. From this vantage point we can have a true and unbiased view of the world around us. Thus released from distortions, and with our humanity made whole, we can seek the higher vantage point that lies in the third dimension above the central point. This is the point of the fifth Element, the Element of Ether. Ether lies beyond the four functions which are immanent in the material world. This is the Element of the fifth and transcendent function, the world of the Divine Self.

The world of the circle projects our inner world outwards so that we can see ourselves. Usually when we first learn to invoke the quarters, we will find some Elements more difficult to invoke than others. These are usually the Elements that represent our weakest functions, those which we use little if at all.

They are the aspects of our personality that we will have to develop if we are to achieve one of the aims of the Mysteries which is to heal the personality of its lopsidedness and make it whole.

The speed with which we acquire the ability to perform different aspects of Wicca will depend in part on the Jungian function that dominates our personality. We will operate best in the area that corresponds to our most developed function.

Thinking people often have difficulty with a system such as Wicca that depends primarily on intuition. At one time there were few predominantly thinking types in the Craft. Thinkers like logical systems and when attracted to the occult tended to join qabalistic groups where they could appreciate Qabalah's complicated and logical philosophy. Some qabalistic groups do very little ritual and many thinking types are content to read about, write about and discuss esoteric ideas without doing much on the practical side. In recent years, as Wiccan writers have given articulate descriptions of some aspects of the philosophy of Wicca, more thinking people have been drawn to the Old Religion. Many ritual magicians have joined Wicca and have espoused Paganism as their religious path. This has produced some interesting cross-fertilizations between the more intuitive and people-oriented approach of Wicca and the intellectual approach of ritual magic.

The skill of thinking types lies in their ability to grasp the rationale behind magic. This enables them to construct effective rituals. They understand, if you like, how to wire the circuit to get energy to flow and how to use symbolism to draw down the right kind of power. While intellectual people may be good at producing the wiring diagram and designing rituals, they are not necessarily good at producing the magical energy needed to perform them. Thinking people often find it difficult to let go of their conscious minds. Traditionally, ritual magicians, who are archetypal thinkers, have needed intuitive or feeling types in order to successfully perform their rites: hence magical partnerships such as Dr Dee and Edward Kelly, and Aleister Crowley and his various *Scarlet Women*.

Intuitives may be less good at writing about Wicca, but much of what the thinkers write will be the fleshed-out bare bones of the inspirations of the intuitive. Intuitives are good at changing levels of consciousness and can usually learn quickly to move into the altered states of consciousness required for clairvoyance and invocation. It is the intuitives' ability to let the arrow of their intuition fly to the Divine centre within themselves that makes them good at invocation. Their intuition takes them onto another level where, to paraphrase Dion Fortune, it is possible to see things of which ye may not tell.

Feeling types are people-oriented. They are excellent at bringing people together in a coven and creating a sense of loving harmony and group identity. In fact, it is essential for either the High Priest or High Priestess of a coven to have a well-developed feeling function if the group is to flourish and develop a strong group mind. Feeling people are excellent too at spotting the talents of others and developing them and they make excellent initiators. They also make very good teachers, because they can adapt their teaching to individuals and will understand each person's difficulties and needs.

Feeling types are also very good at finding out what people are really like. This is indispensable for a coven when deciding whether or not to consider someone for initiation. However, feeling types are not very good at turning anyone down. It is best for the feeling type to explain what someone is like and for others in the coven to make the decision about whether or not to accept them. Otherwise, the coven could find itself full of all sorts of waifs and strays who are not really suitable, but whom the High Priest or High Priestess could not quite bear to turn away. Feeling people are also good at healing. This is not so much the healing of broken bones, but illnesses which arise from emotional imbalances within the individual. The feeling person can detect these and use their healing insights to rebalance the individual.

Sensation types have a flair for natural magic that uses the hidden properties of natural things. This is the magic of herbs, crystals, incenses etc; in fact, the traditional craft of the Witch. Sensation function people often have an innate sense of physical beauty and can create beautiful temples and artefacts. They are down to earth and their common sense is invaluable in the face of all the intuitives who flock to systems such as Wicca. It is the sensation people who remember all the practicalities; that it's five minutes before the start of the initiation and no one's found the blindfold yet; that on Samhain it might be a good idea to find the matches to relight the candles before we plunge the circle into pitch darkness; and on a more prosaic level, whose turn it is to do the washing up.

The magical weapons that are associated with the four Elements symbolize the qualities of the functions. The weapons of sensation are the Earth symbols of the pentacle and the shield, which are used to guard and protect us. In the circle, the pentacle is used to protect us against outside forces that seek to enter. It is also used to focus the power of a spell in order to earth it and bring it into manifestation in the world. One of the things our sensation function protects us against is a lack of reality. Sensation people are practical and realistic. They see what needs to be done and can bring together the disparate ideas, wishes and dreams of the other three functions and turn them into reality. Raising a great deal of power for a spell is no use whatsoever if that power does not reach its destination. Similarly, all the bright ideas, high ideals and flashes of insight of the other three functions are no use if they cannot be bound together and the necessary steps taken to put them into action.

Both the spear and the arrow, weapons of Fire, can be sent high into the sky to travel long distances at great speed in order to reach another place. This is how intuition operates. Thinking starts off at one point and follows a logical step-by-step progression until it reaches its destination. Intuition travels quickly in leaps and bounds. The arrow of intuition flies into the air and it is as though it touches the Heavens and comes back to Earth with a bit of the Divine attached to it. Intuition can travel in two dimensions at once, achieving both height and distance. It can reach levels of consciousness that the thinker, steadily walking to his goal step by step along the ground, can never reach.

Once we have obtained information through sensation or intuition, we must use our judgmental functions, *feeling* and *thinking*, to enable us to act upon it. Our thinking function is best for dealing with things which work logically. Feeling decisions do not work very well when dealing with computers and machinery. The feeling person will be convinced that if you speak to the machine nicely it will respond; though just to confuse the issue, sometimes it does! Thinking is a logical and analytical function and impersonally chooses the basis of cause and effect. This is the task of the athame and sword, weapons of Air. These are powerful weapons which cut and separate out what is good from what is bad.

Feeling types understand people much better than thinking types because much of human behaviour is based on feelings rather than logic. The cup, the weapon of Water, is a vessel and a container that preserves and cherishes what is sacred. Feeling decisions will take into account what is important to people and will not ride roughshod over them. Feeling is the function that prompts us to sacrifice ourselves for others; something that our thinking function finds very illogical. When we want to find out about ourselves or to clarify what is important and what is not, we can go to the feeling person and drink of the cup of his or her wisdom and so come to understanding. The feeling person makes us realize that we are important and worthwhile. With that inspiration and refreshed from the wine of the cup, we will go forth and seek the best within ourselves and so find our own Holy Grail.

Jung believed that as we grew and developed, so too would our personality. As children our lives are dominated by one of the functions, so that our personalities are very one-pointed. As we approach puberty a second function emerges. In adulthood a third function should emerge, usually around middle-age. The mid-life crisis is often a result, forcing us to re-evaluate our lives and find them in some respects wanting.

Many people never reach this stage and remain fixed in their adolescent personalities; sometimes because they refuse to acknowledge the changes that are trying to take place within them and try and thrust a new function back into the unconscious. Others go further and access their fourth function, the one that is most elusive. To be balanced and to create the perfected Self, we must learn to use all four functions.

This does not mean that we will all use all four functions equally and emerge with the same personalities. We will continue to be true to our dominant type, be it feeling, sensation, intuition or thinking, but we will be able to use the other functions when appropriate. The fourth function is always the function that is opposite our dominant function. If we are sensation types, our intuition will be the last aspect of ourselves to appear. If we are thinking types, then our feeling response, our ability to relate to others, will be the last aspect of ourselves that we master.

Interest in Wicca often awakens when we are going through a period of transition and a new function is emerging into consciousness. This can happen in teenage years as the second function emerges, or at the stage of the mid-life crisis. Astrologically, the mid-life crisis is associated with the Uranus semi-return. This is when the planet Uranus moves opposite the position of Uranus at the time of our birth. For many people the mid-life crisis can occur earlier as we fulfil the goals and ambitions of our youth and seek new challenges.

We are likely to enter Wicca with two or at most three of our functions operating. We will therefore experience our own growth and change while in Wicca, and also the effects of the growth and change of others in our covens. This is particularly so because Wicca, like other esoteric systems, accelerates personal growth in what ritual magicians often call the *hot house of the Mysteries*. Those of you who are familiar with Qabalah will remember the saying *The vices of the sephira always manifest before the virtues*. This is also true of the psychological functions, which have negative as well as positive sides. Bringing new functions into consciousness is like learning a new skill. Initially, when we start trying to walk after having spent our first few months crawling, we are liable to be very wobbly on our legs and fall flat on our faces!

When people first start trying to use their thinking function they are liable to be somewhat over-impressed by their new-found intellectual powers and to believe everything their logic tells them is true. They may also want to convince others of this. If the sword, the weapon of Air, is used badly, it can injure others. Similarly, the thinking function used in a negative way can be divisive and hurt other people. The great danger for the thinking person is to think that they alone are right, that everyone else is wrong, and that it is their job to tell them so. When our thinking side emerges we can become very critical of others and a negative influence in a group.

When people first develop intuition, they are unlikely to be very discriminating about their sources. They may decide that they are in contact with the inner planes, whether they see these in traditional terms as *the masters* or follow the modern predilection for extra-terrestrial intelligences. Intuition is not as accurate as thinking. It is almost as though the arrow is sometimes blown off-course by the wind and does not land in the right place. Sometimes it does not quite reach the sky and falls to earth without capturing part of the Divinity. However, at first, we may not realize this and we can mistake our random ideas for Divine inspiration.

The negative side of feeling bears similarities to the negative qualities of the astrological Water signs. The receptiveness of feeling can make us interested in other people's lives to the exclusion of our own with the result that life passes us by and we do not grow and evolve. When we first develop feeling, we are likely to become too interested in the lives of others. A desire to counsel and help can be perverted into a feeling that we know what is best for others and it is beneficial if we manipulate them into doing it. When we first develop feeling, we may fall in love with totally unsuitable people and make ourselves miserable and a pain to our long-suffering Wiccan friends.

When sensation first emerges we may develop for the first time a desire to make things and to learn more about the *craft* side of magic. We may also learn to appreciate for the first time the beauties of the natural world around us. On the other hand we may go through a crisis with Wicca and decide that the material reality is the only true one and that we have been spending our time in airy-fairy nonsense. Often the sensation function awakens in us a desire to do something practical in the world. It can even be beneficial to go away for a time in order to achieve this before we turn our attention again to our inner growth. The emergence of the sensation function is often a time when we have to sit back and evaluate where we are in the world and to realize that there are many levels of reality and all are equally important.

The emergence of new functions causes problems in groups because at first we are not very good at using them. A different kind of problem arises however when we start to become skilled at using our new function. Whenever we come together in groups, whether Wiccan covens or football teams, we tend to specialize in certain areas which then become *ours*. If others become equally skilled in *our* area, this can be very threatening and we may resent it. This is not to paint a negative picture of psychological growth. However, it is important to realize that the birth of a new part of ourselves into consciousness, although very worthwhile in the end, is not without some labour pains.

Finding and balancing the functions

How can we detect our dominant function? You may find that as soon as you read one of the descriptions, it leaps out at you and you recognize yourself. If this is not the case, one clue will be in the way in which we first invoke the quarters. Usually, we find one Element more difficult to invoke than others. This Element is likely to be where our fourth and least developed function lies. Our dominant function will then be the Element of the quarters on the opposite side of the circle. Our astrological birth charts will also give us clues about our dominant functions, but unfortunately the dominant function does not relate to the natal chart in a straightforward way. For some people the dominant function is the Element of their Sun sign; for others it is the Element of the Ascendant, the ruling planet or the majority of planets in their chart.

The four functions and their associated skills can be developed in two ways. The essential way is to use the four functions in our Wiccan and everyday lives. Our sensation function will develop as we learn to make things with our hands. There is an old Wiccan and magical tradition which states that we should make all our magical tools ourselves. In part, this is to imbue them with our own etheric energy which is imprinted on objects that we handle frequently. The other purpose is to ground all those intuitive people who enter magic and make them deal with the everyday world of matter. Intuition is no use at all when trying to make and shape a hazel wand. However, it may be useful in sending us off to look in just the right place to find a piece of wood with just the right potential!

If we wish to develop our thinking, then we should get to grips with the intellectual side of Wicca. We need to read books and work out for ourselves the rationale behind its practices. If we want to develop our feeling function, we should learn to listen to and care for others and perhaps undertake training in counselling skills. If we want to develop our intuition, we should practise with the various divinatory systems.

Another way of developing the functions is by meditating on the four Elements. This may seem a more glamorous way of self-development than the more practical suggestions above. The former are however essential if we are to become balanced people in everyday life as well as in a Wiccan circle. While the latter is spiritually beneficial, we will gain more practical benefits from participation in Wicca if we are able to use what we have learned to make ourselves more successful, well-balanced, likeable and interesting people all the time, not just at esbats and sabbats.

The most important piece of magic we will ever do is the magic we do on ourselves. This is a magic of transformation. The rounding of the personality is one of the major aims of Wicca and of all systems of magical and spiritual development. From this solid foundation of the circle cross – the cross of the four functions within the circle of the Self – the spiritual growth and psychic and magical powers that enable us to climb new heights will spring.

Animus and Anima

In undergoing initiation, we open ourselves to the world of the unconscious and its inhabitants. In our waking consciousness, we are unaware of this hidden part of ourselves; but the voice of the unconscious speaks to us, sometimes directly and sometimes through figures who appear in dream and vision. One of the effects of the first degree is to activate powerful archetypes within our psyches. Archetypes are symbolic forces that appear to us in dream and vision. They are parts of ourselves and yet separate, something which at first is hard to understand. What we think of as ourselves is in reality only a small part of us. Beneath the everyday layer of waking consciousness is a sea of vastness which we must explore.

The Goddess and the God manifest to us in dream and vision through what are known as the *dominant archetypes*. Two major archetypal figures important at this stage of initiation are the archetypes of the opposite sex. Jung called these the *Anima* and *Animus*. For a woman, the *Animus* is the male part of herself. For a man, the *Anima* is the female part of himself, which traditionally male poets thought of as the Muse. How can part of a woman be male and part of a man female? Carl Jung saw the Anima and Animus as innate and biological. Each sex contains genes of the other.

> Just as every individual derives from masculine and fem-inine genes, and the sex is determined by the predomi-nance of the corresponding genes, *so in the psyche it is only the conscious mind, in a man, that has the masculine sign,* while the unconscious is by nature feminine. The reverse is true in the case of a woman.[1]

For both sexes, the Animus and Anima are a source of crea-tivity. For a woman, contact with her Animus gives her the creativity that is associated with the Element of Fire. It is the creativity that inspires us to do things, to be active in the world, to start crusades. Joan of Arc was a woman who was inspired by her Animus to save France from the English. If, as a simple peasant girl in a male-dominated age, she had allowed her con-scious mind to examine this idea critically, she would never have thought that she could succeed. Ignoring this, however, she obeyed her Animus, donned men's clothing and rode off to her destiny. Interestingly, in male-dominated societies, the don-ning by women of male clothing is considered very threatening because it upsets the established power structure. In Medieval Europe, female Witches were often thought of as wearing men's clothing and evidence of this was seen as a sure proof against them.

For a man, his Anima brings the creativity of Water. This is not the creativity of the doer, but the creativity of the artist. It is the creativity that inspires us to compose music, paint pictures, write poems and use the visual imagery that is the key to the ability to do magic.

Masculinity is still more valued in society than femininity and men can be more nervous of getting in touch with their contra-sexual side than are women. Fortunately, men who are attracted to Wicca can usually overcome this problem and, speaking as a female Witch, one of the great bonuses of Wicca is the deep non-sexual friendships which women can form with men who understand and value the feminine psyche.

The subject of male initiation has been much debated in recent years. The poet Robert Bly in his book *Iron John*[2] explores the need for young men to be initiated in the material world by older men. This is an important aspect of male initiation, but it is only the beginning. Beyond initiation into the material world lies the initiation of the Goddess. This is initiation into the world of the inner, the world of spirit. Only when we have mastered both worlds are we whole. The esotericist Dion Fortune wrote:

> There is a turning within of the soul
> whereby men come to Persephone;
> they sink back into the womb of time;
> they become as the unborn;
> they enter into the kingdom where She rules as Queen;
> they are made negative and await the coming of life.
> And the Queen of Hades' cometh unto them as a bridegroom,
> and they are made fertile for life
> and go forth rejoicing,
> for the touch of the Queen of the kingdom of sleep
> hath made them potent.[3]

This stage in a man's individual development is that of the son/lover whose role is to revere the Goddess, but although reverence for the feminine principle never lessens, it is important for the man that regard for the feminine within does not become over-emphasized and negate the masculine. The spiritual journey of initiation is a process of bringing all our qualities into play and not the achievement of the opposite at the expense of the original.

An example of this can be found in society with the experiences of the New Age man. Although many couples have experimented with role-reversal, with the father taking a greater responsibility in terms of the caring and nurturing roles traditionally ascribed to the mother, it is not in itself a total solution if, by doing so, the male qualities and instincts are artificially suppressed. Again it is perhaps a necessary stage in redressing the balance, to counteract previous behavioural patterns but, following this, a new stable balance has to be struck, where both the feminine and the masculine are given their due. In Wicca, the aim is that exploration of the feminine mysteries will for a man develop a new and more enlightened male role, in which both thinking and feeling are given their place and feeling is seen not as the sole province of the priestess and the Goddess, but an important part of the male world. The ultimate task of the Wiccan priest is to realize within himself the qualities of the God and in doing so he accesses the creative force of his own Godhead: for was not Pan the Player of the Pipes?

The persona and change

The words above the door to the temples of the Mysteries are *Know thyself.* In setting out on our initiatory journey, we all seek such knowledge, but the journey is hard and can be painful. In the Jewish myth of the Garden of Eden, it is Lucifer as the serpent who tempts Adam and Eve to eat of the Tree of Knowledge. By their subsequent actions when they did, the myth shows us that the knowledge which the Tree gave was consciousness, the knowledge of one's own existence. Once Adam and Eve had eaten the fruit of the Tree, they became aware of themselves, and perhaps more importantly, they became aware that they could be seen by one another. They were exposed.

Adam and Eve could not cope with this level of truth and covered themselves with leaves; that is, they hid behind the mask of the persona. When we enter Wicca, we must return once more to that state of spiritual nakedness, which existed before Adam and Eve covered themselves, but without losing their hard-won prize of consciousness. We must have the courage to see the truth and not to hide from it. We must see our own bodies as they are and let others see them. We must also see our own souls as they are, our innermost being, and let others see this too; for only when we know ourselves can we progress.

In the first degree initiation, the persona is symbolically stripped away, but one of the pitfalls of this can be to replace the discarded persona with another more exciting one – that of the Witch. The word *Witch* is very alluring; more so perhaps for a woman than a man, for whom there are fewer glamorous historical role models. For a woman, the word *Witch* has the negative connotations of the hag. It also has very glamorous associations – those of power, mysteriousness and sexual allure – Morgan le Fay, Vivianne Lady of the Lake, Circe. For women, it can be all too easy to identify with the persona of the Witch. Many women go through a stage of adorning as much of themselves as possible with occult jewellery and enhancing their *Witchy* image with exotic clothing and make-up.

Although traditionally Witches were both men and women, in the popular mind Witches came to be thought of as female. There is therefore no real stereotype of what a male Witch should look like. Men tend to either escape this stage completely or to take the other course and dress in black polo neck sweaters and large dangling pentacles rather like the classic Satanist in a 'B' movie.

When someone is first initiated, this in itself is no bad thing. We must come to terms with ourselves as Witches and openly advertising ourselves as such is one of way of doing so. Where it becomes negative is when it goes on for too long and people identify so strongly with the persona of Witch that they become ciphers and symbols and no longer themselves. The more strongly we advertise ourselves as Witches, the more we will be treated as Witches by others, and as nothing else. They no longer see us but see only their concept of the Witch – whether good or bad.

If we enter Wicca with our partners, as many people do, there may be changes in our relationship with one another. Men who have been used to being the successful and dominant partner in a relationship may find that their partner is better at magic than they are and more quickly gains an intuitive understanding of Wicca. In Wicca, women have high status and, for some women, it may be a new departure to be treated in this way. The dangers to the Ego are obvious. Very masculine men may also find some difficulties at first in adjusting to not being treated as a superior sex. If a couple has been accustomed to playing stereotyped sex roles, their relationship will have to adjust to the new status which Wicca accords women.

There can also be problems if we are in a relationship and our partner does not enter the Craft with us. Relationships can founder if one partner meets new people, grows, changes and makes new friends, and the other partner feels shut out. All this requires thought and care to ensure that a good relationship is strengthened and not threatened by one partner's growth.

Frequently when people enter the world of magic and Wicca, they expect to encounter spiritual dangers in the form of exotic-looking demons brandishing swords. Would that the pitfalls were as easy to spot as this! The dangers are much more subtle. What we raise when we enter Wicca are the archetypal forces within, the powers of good and evil which spring from inside us and with which we must find reconciliation. Jung writes:

Although everything is experienced in image form, i.e. symbolically, it is by no means a question of fictitious dangers but of very real risks upon which the fate of a whole life may depend.[4]

In the ancient Mystery schools, candidates for initiation were either trained for the priesthood from an early age and were thus properly prepared; or they were mature men and women who were seeking greater meaning in their lives. Many esoteric traditions have turned away the young, refusing to consider people before their mid-thirties. In Wicca, however, many would-be initiates are in their twenties. I was nineteen when initiated.

The danger for a young person who becomes interested in spiritual growth too soon is that it can hinder rather than facilitate his or her development. It can become a means to escape from the demands of life rather than facing them. To become immersed in the spiritual quest is one way of avoiding growing up and coming to terms with the demands of the material world. There is a danger that, as Jung puts it, a young person *regresses to the mythical world of the archetypes*,[5] into a life of fantasy.

Myth and ritual speak to the intuition and the imagination, faculties that often act to compensate for the deficiencies of reality. As teenagers, we fantasize that we have loving husbands when we are fat and spotty and no one asks us out. We fantasize that we are noble war lords when we are rather over-civil civil servants. We fantasize that we are rich and successful as we labour in boring factories. Fantasies are what produce all creative work, but alone they are worthless, something must be done with them.

Wiccan myth and ritual address the world of the imagination and channel it, giving it form and place. Ritual acts not as a substitute for reality, but as a pattern for it. By enacting the ritual dramas of the Gods, we activate these archetypes so that they manifest in our own lives and psyches. In enacting ritual, we are enacting a prescribed form of journey to human growth that overcomes the deviations of individual maladjustment. Ritual grounds the journey of the spirit into the world of the actual. It brings the journey out of the realm of personal fantasy into the world of the group; our inner world must be confronted by others.

In Wicca, we are not offering a substitute for reality, but an enhanced and enriched reality. Young people who wish to enter Wicca may be surprised to find that the first magical task their potential coven leaders set them is to go out and get a job or, if this is impossible, at least to do some voluntary work in the community which will connect them with the everyday world about them.

In some respects, though not all, the spiritual journey is easier for older people; but for young people in whom the archetypal forces have been wakened, the answer is not to forget all about this until mid-life. There are dangers in Wicca, as in all the spiritual, religious and magical paths; but like all dangerous journeys it does not mean than it should not be undertaken. One of the benefits of Wicca is that it exposes us to what Jung called the *divine archetypal drama*, the world of myth. For those whose psyches have become open to the archetypal powers, it is important that they do not retreat to a secret fantasy life, but seek to ground their experiences in the outer world of reality and to make them meaningful on the material plane. The seasonal rituals, the initiations, and even the simple magic circle in which Wicca operates, externalize what is happening in the unconscious and allow us to see it, to understand it, to come to terms with it and to grow.

Wicca is therefore an adventure, an adventure deep into the realm of our own spirit and Godhead. It is a most difficult journey, but the journey which at some point in our incarnations we must all begin to undertake. It is a journey of light and darkness, of laughter and love, but also of pain and desolation, but who can turn from the quest for the Grail when the Grail itself calls?

Notes

1. Carl Jung, *The Collected Works of C.G. Jung* Vol 9, Part 1: *Archetypes and the Collective Unconscious*, p175, paragraph 294 Routledge and Kegan Paul, 2nd ed, 1968.
2. Robert Bly, *Iron John: A Book about Men*, Element Books, Shaftesbury, 1991 (UK Edition).
3. Dion Fortune, *The Sea Priestess*, p202–3, Aquarian, Wellingborough, 1989.
4. Carl Jung, *Archetypes and the Collective Unconscious*, p39, para 82.
5. Carl Jung, *The Collected Works of C.G. Jung* Vol 5: *Symbols of Transformation*, p308, para 466, Routledge and Kegan Paul, 2nd ed, 1967.

8

The Goddess: Wicca and the Feminine

Wicca worships the Goddess, the Divine feminine who has been much neglected and abused in the recent religious past. The Goddess is now awakening for both men and women as we enter the New Millennium. The Goddess in Wicca is seen as *Gaia*, the Earth itself, and is immanent or in-dwelling in creation. The Goddess also pre-exists her creates and transcends it. As the Tantric scriptures say:

> She lives in the bodies of all living creatures wherein She is present in the form of energy, even in such lifeless things as rocks and stones. There is no place where the Mother is not.[1]

The Goddess is known by many names and can be seen as having many aspects, but essentially she is *One*, the eternal feminine, the Divine *She*. Many covens honour the Goddess under her Celtic names of Cerridwen or Bride, but the most frequently used name is Aradia. In Northern Europe, some Witches use the ancient Vanir Goddess name of Freya. In Finland, Witches honour the beautiful forest Goddess Mielikki, the *Foster-Mother of the Bear* who intoxicates and delights the senses. These many names for the Goddess do not imply that Witches are worshipping many Goddesses. A Wiccan priest will say in the rite:

> Listen to the words of the Great Mother,
> who was of old also called amongst men:
> Artemis, Astarte, Dione, Melusine,
> Aphrodite, Cerridwen, Diana, Arianrhod, Bride,
> and by many other names.

The various names are seen as different aspects of the Great Mother Goddess who is universal and present in all cultures and at all times.

In Wicca, the Goddess is commonly seen as having three major aspects. These are called the Virgin, Mother and Hag or Wise One. The *Virgin Mother* aspect of the Goddess is associated with the waxing Moon and the Virgin Mary in Catholicism was often depicted as standing on the Moon with seven stars above her head. The second aspect is the *Lover-Mother*, the sexual Mother. The third is the *Dark Mother*, the *Hag* or Wise One, who appears in some older Christian churches in the guise of the Black Virgin. The Goddess must contain all three aspects – Virgin, Lover-Mother and Hag – if she is to provide the model of psychological wholeness that must be the goal of woman and man.

Aradia is the principal name by which the Goddess is known in Wicca today. She has many of the attributes of the Egyptian Goddess Isis whose worship had flourished around the Mediterranean and beyond immediately before the Christian era. The Goddess Aradia of the Italian Witches was seen as loving humanity and a saviour figure of the peasants who would protect them against oppression. She was a teacher of the magical arts and, like Isis, she was the product of an incestuous brother/sister marriage. Aradia's lineage made her the daughter of Diana the Goddess of the Moon by an incestuous relationship with Diana's brother Apollo, the God of the Sun. Other aspects of Isis are similar to the Wiccan Goddess. Isis was the great initiator. In an inscription found in the Greek islands, her words were:

I have revealed to mankind mystic initiations,
I have established the Gods' temple.[2]

She was also the *Queen of all Witcheries*, for Isis was the great
sorceress. She was also the great healer, who in many of her
temples was partnered by Asclepius, the Greek God of healing.

The Virgin Mother

In Wicca, the word *Virgin* means something very different from
common usage. This is not Virgin in the sense of non-sexual,
but Virgin in the sense of a woman not owned by or needing
man. This is the aspect of the Goddess which emerged before
human beings were aware of the relationship between motherhood and sexuality. It is the stage where woman alone is the
creatrix and the role of the man is unimportant. The God is her
son-lover but he does not impregnate her and he is dispensable.

Wiccan ritual makes much use of *charges*. These are pieces
of ritual poetry or prose whereby the priest or priestess speaks
as the God or Goddess. Charges in Wicca frequently have two
slightly different messages, one for a woman and one for a man.
Here is a charge that speaks to a woman to say what she can
become, not for the sake of a man, but in order to find her Self.
For the man it is a message from the Anima, his inner feminine,
his Muse. It speaks of the strength and creativity which access-
ing his feminine will bring to him.

The Creation Charge
high born, full-blooded and lusting free am I;
the wind is my voice and my song.
high and low,
breeze and whirlwind,
soft and sweet,
loud and shrill,
wild is my will,
and impetuous my desire.

I take whom I will;
no man can refuse my love and live.

And he to whom I have revealed myself,
is the blessèd of men.
He has won the favour of the High Gods,
and who shall refuse the behest of the Gods;
for you are but leaves,
blown upon the wind.

I am thy Goddess;
before the beginning of time was I.
I made the mountains into peaks,
and laid with soft grass the valley and the meadows,
Mine was the first foot which trod upon the Earth,
and where I walked there sprung forth flowers,
and mine was the voice that gave rise to the first song,
and the birds listened and heard and made return.
In the dawn of the world I taught the sea its song,
and mine were the tears that made the first rains.

Listen and hear me;
for none can escape me.
It was I who gave birth to you,
and in the depths of my earth,
You will find rest and rebirth,
and I will spring you forth anew,
a fresh shoot to greenness.

Fear me,
love me,
adore me,
lose yourself in me.
I am the wine of life,
I stir the senses,
I put song in the heart and on the lips of men;
before the battle I give my strength,
I am the Power.[3]

In the *Creation Charge*, the Goddess speaks as the creatrix of
the Earth, as the inspirer, as birth and death, the beginning and
the end, the first and last of the Gods of this world. For a
woman, the charge says: *You are the creatrix; you have need of*

no other. For a man it says: *I am the creatrix; you have need of me.* Society teaches woman dependence and man independence. To know wholeness, we must each learn its opposite.

For a man, the Goddess is the Anima, that all-powerful, frightening and beautiful figure who beckons him from the portals of his unconscious to make the heroic journey into the psyche to find the Grail, the Divine essence of himself. In our Spring Equinox festival the priest invokes *Diana Huntress of the Woods* as:

Lady of the word of power, who makes the shadows flee.

This aspect of the Goddess is frequently called *Isis Urania.* She is transcendent, pre-existing both material creation and time itself. She is the inspirer of man, but he is nothing to her. He is but *a leaf blown upon the wind.* She is the unattainable and man's only role is to worship, revere and to receive whatever gifts she chooses to bestow. Jung believed that the Urania type of mother-image predominates in masculine psychology:

... the man identifies with the son-lover on whom the grace of Sophia has descended, with a *puer aeternus* or a *filius sapientiae.*[4]

It is true that many men cleave more to the Queen of Heaven that to the Queen of Earth. We tend first to love what is most beautiful and on the surface this is always the young woman in the flower of her womanhood. She is the young woman who is not possessed by man, but who lures him to pursue her, to hunt her down, to make her his. At the Spring Equinox the Goddess charges:

Spring Goddess Charge
Hear then the words of Diana the Moon,
the Bright Virgin.
Changing but unchanging,
my mystery is unanswerable,
but solve ye that mystery.
My nature is unknowable,
but strive to understand me.

141

> Darkness and light are met within me.
> I flee from thee, but lure thee on;
> I seek for thee, but hide my face;
> I speak to thee, but my words are silent.

For some men, the lure of the chase and the brief moment of conquest are the end. Having captured the star, having brought the Queen of Heaven down to Earth, the man no longer wants her. Face to face she looks too ordinary. It is the unattainable that he desires. The *puer aeternus* or *eternal youth* is a Peter Pan who has decided never to grow up and never to face the consequences of his own sexuality. This is the *Don Juan syndrome* where a man cannot mate with a real woman; for as soon as he possesses her he despises her. It is the promise of the Goddess he seeks and not its fulfilment. If a man is to find his own Divinity, he must cease to be the son and become the husband and father, not *Peter Pan*, but Pan the Phallic Lord; for it is through mating with the Goddess that a man becomes a God and a King.

The Lover-Mother

The second aspect of the Goddess is the Lover-Mother. She is the full Moon, Paradise, the cup, the Grail, the Motherland, Earth, the pool of still water, matter, the ploughed land, the cornucopia, the rose, the lotus, the magic circle, the cauldron. This is the woman who has known sexuality and carries a man's seed within her womb. Here the Goddess has descended to Earth. At this stage the concept of the *hieros gamos*, the Sacred Marriage, develops. Now the man's role is important; for it is he who fertilizes the woman and the land and without him both are barren.

The transition to the second aspect of the Triple Goddess is symbolized by the appearance of the Goddess' daughter. Demeter begets Kore who is also known as Persephone. Demeter's origins lie in the Great Mother Goddess who creates alone, but Kore is different. She too bears a child, but the child has a father; for Kore is wedded to Hades the Dark Lord of the Underworld.

In Wicca, the Kore figure is Aradia, the Goddess of the Earth, the daughter of the brother/sister marriage of the Moon and the Sun. These are her words.

The Aradia Charge

I am Aradia,
daughter of the sea
and daughter of the wind;
daughter of the Sun,
and daughter of the Moon;
daughter of dawn,
and daughter of sunset;
daughter of night,
and daughter of the mountains.

And I have sung the song of the sea.
and I have listened to the sighing of the wind;
I have heard the hidden secrets of the Sun,
and I have drunk of the tears of the Moon;
I have seen the beauty of the dawn,
and the sorrow of the sunset;
I have lain 'neath the darkest dark of the night,
and I have beheld the might of the mountains.

For I am stronger than the sea,
and freer than the wind;
I am brighter than Sun,
and more changing than the Moon;
I am the hope of the dawn,
and the peace of the sunset;
I am more mysterious than night,
and older than the mountains,
older than time itself.
For I am she who was,
who is,
and who will be;
for I am Aradia.[5]

Aradia begins as *the daughter*. She is immanent in creation, the product of the forces of nature, but she goes forth to seek experience of the world. She learns the song of the eternal sea, the life force. She knows pain, the *sighing of the wind*, and the *sorrow of the sunset*. She knows the darkness of fear and despair, the *darkest dark of the night*. Then finally she comes to the mountains; the high place of the Self that transcends the world of matter.

In the *Aradia Charge*, we have an image of the Goddess who has glimpsed a Self that is outside time and matter and endures forever; but she is not yet that Self. She has experienced what Carl Jung called a *partial rebirth*. Her Ego has been strengthened and renewed. She is in full realization of its power, with the strength which comes from the certainty that she has an eternal core that will never die. However, Aradia still defines herself by the qualities of others, compared with whom she is *stronger, deeper, wider, more mysterious, older*. She still measures herself against outside criteria, the criteria imposed by others.

Like Aradia, Kore suffers pain and anguish. She is stolen away from the world she knows and loves by the forces of darkness. In experiencing these things, however, she learns the secrets of life and death and finally she eats willingly of the pomegranate, the seed of Hades. As this sexual symbolism tells us, now she knows sexuality. She is no longer the unattainable Virgin, but woman as she truly is, a Queen in touch with her own physical nature and sexual desire.

Daughter figures such as Kore are figures of the threshold, figures of transition. First they are the Virgin aspect of the Goddess and then the Lover, but they are not wholly either. To find a true Lover-Mother image of the Goddess, we can turn to the Celts and the story of Maeve Queen of Connaught.[6] Maeve has entered English literature in Shakespeare's *Midsummer Night's Dream* as Mab, Queen of Fairies. However, her origins are in pre-Christian Celtic Ireland. As Queen of one of its ancient kingdoms, she led her troops into battle and boasted that she could best thirty men a day – in the battlefield or in her bed. This is the true image of womanhood that is hidden behind the veil of the Virgin, the image of the Queen. This is not the Goddess who flees a man, but the Goddess who summons him to her bed to serve and impregnate her.

This Goddess seeks not a distant adorer, a son-lover, a puer aeternus, content to worship forever at her feet. What the Goddess seeks is a whole man, who has comes to terms with the demands of the outer world. Wicca is not a flight from reality, but a grounding in earth. This is both the earth of the material world and the earthy realities of mature sexuality. What kind of man dares to want a woman whose sexuality may be stronger than his? According to Maeve this man must be neither selfish, timid, nor jealous. He must be as generous and brave as she. This is the woman who has sexual expectations, not the Heavenly Virgin who is content with only adoration. This is the Goddess before whom a man might fail. This is not the Isis Urania Goddess of the son-lover. She is not for princes, but the mate of kings.

Jung writes that the mate of the Earth Mother is the phallic God – *the god of revelation*[7] – whom in Wicca is worshipped as Cernunnos. Small wonder that many men flee; for who can face the huntress and who dares to take the part of the God of Revelation? But the purpose of the fleeing hind is to lead the hunter hero to a clearing in the forest, a place of realization in the tangled world of the unconscious mind. Here, beneath the light of the full Moon, he is confronted by the naked beauty of the full Moon Goddess. This is Isis Urania come down to Earth and seeking his seed within her, so that she may transform herself from the unobtainable Virgin to the Mother of all living, Queen of Earth now as well as of Heaven.

The Lover-Mother gives the Goddess duality, daughter and mother, Demeter and Kore. Jung writes that:

> Demeter and Kore, mother and daughter, extend the feminine consciousness both upwards and downwards. They add an *older* and *younger*, *stronger* and *weaker* dimension to it and widen out the narrowly limited conscious mind bound in space and time, giving it intimations of a greater and more comprehensive personality which has a share in the eternal course of things.[8]

Demeter and Kore can give us only an *intimation*, a hint of what is to come. For a woman, the Goddess is a symbol of the wholeness that lies beyond the confines of the Ego. The Goddess is ultimately the Self; that to which she aspires and that which essentially she is. However, in order to find the Self, we must first have a strong Ego. It is this aspect of the Goddess which is represented by the Lover-Mother. Demaris Wehr, Professor of the Psychology of Religion at Boston University, in her book *Jung and Feminism*,[9] writes that many women today have had their Egos undermined by the low value which society places on the feminine. Vesting the Divine power solely in a masculine God reinforces internalized oppression of women. Demaris Wehr believes that sexism is particularly damaging to women.

> It is particularly wounding to women because women are the ones who stand outside the definition of the fully human ... Because this is ... reinforced constantly ... in religion, in psychology, in popular culture – women find many difficulties in claiming adult status, responsibility, authority.[10]

Sexism prevents both men and women becoming who and what they really are because some behaviours are outside the scope of what society accepts as masculine or feminine.

To feel secure enough to let go of its grip, the Ego must first experience a sense of power and control. In Wicca, women learn to value the feminine and, where necessary, to grow and nurture the Ego which has not been taught to value itself. One of the most important things which Wicca teaches a woman is a sense of control over her own destiny which she may not have learned in the outer world. In the magic circle, sacred space is cast anew for each rite. It is woman who has ultimate power. In taking on the role of priestess, a woman demonstrates for herself her own inner power and for other women provides a much needed role of strong womanhood to which they can aspire. When she has experienced this sense of power, a woman's Ego can become strong and from this position of strength she can move forward.

The image of women offered by Wicca is one of wholeness and strength. The priestess is seen as possessing qualities that have traditionally been monopolized by men: *Word, Power, Meaning and Deed*.[11] By absorbing these qualities and by developing self-confidence and a sense of identity of what it is to be a woman, women are better able to integrate into society. They are also better able to form relationships with men and to understand the role a woman can play in assisting a man to become a man.

When she has experienced this sense of power, a woman's Ego can become strong and from this position of strength she can move forward. Myths often talk of the hero's journey, the heroic quest. This quest is found in many of the myths and symbols of Pagan mythology and it is women and not just men who make it. Demaris Wehr points out that:

> Symbols have both psychological and political effects, because they create the inner conditions ... that lead people to feel comfortable with or to accept social and political arrangements that correspond to the symbol system.[12]

In Wicca, women learn to reject beliefs and philosophies that oppress women and to seek roles through which they can function as whole human beings realizing all and not just part of their inner qualities. A woman enters the circle, the world of the unconscious, the underworld, as a Virgin and emerges a Queen. Kore or Persephone represents the Ego of woman. She descends to the Underworld as a cipher – Demeter's dark-eyed daughter, Hades' doe-eyed bride – but there she finds her destiny. She is no longer the Virgin princess but Queen of the Underworld, wielder of the sceptre of power.

In the dual Goddess, Kore and Demeter, one part of the Goddess is still hidden. The Moon has reached fullness, but is not yet waning. The missing element is hinted at in the qualities of the Mother and Daughter. In Greek temples, the sacrifices to Demeter were not made on the altars which stood open to the Sun. They were poured into holes that went deep beneath the Earth and it is in the Underworld that Kore finds her destiny. The Underworld is the realm of the third aspect of the Goddess. To find the Self we must encounter the Dark Mother. It is the Grandmother, the Hag, who holds the answer to the *greater and more comprehensive personality.*

The Dark Mother

For a man, mating with the Lover-Mother represents a transition to manhood. Here a man finds his own sexuality. He ceases to be Herne the Hunter, Lord of the Greenwood, and becomes the Phallic Lord, the second aspect of the God that arose in the human psyche. He becomes a Sun King and father and leaves behind forever the role of prince and son. Jung writes that the hero often fears this transformation and this is so, for he does not know what the consequences will be. In our Midsummer rite, the Goddess calls the God to:

> leave the greenwood of your youth
> and bear the burdens of a King and Man.

But the God does not wish to sacrifice his youthful freedom:

> I married thee, my Love,
> and not thy land.
> I roam the woodland wild,
> the deer my companions and the birds my friends.
> The greenwood is my home and not the seat of kings.

There is also another reason why the Ego recoils from the burdens of kingship:

> I fear to take this kingship;
> for before me I see,
> darkness and pain
> and blood upon the corn.
> The shadow of my death.

At Beltane, the God has married the Goddess, but he has not forsaken his woodland home for her circular clearing, the world of the tribe and the village, the world of responsibilities. He fears to enter the circle, for within it the Goddess herself may change and it is this transforming aspect of the feminine which men often fear. Many of the images of the Goddess are really images of transition. Many transformations are positive. The lotus in its Virgin white purity can become a symbol of sexuality. The Virgin hind may give herself to the hunter. The fearsome Hag may transform herself into a beautiful maiden.

Other transformations are less pleasing; for always lurking behind the Lover-Mother is that third aspect of the Goddess which is feared by man. 'Sacrifice yourself for me,' says the Goddess, but it is she who is the sacrificer. This is the Hag, the wielder of the sickle, the destroyer. The hare of the full Moon Mother is a shape changer who beneath its rays may lead the hunter to the swamp or to the cliff edge and so to his doom. The bow and arrow of the Virgin may be turned against the seeker and take his life. Lured to the magic circle by the full Moon Mother, she may curse those who enter by turning them into swine. The Goddess does not deceive him. His contra-sexual self, his Anima, knows that she leads him to his death; but only through death can life be renewed; only through death comes rebirth.

> Dark in truth is the fate of kings,
> for when the harvest comes,
> he who is wed to the people
> must die for the people,
> that power may be renewed within the land.
> But the fear of the shadow is greater than itself,
> for from the ashes of the fire,
> the phoenix is reborn,
> and out of death comes forth new life,
> though in another form.
> Out of love for myself and our child,
> will you share this, the fate of kings,
> and embrace this destiny for us all?

The Goddess asks him to *embrace this destiny for us all*. The Anima asks for the hero's Ego death, for only through this sacrifice of the image of ourselves as we think we are can we find the Self we truly are.

For a woman, Hecate is the Wise Old Woman who guides her to herself. This is a role that in older societies would have been played by a real Old Woman, a wise woman, a grandmother, a Witch. In Wicca, women are given the titles of *priestess, Witch* and *queen*. Kore is the priestess who journeys to the underworld. There she is crowned queen, the equal of her mother Demeter. As Mistress of the Underworld, she is Hecate the Witch and the secrets of life and death are hers. In Wicca, we must value the Witch, that person most abused; for it is she who will show us the way to our destiny. Her Witchcraft is neither black nor white, for what she reveals is beyond morality. It is the knowledge of good and evil, the knowledge of the life itself.

Hecate is the most difficult aspect of the Goddess for both men and women to understand. It is easy to love what is beautiful like the Virgin Kore. It is easy to love what is powerful and strong like Maeve the Queen. It is not so easy to love what is old and weak, a woman no longer fertile, who has given over her worldly dominance to others. Hecate teaches us an important lesson: that the feminine should be valued for itself. This is not because it brings sexuality or power, but because deep within the feminine there is an eternal wisdom; for Hecate is also the High Priestess, the keeper of the Mysteries.

Hecate is not the priestess whose quest is inner knowledge, but the High Priestess who has found it and imparts it to others. For a man, the Virgin aspect of the Goddess is an initiatory priestess who brings him across the threshold of the psyche into the world of the unconscious. However, it is Hecate who sits enthroned before the Veil of the Temple as the High Priestess, the card in the tarot which is ruled by the Moon. To reach daylight on the other side of the veil, we must all become at one with the Dark Mother of night.

Mother of Mystery Charge

I am the Mother of Mystery;
all places, all times, all seasons are alike to me.
You have sought me in the wind amongst the trees,
in the flowers amongst the grass,
in the streams amongst the hills,
in the waves upon the ocean.

Like unto the sea am I,
gentle and calm,
fierce like thunder;
changing am I but unchanging.
You sought me in a whisper in the shadows,

and I was there.
You sought me on the mountain top,
and I was there.
All the peoples of the ages,
they have sought me,
they have found me,
and ever changing was my face.
In the silence of the night they call me,
and I take them to my embrace.[15]

The embrace of the Dark Mother is death. Sometimes the death of the Ego is violent and we succumb struggling. Sometimes the old life slips away quietly one night, taken by the embrace of the Dark Mother. We find that we have entered a new kingdom of untold expansion of consciousness, never more to return.

The Triple Mother

Wicca honours the Goddess as Mother, but also the Goddess as Wise Woman and Woman of Power. Women are enjoined not to be passive vessels at the disposal of men, but women in control of their own destiny. For both woman and man, the ultimate image of the Goddess is the Triple Mother whose aspects are reconciled in One. She is the Moon who is ever-changing, but ever the same.

Autumn Goddess Charge

I am the waning moon,
the Goddess who is fading from the land.
In the Springtime I sought my Lord,
and I mated with him beneath the trees and stars.
At Beltane I wed my Lord,
beneath the first blossoms of the hawthorn tree.
And in the Summertime I ripened the apples in the orchards,
and the fruit grew round and strong,
like the seed within my womb.
At the corn harvest I cut down my Lord,
that by his death our people might be fed.
And now in the Autumntime,

I descend beneath the earth,
to dwell with my Lord in his dark kingdom,
until our child is born.
At the Winter Solstice I will bring forth the child
and renew your hope,
and at Imbolc I myself will return,
to renew the land.
I leave you, but I return to you.
When you see my power fade,
and the leaves fall from the trees;
when snow obliterates like death,
all trace of me upon the Earth,
then look for me in the Moon,
and there in the heavens you will see the soul of me,
soaring still amongst the stars.
And in that darkest time,
when the Moon is covered by shadow,
and there is no trace of me in Heaven or on Earth;
when you look outward
and your lives seem cold and dark and barren;
let not despair eat at your hearts.
For when I am hidden,
I am but renewing;
when I am waning,
I am making ready for return.
Remember my promise and look within you,
and there you will find the spirit of me,
awaiting those who seek;
for by the well-spring of your being,
I await you always.
I am Diana in Heaven,
and on Earth, Persephone,
and within you that dark Hecate.
Triple am I,
the One in Three;
my body the Earth,
my soul the Moon,
and within thy innermost self,
the eternal spirit of me.[14]

Here the Goddess is Earth, Moon and Spirit. In the Triple Goddess, a woman finds the reflection of her true Self and a man the true image of his inner feminine. The Goddess is then complete. She is no longer *Isis Urania*, the unattainable Moon, or Queen Maeve who dominates, or Cybele the Great Earth Mother who devours, but all these and more. She is Isis the Triple-Mother who is seen first in the outer world. Only finally, when that has been stripped from us, do we find her in her true home, the inner world of a man's soul and a woman's spirit.

Notes

1. Quoted in Arthur Avalon (Sir John Woodroffe), *Shakti and Shakta*, p732, Dover, New York, 1978 ed (originally published 1918).
2. W. Peek, *Isishymnus von Andros und verwandete Texte, Cyme*, 22-4, *Ios*, 19-21, Berlin, 1930.
3. Vivianne Crowley, Beltane, 1982.
4. Carl Jung, *Archetypes and the Collective Unconscious*, p106, para 193.
5. Vivianne Crowley, 1968.
6. Merlin Stone, *Ancient Mirrors of Womanhood*, pp67–9.
7. Carl Jung, *Archetypes and the Collective Unconscious*, p106, para 193.
8. Carl Jung, *Archetypes and the Collective Unconscious*, p188, para 316.
9. Demaris Wehr, *Jung and Feminism: Liberating Archetypes*, pp101–3, Routledge Kegan Paul, 1988.
10. Demaris Wehr, *Jung and Feminism: Liberating Archetypes*, p15, Routledge Kegan Paul, 1988.
11. Emma Jung, *Animus and Anima: Two Essays*, p20, Spring Publications, Zurich, 1957.
12. Demaris Wehr, *Jung and Feminism: Liberating Archetypes*, p22.
13. Vivianne Crowley, 1982.
14. Vivianne Crowley, Autumn, 1984.

9

The God: Wicca and the Masculine

In caverns deep the Old Gods sleep;
but the trees still know their Lord,
and its the Pipes of Pan which call the tune,
in the twilight in the wood.
The leaves they dance to the Goat God's tune,
and they whisper his name to the winds,
and the oak tree dreams of a God with horns,
and knows no other king.[1]

Wicca is often thought of as Goddess religion and the popular image of a Witch is female, but this is only part of the truth. Wicca honours not only the Goddess but also the God and in Europe, until recently, men considerably outnumbered women in Wicca. In Wicca, the God is worshipped in many forms, but his principal form is that worshipped by our earliest ancestors – the Horned God. The first known representations of the God were made 12,000 years ago in Palaeolithic cave paintings in Spain and France. These show a horned hunting God who is part animal and part man. The species of animal varied. In La Pasiega at Santander in Spain, there is a bison-headed man playing a musical instrument; in the Caverne des Trois Frères at Ariège in France, a man in antlers and deer-skin; and at Forneau du Diable in the Dordogne in France a goat-horned figure.

Although newer Gods emerged, the Horned God remained a dominant force and he was still present at the dawn of the Christian era in the form of Pan and other Horned Gods. His continued existence 10,000 years after the first cave paintings appear is a reflection of the power of this archetype in the human psyche. Horns were seen as a sign of Divinity and in Babylon, the more horns the Deity wore, the greater his or her importance. The Goddess Ishtar had seven. When Alexander the Great took the throne of Egypt and declared himself a God, he had himself painted wearing the horns of the Ram-God Amoun. In the *Koran*, Alexander is called *Iskander Dh'l Karnain*, *Alexander the two-horned*, and this name is preserved in Alexandrian Wicca where the God is called *Karnayna*.

In Gardnerian Wicca, the name of the God is Cernunnos, the Gallo-Roman version of the Horned God whose altar was discovered under the site of Notre Dame cathedral in Paris. The name Herne is also used. This and variations of the name appear in many place names in Britain, including Cerne Abbas in Dorset in southern England, which is the home of the phallic hill figure known as the Cerne Abbas Giant.

Cernunnos and Herne are both Celtic in origin, but the God of Wicca has also absorbed some of the characteristics of the God Odin or Wotan of our Norse and German ancestors. At Samhain, the Festival of the Dead, the God is invoked as *Hornèd Leader of the Hosts of Air*. This is a reference to Odin as Leader of the Wild Hunt. This synthesis was natural in the British Isles where successive waves of invaders brought with them similar and overlapping deities.

With the advent of Christianity, many Pagan deities were absorbed into Christianity, but the Horned God was largely suppressed. He was threatening – sexual and animalistic. Christianity was a religion of the day, not the night; of temple not of forest. It was seeking to consolidate the dominance of rational Apollonian consciousness in the face of the unconscious Dionysian desire to return to the ways of the wild and to shed the burden and the loneliness of individuality by returning to the oneness of the group mind. Christianity equated sexuality with darkness and evil, and equated the Horned God, the leader of the Dionysian rout, the Lord of the Dance, with the Devil. Nevertheless, the image of the Horned God has endured in human history through centuries of repression and calumny.

The Horned God survived in many ways. In folklore, he became Robin Goodfellow and Puck, mischievous spirits who could be helpful to humans if propitiated, but who would play spiteful tricks if not. Puck appears as a main character in Shakespeare's play set on a sabbat, *A Midsummer Night's Dream*. Robin Goodfellow is associated with that other figure of folklore, Robin Hood, who like the Goddess Aradia was a saviour and champion of the people against the oppression of the nobility. In Northern Europe, the God's image also endured. As the Green Man he still appears in folklore celebrations and in Britain his image often hangs above the door of those temples of Dionysus so beloved by Pagans – pubs!

The God was sleeping, but in the collective unconscious of humanity, within us in the storehouse of memory and myth, he lived. The God of Wicca is no distant, abstract, cerebral God who lives in some cloud in the sky. He is the God of the ever-renewing, ever-growing force of life itself. The God is energy and change, truth and paradox, hunter and warrior, father and carer, servant of the Goddess and King of the land. His body is that of a man, but his feet are hooves and his antlers or horns reach up to heaven, capturing within them the power of the Sun and the stars. He is strong and powerful; but we need not fear him.

The year's round

The God is perceived as primarily dual – a God of summer and a God of winter. At some stages he is *Pan-like*, both in the sense of being mischievous and Puck-like, but also in the sense of creating *Pan-ic*. With his summer aspect, we find him honoured as the Green Man, the Sun King and the Corn King. In his winter aspect, the God is honoured as the Hunter, the Shepherd, the Healer and the Lord of the Underworld. He is also honoured at Winter Solstice as the Child of Promise, the reborn Sun. He is the Lord of Light as well as the Lord of Death. How can all these aspects be reconciled and how can they form part of, and fit in with, the feminine symbol of the circle?

The circle is a symbol of wholeness. With its cyclical nature, the image of the womb, the never-ending, eternal rhythm, it is quite difficult to see how the male principle, which is represented by a straight line or an arrow, can be fitted into this with any degree of harmony. In myth, it is the female who is never ending, while the male is renewed through the birth of a new generation, the creation of the *Child of Promise*. The God passes this way but once and must leave it to the next generation to build on what he has achieved; embodying Nature, the Goddess however is restored and renewed and is eternal.

The symbol of the circle works simultaneously on many different levels. Apart from being the feminine principle, the directions of North, East, South and West and the Elements associated with these (Earth, Air, Fire and Water respectively) can all be placed around the circle; as can the psychological functions of Sensation, Thinking, Intuition and Feeling, which superimpose on the circle the pattern of the balanced personality. Journeying within the circle therefore becomes a journey towards *individuation* – the term which Carl Jung used to describe the process of becoming who and what we really are.

The year journey of the God

We have talked about the Goddess in terms of the lunar cycle. Here we will talk about the God in terms of the solar cycle. This is not to say that the Goddess does not partake of the solar cycle or the God of the lunar, but we have used these as starting points. In addition to its other symbolism, the circle can be seen as a symbol of the annual solar cycle of the sabbats. The four solar sabbats of the Spring Equinox, Midsummer, Autumn Equinox and Yule are placed at the cardinal points of East, South, West and North. The four Celtic festivals are placed between them, with Imbolc or Candlemas being placed at the north-east; Beltane or May Eve at the south-east; Lughnasadh or Lammas Eve at the south-west; and Samhain or Hallowe'en at the north-west.

157

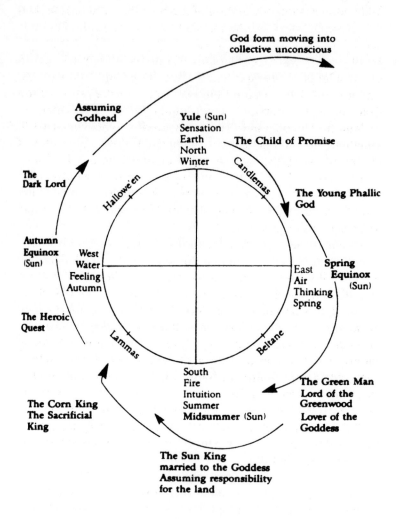

God form moving into collective unconscious

Assuming Godhead

Yule (Sun)
Sensation
Earth
North
Winter

The Child of Promise

The
Dark Lord

Hallowe'en

Candlemas

The Young Phallic God

Autumn
Equinox
(Sun)

West
Water
Feeling
Autumn

East
Air
Thinking
Spring

Spring
Equinox
(Sun)

The Heroic
Quest

Lammas

Beltane

South
Fire
Intuition
Summer
Midsummer (Sun)

The Green Man
Lord of the
Greenwood
Lover of the
Goddess

The Corn King
The Sacrificial
King

The Sun King
married to the Goddess
Assuming responsibility
for the land

The sabbats are a journey. The Spring Equinox celebrates the mating of the Goddess and the God. Beltane celebrates the coming of Summer and the marriage of the Goddess and God. Midsummer is the celebration of the Sun, the Lord of Life, and the coming of the God into his maturity and kingship. Lammas celebrates the harvest, the sacrifice of the God, which is necessary to fertilize the land, and his death which liberates him to the challenge of conquering a new kingdom – that of the Underworld. The Autumn Equinox celebrates the return of the God from the Underworld as a conquering hero who comes to reclaim his Queen and to take her with him to his Underworld kingdom. Samhain is the feast of the dead, when the worlds of matter and spirit draw close to one another and the dead may pass to and fro through the veils. Yule celebrates the birth of the young Sun God and at Imbolc the God releases the Goddess from the Underworld so that she may re-emerge into the world as Virgin once more.

Annual cycle or lifetime round? It operates on both levels. The developing God, although linking in with the Goddess on the annual fertility cycle, is also progressing around the circle on a lifetime quest. Jung calls myth that which is not objectively true, but is psychologically true: *the bridge to all that is best in humanity*.[2] It is this inner reality that our ancestors portrayed in ritual. The method of portrayal was to use allegories found in Nature; for it was in part through observation of the cycle of birth, death and rebirth in Nature that human beings understood that this too was their own fate – to be born, to die and to live again. The experience conveyed by the cycle of the seasonal rituals is that of transcendence – a sense of the enduring Self which though part of the Wheel of Life and Death is yet beyond it. Jung writes that:

> The initiate ... takes part in a sacred rite which reveals to him the perpetual continuation of life through transformation and renewal. In these mystery-dramas the transcendence of life ... is usually represented by the fateful transformations – death and rebirth – of a god or a godlike hero. ... The initiate who ritually enacts the slaying, dismemberment, and scattering of Osiris, and afterwards his resurrection in the green wheat, experiences in this way

159

the permanence and continuity of life, which outlasts all
changes of form and, phoenix-like, continually rises anew
from its own ashes.[5]

Through participating in the seasonal rituals, we come to terms
with the processes of ageing and death. We understand that
they are but part of the life process that is eternal. The sabbat
round is a wheel which can be entered at any of its spokes. Here
we will start at the Spring Equinox where the God is at his most
Pan-ish. At Spring, he is the Lord of the Greenwood and lusting
free; probably rutting everything that moves! He is a symbol of
youth, a symbol of instinct in tune with Nature. At this stage of
his development, he is in tune with animals and is himself at his
most animalistic. The image of Pan, with horns but human
trunk and goat legs, captures this. He is free, careless of
responsibility, the adolescent coming into maturity, roaming
the forests and heathlands.

At the Spring Equinox, *the light equals the darkness.* This can
be taken both as a representation of the Goddess meeting the
God, and as an emblem of the God's evolution. He is at the
equipoise between unconscious animalism and growing conscious awareness. It is at this festival that he impregnates the
Goddess; but although coupling with her, he does not stay with
her. He continues roaming the greenwood as the Horned
Hunter.

The next festival is Beltane. It is during this ritual that the
God recognizes his responsibilities to the now pregnant
Goddess and the ritual is predominantly a celebration of their
marriage. Although the God remains very much Lord of the
Greenwood, he has begun to evolve from his Pan state, the
purely instinctual, into forming a specific relationship with the
ability to love an individual.

The God has begun the evolutionary climb from the sacral
chakra – the realm of unbridled sexuality – to the solar plexus
chakra which is the realm of personal emotions and love. He
has evolved from a predominantly instinctual unconscious state
to a human state where he can form a loving relationship.
Although he is still very much Lord of the Greenwood, he
begins to take on a much more Shepherd God role. He has
begun to feel for others. He has passed from the realm of the

son to the realm of the lover. He has assumed the role of ithyphallic Hermes, the impregnator of the Goddess.

At Midsummer, a great change comes over the God in terms of the role he is required to undertake. At Beltane, he marries but remains relatively free. At Midsummer, he has to accept the consequences of his actions and take on the responsibilities which the marriage has occasioned. The Goddess is now pregnant, a mother as well as a queen, and has need of the support and love of the God. The Goddess asks him to help her care for the land which is, of course, an aspect of the Goddess he has married.

> Beneath the blossoms of Beltane,
> you came forth from the woods to claim me,
> and to own your child;
> and you pledged yourself to me in life and death.
> Now the power within me which nourishes the land,
> Turns inward to protect and grow our son,
> and I can no longer rule alone.
> Though it was for myself that I loved thee first,
> my people too have need of thee ...
> Will you help me now to rule my people,
> and share with me my kingdom's crown;
> will you leave the greenwood of your youth,
> and bear the burdens of a King and Man?

At this point, the God can no longer roam free. In taking responsibility for the land, he accepts responsibility for the people within that land. It is not from a desire to gain power, but from love of the Goddess.

> I did not think when first we met,
> to what end it would lead;
> but if this is thy will,
> then so mote it be.
> I will take thy people as my people,
> and lay down my greenwood freedom,
> to wear a kingly crown.
> And I will be bound to thy people,
> their servant and their king.

The God thus evolves from the ability to form a single relationship with a woman to a wider compassion. He has become the strength on which other people depend. He has moved from being Lord of the Greenwood to a Sun King. In becoming the Sun, the God has become energy or fire. The making of fire has always been a sacred act surrounded by taboos and fire itself was considered to belong originally to the Gods, not to men. The Gods were also less than keen to part with it. In the Greek legend, fire had to be stolen from heaven by Prometheus and he suffered badly for his temerity; for the fire which Prometheus stole was not physical fire but spiritual fire, the fire of consciousness which makes us human and not animal and awakens in us the Godhead.

Prometheus suffered terrible torments for his transgression in gaining consciousness. He was doomed to be forever chained to a rock and his liver torn by eagles. By awakening into consciousness he saw for the first time the fullness of the human condition. We have consciousness, the powers of the Gods. Through consciousness we experience joy but also anguish. To be conscious is to see and as those who have had their sight restored after being blind from birth have testified: all that we see is not beautiful. At Midsummer, when the Goddess asks the God to forsake the woods, she is asking him to forsake the Dionysian aspect of himself which is half animal and half man and to become wholly human, a king. She is asking him to become conscious and to leave the world of the *Dionysian rout*, the animal world where there is no individuality and no separation of consciousness from Nature.

For a woman, the second aspect of the Goddess, the Lover-Mother, represents the strengthened Ego that is capable of making choices. For a man, it is the Sun King aspect of the God which plays this role. At Midsummer the God is offered kingship and consciousness, but the price is to know the anguish of his own physical mortality. No man finds this an easy path.

> Once long ago, My Love,
> when we were first young,
> beneath the budding trees of Spring,
> you gave me the cup of life to drink
> and gave me yourself in equal measure.

I promised myself to you then for ever;
that whatever you sought, I would give;
whatever you asked, I would perform.
But I married thee, My Love,
and not thy land.
I roam the woodlands wild,
the deer my companions and the birds my friends.
The greenwood is my home and not the seat of kings.
If I share thy crown I must live for thy people;
no more for myself, for you and my child.
And I fear to take this kingship;
for before me I see,
darkness and pain and blood upon the corn –
the shadow of my death.

The gaining of consciousness brings us into the realm of judgement, the moral realm, where it is possible to do both good and evil. With consciousness comes an awareness of alternative courses of action and the possibility of choice. The Sun therefore contains an inherent ambiguity; it brings life but it also brings death. It gives us the power to do good and the power to do evil.

The God responds to the moral challenge of kingship and develops compassion, wisdom, justice and the power to heal. The idea of the King's touch being the healing touch has endured until relatively recently and continues still in our unconscious. In chakra terms, the God has moved from the solar plexus, a chakra associated with personal love, to the heart, which enables him to begin experiencing the qualities of universal compassion and a wider, less selfish love.

The taking on of kingship, the stewardship of the people, begins to open up the God's thinking function. Now he will be called upon to administrate and arbitrate; to make decisions involving others; to apply wisdom and justice; and to become the figurehead, the representation of the land and also its upholder. Joseph Campbell writes in his book on the male initiatory journey, *The Hero with a Thousand Faces*:

Just as the traditional rites of passage used to teach the individual to die to the past and be reborn to the future, so the great ceremonials of investiture divested him of his private character and clothed him in the mantle of his vocation. Such was the ideal, whether the man was a craftsman or a king.[4]

This kingship is gained when the God is at his prime, only half way round the circle and at the half way stage of his life. He is at his most materially successful and at his most dominant. It would appear, both in terms of the God's progress, and in most men's, that this in itself produces a dilemma. From the vantage of this material high point, there can appear to be no further upward path. Powers at their prime can only weaken, albeit very gradually. The view from the top is to see a continual surging, waves of challenges from younger men, all committed to achieving their destiny and taking his place.

In earlier times it was imperative for a king to be at his peak in terms of both mental and physical strength. Sir James Frazer in The Golden Bough explored the concept of the seven-year king. After seven years on the throne, the king is sacrificed and his blood spilt upon the earth to revitalize and restore the land. Here the blood is seen as the carrier of the solar energy of the lifeforce. By spilling it on the ground, the sacred marriage is enacted in another fashion, the solar energy and earth force are joined as one: *The Sun has come down upon the Èarth.*

The sacrifice of the king is celebrated at the festival of Lammas. The Sun king, over the seven years of holding stewardship of the land, has developed compassion and an awareness of the greater good beyond personal interests. He accepts the inevitability of the ultimate sacrifice and is cut down by the Goddess, who now appears as Hecate the wielder of the sickle. Jung writes that:

The god-hero symbolized by the spring zodion (Aries, Taurus) ... having passed beyond the summer solstice is himself overcome as if by an unconscious longing for death. Nevertheless he is divided within himself, and his descent and approaching end therefore seem to him like evil designs of the sinister mother who secretly lays a poisonous snake in his path to undo him. The mysteries, however, hold out the consoling promise that there is no

contradiction and no disharmony when life changes into
death: The bull is the father of the dragon and the dragon
is the father of the bull.[5]

There is a message here for us all. If we can accept the penalty
of consciousness and face our own physical mortality, we
discover not death, but life. After the God has been cut down at
Lammas, he rises again; not to rejoin his old life, for that is over.
He must leave the world of men and journey to another place.
His realm is now the realm of the Gods. Consciousness takes us
on a path which makes us feel separate and alone; but if we
climb the lonely mountain and emerge above the cloud layer
that obscures our vision, we find that we are not alone. Others
have also arrived at that same place. We have then tran-
scended our separateness and entered the unitive reality where
we experience the joy of unity on a higher level, both with one
another and with the cosmos itself.

Both for the God and for us as human beings, the willing sacrifice is the most difficult. For men in modern life, the sacrifice
is not normally so dramatic as that of the Corn King; but there
is a very strong sense in a man's mid-life crisis of wanting to
give things up in order to develop further. Failure to make this
sacrifice leads, in mythological terms, not to immediate dis-
aster but to corruption.

Joseph Campbell explores this in *The Hero with a Thousand
Faces*, through the legend of King Minos of Crete. King Minos
rules a sunlit isle set in the sparkling sea, but in the labyrinth
beneath the painted palace lurks his Shadow personified by the
Minotaur, his own half-human and half-beast son, to whom the
Athenians must send a tribute of human sacrifices every seven
years. The youths and maidens of Athens who are sacrificed in
Minos' name have become a substitute for the king himself.

In the rites of Midsummer, by accepting the kingship, the
king is set apart. The mark of Godhead is upon him. His destiny
is written in the Heavens. If he accepts his fate at Lammas, he
moves on to Godhead. If he refuses, he becomes a dangerous
tyrant. The vocation of a king is to live and die for his people;
but there is always the possibility of *the sacrilege of his refusal*.
The God may choose to keep the power of kingship rather than
return it to the Goddess who gave it to him. He may choose to

reject the path ordained by the wider community and become reactive and defensive and, as his attempts become more desperate, so does he become more corrupt, more tyrannical. As Joseph Campbell explains, the king becomes the dangerous tyrant *Holdfast* – out for himself.

> The inflated Ego of the tyrant is a curse to himself and his world – no matter how his affairs may seem to prosper. Self-terrorized, fear-haunted, alert at every hand to meet and battle back the anticipated aggressions of his environment, which are primarily reflections of the uncontrollable impulses to acquisition within himself, the giant of self-achieved independence is the world's messenger of disaster, even though, in his mind, he may entertain himself with humane intentions. Wherever he sets his hand there is a cry (if not from the housetops, then – most miserably – within every heart): a cry for the redeeming hero, the carrier of the shining blade, whose blow, whose touch, whose existence, will liberate the land.

The original hero failed and turned into the tyrant. A new hero is needed to vanquish the tyrant.

In Jungian terms, the sacrifice we must make to evolve to our true destiny is the sacrifice of the Ego. It is the Ego that stands in the way of finding the Godhead within us. It is the bar to further self-discovery and the journey towards individuation. The Ego, the ruler of the conscious mind, suppresses all that it finds displeasing, distasteful and unadmirable. All this is kept both firmly and furtively locked away in the unconscious; just as King Minos of Crete locked up the expression of his guilt and failure, his half-human and half-beast son, the Minotaur, in a specially-constructed labyrinth.

In Wicca, the Corn King accepts his fate. At the Beltane rite, he placed his ring on the Goddess' finger and said:

> This is my fate and thus my will.
> I give to thee this, my ring,
> and pledge myself to thee in life and death.

The God's feelings are mixed, but he accepts what must be. He sacrifices himself for the land. By sacrificing material success and power, he descends into the Underworld – an externalization of the inner process of descent into the unconscious. Until Lammas, he had been the Lord of Light and life, developing the male side of himself in the conscious world. Now he becomes the Dark Lord, the dread Lord of Death, as he opens himself to the realm of his unconscious.

In myth, the journey that is undertaken after Lammas is portrayed as a quest which takes the hero into a darkness peopled by monsters and dragons. It is a nightmarish world of distortion. It parallels the distorting effect that the unconscious can have on our anxieties when we do not face them, but push them away out of sight. On the threshold of consciousness they lurk, growing more grotesque and more powerful as they feed on our fear.

These demons and dragons all have to be faced, fought and vanquished. This is the journey that we commence at initiation. In myth there is often a wise person to guide us, a representation of the Self, and magical weapons and charms which bring us appropriate aid. The initiatory quest is to find the Grail, the symbol of the Self. Unsurprisingly, the way is full of hardship. The hero is often at the very point of failure before finally winning through. The secrets of the unconscious are not easily won.

In the male initiatory journey, the quest is often to free a beautiful princess who is imprisoned against her will; a powerful symbol for the male's treatment of his Anima! In Wicca the festival after Lammas is the Autumn Equinox where the God returns from his quest, but only momentarily. Now his kingdom is not of the Earth but of the Underworld. At this time, some covens celebrate the Legend of Kore or Persephone and Hades. The King of the Underworld kidnaps the Goddess, who descends with him beneath the Earth to share his throne. Her mother Demeter is grief-stricken and goes in search of her daughter. Without the Goddess to care for the land, all growing plants wither, the earth grows cold and barren, and we have Winter.

Here we have an interweaving of different myths. The Kore–Persephone myth is a re-telling of an older story which helped to explain the season's change. That which was fruitful was now barren; not dead, but resting before the renewal of the Spring when the annual cycle begins again. In terms of the God's development, it is implicitly recognized that, whether the female is the object of his quest or whether she must be taken with him to enable him to achieve it, his goal cannot be achieved without the involvement of the feminine. A man has to recognize the feminine within him if he is to be whole.

As the God has need of the feminine, so too does the Goddess need the God. For a woman, entering into the right relationship with the God is important because she can then realize within herself those qualities which are associated with the God. She can absorb into herself the qualities which she has projected onto her Animus. This involves interacting with the outer world and embarking on the heroic quest. An ancient form of this heroic quest is found in the story of the ancient Egyptian Goddess Isis. Isis' husband and brother Osiris is slain by their brother Set who scatters his body across the land of Egypt. Isis must go in search of the body so that Osiris may be brought to life once more. The task of Isis is that of all women: to bring into consciousness the unrealized aspects of herself. In order to do so, Isis, like all women, has to undertake a heroic journey, a quest to find her Animus, her male self.

Samhain or Hallowe'en follows the Autumn Equinox. Now the Goddess is with the God in the Underworld. The land above grows barren, but within her womb is the seed of the God, the seed that will bring new life. Samhain is the night when the spirits of the dead roam free. The God and the Goddess are at this stage happily united in the Underworld as equals and she exhorts him as *Summer is Dead* to *Feast with Death*. This, in terms of the God's development is the point where, with the help of the Goddess, his Anima, he has been successful in exploring and winning the battles within his own unconscious, and he can move to a wider stage and begin to embrace and participate in the whole collective unconscious. The evolution he undergoes mirrors the earlier part of his life when he evolved from the love of an individual to a broader-based, compassionate love. In both cases he begins with the part and uses the experience to embrace the whole. He is now wholly Divine and has evolved beyond animal and beyond man into the realm of spirit, the realm of the transcendent Godhead.

Earlier we talked of the feminine as a circle and the masculine as a straight line, the arrow which flies but once. New hope comes from the next generation. The God will be reborn through his son. At Yule, a solar festival, the son is born. The sabbat is a celebration of the Child of Promise. At this festival, the old God must come to terms with the implications of parenthood. For each new birth brings us a little nearer to death. At Imbolc or Candlemas, the people plead for the return of the Goddess from the Underworld to renew the Earth.

> O Great Lord of Life and Death,
> our Lady is lost to us who makes all things to be,
> our hearts are in darkness,
> about our hearths no joy abounds,
> and barren is the land where once she walked.

The God releases the Goddess from the Underworld.

> Then She shall come forth,
> who is light of my darkness,
> I shall restore her to you,
> whose love is life to me,
> I hinder not her return;
> for I see that without her all must perish.

Knowing that with his failing powers he can no longer hold her, the God allows the Goddess to return to bring fertility to the Earth. For the Child or Promise, this is a key stage. He has to be separated from the mother at a certain age, which in terms of the God cycle (see diagram) is seven, in order to be initiated into the male mysteries.

Having been taught all the old God knows, then eventually they must meet as men and fight. This is the battle of the dark and the light, the old and the new. The new God has to prove himself worthy and the natural successor and heir in order to come forth from the Underworld and into the light of consciousness, the world of men. It is the re-enactment of the old bull/young bull tussle and, although the old God still has reserves of power, experience and guile that might defeat the new, it is a fight he has to lose. This is the last great sacrifice which he must make in order to be released into the transcendent realm, the collective unconscious, free forever from the Wheel of Rebirth.

Notes

1. *The Pipes of Pan*, Vivianne Crowley, 1969.
2. Carl Jung, *The Collected Works of C.G. Jung*, Vol 5: *Symbols of Transformation*, p231, para 343, Routledge and Kegan Paul, 2nd ed, 1967.
3. Carl Jung, *The Collected Works of C.G. Jung*, Vol 9, Part 1: *Archetypes and the Collective Unconscious*, p117, para 208, Routledge and Kegan Paul, 2nd ed, 1968.
4. Joseph Campbell, *The Hero with a Thousand Faces*, p115 Bollingen Series, Princeton University Press, 1972 (originally published 1949).
5. Carl Jung, *Symbols of Transformation*, p384, para 596.

10

Invoking the Gods

To our Pagan ancestors, the Divine existed both within and out-side manifest creation. It was the eternal ever-becoming life force immanent or in-dwelling in human beings and in Nature. It also pre-existed the material world and created it. The knowl-edge of the Divine within us was one of the secrets of the Mysteries and of the esoteric or inner side of most religious tra-ditions. The ancient Egyptian texts of the *Book of the Dead*[1] or, to give it a better translation, *The Book of Coming Forth by Day*, spoke of the soul *becoming Osiris* as it made its journey through the kingdom of the dead after bodily death. In the after-life, we would become as the Gods. This knowledge was and is a source of great strength to the initiates of the Mysteries.

In Wicca, we bring the individual into contact with the Divine part of his or her psyche through invocation. Invocation involves a technique similar to that known in magic as *assump-tion of god forms*. In some traditions, a priest or priestess will not participate in invocation until after the second degree. In others, particularly where second degree Witches are respon-sible for training new initiates, they will begin to practise invo-cation during their first degree.

The Divine within

When we invoke the God or Goddess, we are effecting a change of consciousness. We move from our everyday waking con-sciousness to a state wherein we are put in touch with the

Divine core of our being. The human psyche has many levels. The first and most familiar level is the conscious mind. This has two aspects. The *persona* is the mask that we present to the world. It is our *front, what we pretend to others that we are.* Our persona may be singular or plural. We may have one mask or we may have a number of different roles which we play at different times – the dutiful son, the efficient businesswoman, the loving mother or father. The masks will change as we go through the transitions from teenage to adulthood to old age; hence all those ex-hippies now in three piece suits!

The *Ego* can be thought of as lying *behind* the persona. It is the face behind the mask; *what we think we are* rather than what we pretend to be. Unfortunately, we are wrong. When we look at our faces in the mirror, we see only part of ourselves. Beneath is another deeper layer. In the mirror of the conscious mind, we cannot see what lies behind the face.

What lies behind the Ego is another part of ourselves that is strongly related to the Ego. This is called the *Shadow*. Most of us (though not all) have sufficient insight to know that we are not perfect; but there are always aspects of ourselves that we prefer not to see. However, we cannot completely ignore these characteristics, so we come to a compromise: we project them onto others. It is not us but other people who have these undesirable qualities that we cannot face. Jung believed that these characteristics form our Shadow.

> The Shadow personifies everything that the subject refuses to acknowledge about himself and yet is always thrusting itself upon him directly or indirectly – for instance, inferior traits of character and other incompatible tendencies.[2]

The *Shadow* is therefore the opposite of the Ego. The Ego is what we think of as our total personality – we are wrong. The Shadow is all the characteristics that we think are not part of our personality – but again we are wrong. The concept of the Shadow is sometimes difficult for people to accept. However, most of us can think of certain types of people who cause us to react with the kind of bristling of psychic fur with which a cat greets a friendly dog. These are the people whom we meet and

Persona, Ego, Shadow and Self

thoroughly dislike for reasons that our friends cannot understand. The Shadow is what is hinted at in the old English nursery rhyme:

> I do not like thee, Dr Fell,
> the reason why, I cannot tell.
> There's only one thing I know well:
> I do not like thee, Dr Fell.

The *personal unconscious* is that part of ourselves which we do not normally access in waking consciousness. The personal unconscious makes itself known through dreams and visions and also in the famous *Freudian slip*. The unconscious is always seen as a place of darkness. It is the place to which in Greek myth Orpheus descended to rescue his wife Euridyce from death; a place which to some people is hell.

Why do people have so many negative images of the unconscious? In part it is because when we start to look into this unknown aspect of ourselves we tend to see first that dark spot lurking in the whiteness of the *Ego*. This is that part of us that we can neither fully suppress in the unconscious nor fully face. It is the Shadow which we would rather not know at all. This is why many people are afraid to look; but we must confront ourselves and own all our characteristics both good and bad.

Our conscious and unconscious minds can be symbolized by the Chinese Yin-Yang symbol. The Shadow is the dark spot in the light of the conscious mind, the fatal flaw, our Achilles' heel.

If you imagine that this is not a flat two-coloured disc but a ball or sphere, you will realize that the dark spot in the white leads like a tunnel into the centre and through to the darkness on the other side. This dark spot is the rabbit hole through which Alice fell and found herself in Wonderland and this too is the entrance to our unconscious. In Wicca, we have to lose our fear of the dark and go down the tunnel into Wonderland. It is only if we can face the Shadow, this *lurker on the threshold*, the guardian who bars the way at initiation, that we see that what the dark Shadow in the doorway protects is a new kingdom full of untold wealth and riches.

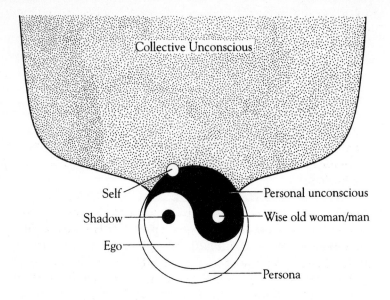

Persona, Ego, Shadow and Self

The light spot in the dark of the Yin-Yang symbol is the archetype of the *Wise Old Woman* or *Wise Old Man*. Here is the entrance to another tunnel, the tunnel to the *Self*. The *Self* is often symbolized in fairy tales as a golden ball which must be rescued from the bottom of a deep well guarded by a fearsome ogre. Another image of the Self is that of a treasure or precious jewel hidden in a cave. Sometimes it is guarded by dragons or fearsome monsters. In *Psychology and Alchemy*, Jung writes of the *treasure hard to find* which lies in the ocean of the unconscious and which only the brave can reach. The *Wise Old Woman* or *Wise Old Man* will often appear in order to help us. This is because this Wise Person is also an image of the Self.

Often we come across the *Wise Old Man* or *Wise Old Woman* in dreams and pathworkings. When we first encounter the Self in this way, we may think that we have met with an inner planes teacher. We are unlikely to recognize this wonderfully wise person as part of ourselves! In a sense, however, we have met a wise teacher; for the role of the Self is to imbue our personalities with the collective wisdom of all human experience and also with the Divine wisdom gleaned at its point of origin.

Beyond the personal unconscious is the collective unconscious.

> In addition to our immediate consciousness, which is of a
> thoroughly personal nature and which we believe to be
> the only empirical psyche (even if we tack on the per-
> sonal unconscious as an appendix), there exists a second
> psychic system of collective, universal, and impersonal
> nature which is identical in all individuals. This collective
> unconscious does not develop individually but is
> inherited.[3]

We can access this collective psyche through dreams. Its con-
tents are also represented in myths. The collective unconscious
is common to all humanity. Even though they are separated by
time and geography, the myths which different human societies
produce are similar. Within the collective unconscious are
archetypes. These are figures which recur constantly in the
myths and religions of all peoples. These archetypes include
the Great Mother, the Sky Father, the Child of Promise, and also
the archetype which Jung called the Self. It is with the material
of the collective unconscious that Wicca works – the Gods, the
Self and the relationship between them. The images of the Gods
represent the Divine forces that move the universe; but they are
also images of our own inner Divinity. In the first degree initiation we are taught:

> Single is the race, single of Gods and of men,
> and from a single source we both draw breath.

When we invoke God or Goddess, we attune ourselves to the
Divine Self within. To identify with a particular aspect of the
God or Goddess and to bring that Divine power into the circle
is one of the aims of Wiccan ritual. In temporarily incarnating
the Divine, a Wiccan priest or priestess is manifesting what is
essentially part of his or her own true spiritual nature. Most
Western religions believe there is an immortal spiritual compo-
nent to humanity, but this is not necessarily seen as being of the
same nature as the Divinity. Wicca takes the approach of the
Classical Pagan Mysteries.

The neophyte, after initiation, is himself lifted up to divine status: at the conclusion of the consecration rites in the syncretistic Isis mysteries he was crowned with a crown of palm leaves, set up on a pedestal, and worshipped as Helios.[4]

Jung saw this as offering enormous psychological pay-offs to the devotee.

To carry a god around in yourself means a great deal; it is a guarantee of happiness, of power, and even of omnipotence, in so far as these are attributes of divinity.[5]

Jung[6] saw the identifications made in ritual as beneficial because myth and ritual lead us to an understanding of the true nature of the archetypes. By temporarily identifying with a particular God or Goddess, Jung[7] believed the worshipper would be led to a true understanding of the nature of the Gods. This realization is a necessary step in the process of *individuation*. Individuation was seen by Jung as originally being the prerogative of shamans.[8] The shaman's initiatory experiences of sickness, pain and the threshold of death, brought him or her to a new plane of consciousness. In the New Millennium, Jung saw individuation as the primary goal of us all – the permanent healing of the division between Ego and Self.

The concept that at our core we are Divine is a difficult one for the Ego to handle. The first encounters with the Self through the processes of invocation may create problems. What is important is that identification with the Goddess or God is *temporary* and that it is not carried into everyday life. Having encountered and appreciated something of the nature of the Self, it is essential that we do not by a process of Ego inflation mistake the operations of our everyday Egos for the inner Divine Self and the promptings of our unconscious for the directives of the Gods. To quote Jung, coming into contact with the Divine part of ourselves creates feelings *even of omnipotence*.[9] Within the confines of the circle, as we speak as the Goddess or the God, this is what is meant to happen. The danger of such mystical experiences is, as Jung points out, that an archetype can *take over* the Ego.

> The archetype appears strange and as if not belonging to consciousness ... if the subject identifies with it, it often causes a devastating change of personality, generally in the form of megalomania or its opposite.[10]

Here the role of experienced group leaders is helpful in guiding us through the rocky rapids of our spiritual journey.

Invocation creates a temporary change within us, but the long-term aim of all spiritual systems is to make this change permanent. When we are invoked on, we make a *bridge* between our everyday selves, our Egos, and the Divine Self. As through invocation we access our Self more and more, this bridge which Alice Bailey in *Esoteric Psychology II*[11] calls the *antahkarana* is made permanent. Ultimately, we cross this bridge and instead of our Ego reaching out to contact the Self, the centre of our consciousness is transferred to the Self.

Our normal state of consciousness is one in which we constantly monitor our behaviour. We are divided from ourselves. We are the looker and the looked upon. As we learn to use both halves of our brain at will, we find that we are able to stand back from the two sides. Maxwell Cade and Nora Coxhead[12] associate this *standing back* with Jung's transcendent function, which he believed existed in the oldest and deepest level of the brain, the brain stem.

The permanent cessation of our inner division is what is implied by Jung's term *individuation*. This can only occur when the Ego and the Self are united and we become centred in the Self. Individuation is associated with a permanent change of consciousness. We no longer identify with any of the four functions of the personality, but with the fifth and transcendent function, the point in the centre of the circle, which is the astrological symbol of the Sun. This is the central point at which the four quarters of the circle cross join; the fifth and hidden Element, Spirit or Ether – the Self.

The Divine without

If the Divine is within us, is it merely psychological, an imaginary construct? Are the outer forms of the Gods real? Do they have meaning? In Wicca, we would say that what lies beyond the images is a Divine reality. Jung wrote:

> Symbols are not allegories and not signs: they are images of contents which for the most part transcend consciousness. We have still to discover that such contents are real, that they are agents with which it is not only possible but absolutely necessary for us to come to terms.[13]

The ancient images of the Gods are not random creations, but true expressions of the nature of the Divine translated into human terms. The Pagan religions are not the creation of one person, but have evolved from the religious experience and wisdom of generations over many millennia. The newer *Religions of the Book*, Judaism, Christianity and Islam, were created by men; men who made their God in their own image. Wicca sees this as a fundamental error. The Divine is both male and female, immanent and transcendent. It manifests through different images and symbols so that we can come to a true understanding of its nature, an understanding that stretches far beyond the understanding of our conscious minds. We therefore treat our ancient Gods with respect and honour. The full nature of the Divine reality is as yet beyond our human understanding. We therefore clothe this multi-faceted reality in archetypal images that are an expression of the truth, but not the full truth; much as we translate complicated scientific laws into simple terms for school children.

The Gods are considered to be expressions of the Divine within humanity. The Gods are also considered to be Divine forces operating in the universe. Whether they are seen as aspects of an impersonal life force, or as cosmic beings with an individuality, will depend on our own inner experiences and each individual will interpret these differently.

In Wicca, our concepts of the Divine can be related to the religious ideas of two groups of Pagan Greek philosophers, the Neoplatonists and the Stoics. The Pagan Neoplatonists saw the Divine as a being who was of a different nature from humanity and who was outside the created world or *transcendent*. The Stoics believed that the universe was itself Divine and that human beings were part of this Divinity. The Divine force was seen by the Stoics as in-dwelling in the universe and in human-ity and was *immanent*. Within Wicca today, most people accept that the Divine is immanent, with some people believing that it is also transcendent and others not.

A transcendent concept of Divinity tends to be accompanied by the idea of *reincarnation*: our individuality endures in a series of physical existences, possibly culminating in non-physical existences. The concept of immanent Divinity tends to be accompanied by the idea of *metempsychosis*: when we die we do not have an individuality that endures, but the life force within us is never lost. It flows back into the ocean of being to reappear in other life forms.

Most Witches believe in reincarnation and an enduring Self that exists before, during and after physical incarnation. In other words the Self is *transcendent* (hence Jung's term tran-scendent *function*). On the other hand, in incarnation the Divine Self inhabits a material body; so the Self could also be said to be *immanent*. In the Pagan view, the microcosm of the human being is a reflection of the macrocosm of the universe, *As above so below*. Just as Divinity dwells in the human body, it also dwells in the planetary body, the Earth. Jung quotes, in *Psychology and Alchemy*, the early seventeenth-century German alchemist Basil Valentinus.

> The Earth is not a dead body, but is inhabited by a spirit that is its life and soul. All created things, minerals includ-ed, draw their strength from the Earth-spirit. This spirit is life, it is nourished by the stars, and it gives nourishment to all the living things it shelters in its womb. Through the spirit received from on high, the Earth hatches the miner-als in her womb as the mother her unborn child.[14]

The devas or nature spirits are the beings who do the work of the planetary Deity. Whether we believe in devas will depend on whether or not we have experienced them but, if our species is to survive, we must learn to live in harmony with the Earth, the Great Mother. Even if we have not had the sense that cer-tain trees, caves, wells and rivers, are sacred and inhabited by a personality, our own lives and the life of our planet can be considerably improved if we accept this as a hypothesis and treat Nature with respect. When Nature is seen as full of conscious entities, and trees and plants, etc, are in every sense seen as living things, then we learn to work in harmony with Nature rather than merely exploiting it for our own ends to the ultimate detriment of the human race and the other life forms which inhabit the planet.

Wicca teaches us to value our planet because it is sacred. It also teaches us to value our own physical selves, our bodies. To digress a little, so far we have talked a great deal about group ritual and less about individual spiritual practice. Those who practise Wicca meditate. We also talk to our Gods in private prayer, but we tend to have few formal prayers. We simply talk to the Goddess or God and ask for assistance, discuss our problems and offer praise as we see fit. Where we do use set prayers, the best ones are usually those which we have created ourselves. However, here is a prayer that I thought I would include because it says something about the value which Wicca places on the immanent aspect of the Divine.

Prayer of Praise to the Goddess

Blessed Be the Great Mother,
Without beginning and without ending,
Blessed Be her temple of pure white marble,
Blessed Be the stillness of her holy place.
Blessed Be the babe who cries to her,
Blessed Be the deer who lift their heads for her,
Blessed Be the birds who fly the skies for her,
Blessed Be the trees which shake and sigh for her,
Blessed Be the leaf that falls for her and nourishes the soil.
Blessed Be the wave which caresses the shore for her,
Blessed Be the sand which succumbs to its embrace,
Blessed Be the shell that is cast up from her,
Blessed Be She, the Mother of Pearl.
Blessed Be the stars which shine like jewels for her,
Blessed Be the Moon in which we see her face,
Blessed Be my spirit which soars the heights for her,
Blessed Be my soul which expands in joy for her,
Blessed Be my body, the temple of her being.[15]

Wicca considers the body to be a gift of the Gods; the vessel of our Divine Self. It must therefore be treated with respect and care. The word *Pagan* means country dweller and humans were not designed for a predominantly indoor, city existence. Wicca considers it important that we do not lose touch with the Earth, but that we find time to get into the country and immerse ourselves in the natural forces around us. If we take time to walk upon the Earth, expose ourselves to sky and Sun, and to absorb the energies of water and trees, then Nature will replenish us and counter-balance the stresses of modern living.

The stance that the Divine is immanent is an antidote that reminds us of an aspect of Deity which years of transcendent monotheism were in danger of obliterating. Christianity can be seen as the triumph of the conscious mind over the realm of Nature. The Gods were no longer to be seen as within Nature, but outside it. Nature was no longer sacred and holy, but the creation of a transcendent father (without the mother). Our conscious minds learned to suppress the unconscious and keep it at bay. The focus of human attention became the world beyond Nature; God lived in Heaven not Earth.

Despite its negative aspects, the transcendent concept of the Divine was a necessary step in human development. The psyche of humanity was no longer solely immanent in Nature. The human mind, developing in consciousness and self-aware-ness, had said:

I am. I exist. I am not my body. I am not my intellect. I am not my emotions. I exist beyond the body, beyond all this.

As we have come to believe that we exist *beyond* what our senses perceive, so too have we come to believe that the Divine also exists beyond the material world. This is not to say these views are right. Some would see it as monstrous egotism on the part of human beings to assert their transcendence over the natural world around them. In Wicca, we are free to form our own views, based on our own inner experiences and revela-tions. It is these which must ultimately determine our beliefs. All our images of the Divine, whether masculine, feminine or abstract like the Neoplatonist's transcendent One are limited by our experience and will evolve as our spiritual understanding evolves. Our images can only hope to give us pointers to the truth.

Invocation

In Wicca, the Gods are always invoked in the circle once this has been cast and purified. Casting the circle creates sacred space, a place where we and the powers of the Gods can safely meet. The Gods manifest in the psyche through what Carl Jung called *dominant archetypes*. These include the images of the Great Mother Goddess, the Horned God, the Child of Promise. These are immensely powerful and the danger is that if we contact them unprepared, they can overwhelm our inner world.

As well as the dominant archetypes, there are also *organizing archetypes*. These are archetypes that surround and contain the dominant archetypes and so create a space where their power can be safely contacted without overwhelming the psyche. In Wicca, two important organizing archetypes are the sacred circle and the four quarters, symbolized by the cross within the circle. This is a symbol of the balanced personality, the goal of all religious, magical and spiritual systems. By coming into right relation with the organizing archetype of the circle, we create *safe space* in our own psyches. The powers of the Gods can then be made manifest.

In Wicca, the Gods are usually invoked into someone of the same sex as the Deity by someone of the opposite sex. For simplicity's sake, I will call the person on whom the Deity is being invoked the *priest* or *priestess* and the person invoking the Deity the *invoker*, but the invoker would also be a priest or priestess. The priest or priestess and the invoker have the principal responsibility for the invocation. However, like all processes in the circle, the end is achieved much more easily if the whole coven reinforces the invoker's actions and assists in the spiralling of etheric energies and the visualization that are part of the process of invocation.

Usually, the invoker will kneel before the person who is to be invoked upon. Both will visualize a particular form of the Goddess or God. The priest or priestess will then open his or her chakras, draw energy into his or her etheric body, and enter the meditative state of consciousness.

Invocation involves the invoker drawing the Divine force into the body of the priest or priestess. At the beginning of the process, it is desirable for the invoker to link his or her etheric energies with the priest or priestess. The invoker can use these etheric links to *inject* the etheric body of the priest or priestess with a particular God or Goddess image and force. To do this, the invoker creates a *spiral* of energy by opening his or her chakras and directing energy from the base-of-spine chakra into the base-of-spine chakra of the priest or priestess. The energy is then drawn back into the invoker's sacral chakra. The invoker then directs this energy back to the sacral chakra of the priest or priestess; and so on up the body until the energies reach the level of the third eye.

At this point, the invoker creates a visual image of the God or Goddess in his or her third eye chakra. The invoker can then *develop* the image, by visualizing it forming at the third eye and crown chakras of the priest or priestess, and then growing larger and descending and enveloping him or her.

The God or Goddess is asked to *descend into the body* of the priest or priestess. Thus, a male invoker will complete a full Moon invocation with the words:

O Mighty Mother of us all,
by seed and root,
by bud and stem,
by leaf and flower and fruit,
by life and love,
we do invoke Thee and call upon Thee
to descend unto the body of Thy servant and priestess.

If the invocation is a long one, then most of the energy spiralling and visualization process can be carried out during the invocation. If the invocation is short, it is important to allow a silent period beforehand to prepare the priest or priestess. This is particularly important when people are new to invocation.

In saying invocations we are performing a *making* and it is important that the words are *charged*. They must be spoken as energized words of power that are directed towards the priest

or priestess using the energy of the throat chakra. The words
should be accompanied by appropriate visualization on the part
of the invoker. This is part of an invocation that we use at the
Spring Equinox which contains a lot of visual imagery.

Spring Equinox Invocation

We invoke thee, O Diana,
Huntress of the wood,
Lady of bright imaginings,
Silver Star of our desire,
Crescent Moon of midnight clear,
Diana the wild, Diana the pure,
Virgin Huntress white as snow;
fair thou art as the music of the harp;
radiant thy smile as moonlight on water;
light thy step as blossom on the wind.
Thy womb is the Cauldron of Creation,
which shall bring forth all hope to men.
O Lady of the Word of Power,
who makes the shadows flee,
turn thy ear Diana,
as we invoke thee.

When words are used to conjure visual images, they act power-
fully on the psyche and take us into a deep state of consciousness where the boundaries of the Self merge into the greater
whole. At this level of consciousness, we can absorb the words
and images that the invoker creates, until we become the
archetypal image which they reflect. This does not usually happen straight away. When people are first invoked on, they may
reach no more than a meditative state of consciousness. With
time, however, deeper and deeper states of consciousness are
reached which take us into *samadhi* and beyond. Here there is
no subject and object, you and I, Self and other, but only a sense
of a vast expansion of consciousness and oneness with the universe. This is Lawrence Le Shan's fourth reality, the *unitive*
reality, where we enter into oneness with others and with the
universe itself.

As we enter these states, much of the brain's higher fre-
quency beta rhythm disappears and with it much of our

awareness of the outside world. All sounds other than the words of invocation tend to fade away and if we have our eyes open, the circle around us will seem to recede into the distance and become very remote. There is often a sense of the body becoming taller and taller, so that the circle seems far, far below. There can also be a sense of the circle and the people in it and even the wider universe itself being somehow no longer external to us but in us. As one person said: *The constellations moved within me.* One invocation asks the Goddess to *pour forth her store of love* and, when we enter a deep invocation, this sense of a loving Divine force or power flowing through us and into the circle is very strong. When we come out of the invocation, our memory of what has happened will be hazy; although as we gain in experience of the process, it is possible to retain greater contact with the outside world if we wish.

Invocation has a strong effect on the crown chakra which is the link between our individuality and the Divine Self. When we are invoked upon, energy from the crown chakra descends into our lower chakras. At first, this energy is likely to descend only as far as the heart chakra and, for most people, it takes many years before the force is able to enter their lower chakras. This flooding of the etheric body with crown chakra energy may be accompanied by a visible change in the appearance of the person who has been invoked. Often, he or she takes on the appearance of the God or Goddess who has been invoked. They may also appear to shimmer with silver light.

When, through invocation, we have entered a deeper state of consciousness, we fuse with the archetypal image and at that moment become the Goddess or the God. The invocation is not something that happens only for those on whom the God or Goddess have been invoked. Carl Jung[16] thought that there were five ways in which the psyche could be renewed, energized and reborn. The fourth of these, *renovatio* or *renewal,* is what happens for those on whom the Gods are invoked. This is a temporary transmutation of our essential nature: the mortal becomes temporarily immortal. The fifth experience, *indirect rebirth*, is what happens for the rest of the group. Jung described *indirect rebirth* as *witnessing the transformation.* The word *witnessing* suggests that the rest of the group merely see something that happens not to them but to someone else; but this is not true of Wicca. At the invocation, all the group are likely to enter the same state of consciousness as the priest or priestess.

Changed states of consciousness can be communicated to others. This is what happens during spiritual healing. This is also the reason why followers of advanced Eastern gurus experience enlightenment through contact with the guru. The role of the priest or priestess is therefore a dual one of changing their own consciousness and merging with the Deity, but also of communicating that changed consciousness to others. One way of facilitating this communication is through a *charge*. A *charge* is a piece of ritual poetry or prose in which the priest or priestess speaks *as the God* or *as the Goddess*. Like the invocation, the words of the charge must be spoken as words of power energized by the throat chakra. The function of Goddess and God charges in Wicca is to convey the true nature of the deity and also to directly address the worshipper. The nature of the message will depend on the worshipper's sex and on the sex of the Deity. If they are the same then the Charge can be seen as a message from the Self to the Ego. If they are different, the message to the Ego is from the Anima or Animus.

The effect of the charge on those in the circle will depend on the invoker's ability to draw down the Divine force, on the receptiveness of the priest or priestess, and on the spiritual development of the worshippers. Those who are experienced in participating in invocation are likely to enter into a deeper meditative state of consciousness and, depending on their sex, will become at one with the invoker or with the priest or priestess. If the Deity is of the opposite sex, it is as though it has manifested to us and answered to our call. We are then in Lawrence Le Shan's *transpsychic reality* where we are united with, but also separate from, the greater whole. If the Deity is of the same sex, it is as though the deity has manifested not only within the priest or priestess, but also within ourselves. We have then entered the *unitive reality*.

There a number of invocations and charges in the *Book of Shadows*, including the *Great Mother Charge* that is used at first degree initiations. After a time, most people find that they create their own invocations and charges which express aspects of the God and Goddess that are most important to them. It is important to know these by heart. Although in the first degree initiation the *Book of Shadows* mentions *reading the Charge*, it is very difficult to read and to speak energized words of power. When we first experience consciousness change, to speak at all is quite difficult, and for most people it is probably impossible to carry out the left-brain activity of reading while remaining in an altered state of consciousness. To use charges and invocations effectively, we must know them so well that it is like switching on a tap. The invocation or charge should pour forth without any conscious intervention on our part, so that we can concentrate on drawing the Divine energy into the circle.

Once we know charges and invocations from the *Book of Shadows*, the next stage is to create our own. Good charges and invocations often emerge from the unconscious as complete entities with no intervention from the conscious mind other than to record them. They also often arrive at unexpected and inconvenient moments such as in the middle of the night, sitting in the bath or driving the car. The latter means saying the charge over and over so as not to forget it before arriving somewhere where one can write it down. No doubt, this amuses one's fellow drivers at traffic lights and gives credence to the traditional image of Witches muttering under their breath!

The final stage is to have no prepared material, but to enter the unitive state of consciousness and then to open the throat chakra and allow the Deity itself to speak through us. What often emerge are some of the most beautiful charges that we are likely to hear and perhaps, like a beautiful flower, their power to move us is enhanced by their ephemeral nature; for afterwards it is rarely possible for speaker or listeners to remember what was said.

Cakes and wine

One way in which the power of the Gods is poured forth into the ritual is through the charges. Another is through the ceremony of Cakes and Wine. This can be seen as the culmination of the invocation of the Goddess and the God. Often it is the priest and priestess on whom the Deities have been invoked who will bless the Cakes and Wine. In the blessing of Cakes and Wine, sacred food and drink are imbued with Divine force to provide us with energy for the spiritual journey that is life. We can then truly feast with our Gods.

The ceremony of Cakes and Wine illustrates the relationship between the male and the female, God and Goddess, in Wicca. It is the priest who holds the female symbol of the cup and the priestess who blesses the wine within the cup with her athame, the symbol of maleness. Here on the inner planes, it is the Goddess who impregnates and energizes. As the priestess sits upon the altar and the priest kneels before her, the priestess gently lowers the athame into the cup as he says:

> As the athame is to the male;
> so the cup is to the female,
> and conjoined they bring forth blessedness.

Here in this sexual symbolism is the relationship between the God and the Goddess: the two Divine forces ultimately reconciled in One.

Following the blessing of the wine, the priest presents cakes. These are often made in the shape of the crescent Moon. They may be on a special plate or they may be offered on the pentacle. The priestess blesses the cakes with the athame and the priest speaks again:

> O Queen most secret,
> bless this food unto our bodies,
> bestowing health, wealth, strength,
> joy and peace,
> and that fulfilment of love that is perpetual happiness.

Some Witches like to bless wine with the athame (the athame, a weapon of Air, is used to bless the cup, a weapon of Water); but use the wand to bless the cakes (the wand as a weapon of Fire blesses the pentacle, a weapon of Earth), thus making the ritual of Cakes and Wine a balance of all the Elements.

The cup and the plate are passed to all in the circle with a kiss. This is the signal for the feast to begin. Food, wine, dancing, singing and talking now follow. The feasting is seen as an integral part of any Wiccan rite; for all rites must contain a balance of reverence and mirth, work and play. This is the last action that takes place before the feast which ends the circle.

Wicca and its Gods

An essential point of any Wiccan circle is that people participate and come to worship the Gods because they want to and because they enjoy it. It is not seen as a duty or an obligation. The relationship that a Wiccan priest or priestess has with the Gods is perhaps best conveyed by the *Great Mother Charge*, the Charge that greets all new initiates.

At the beginning of the Charge, a priest speaks and tells the Goddess's children to hear her:

The Great Mother Charge

Listen to the words of the Great Mother,
who was of old also called amongst men:
Artemis, Astarte, Dione, Melusine,
Aphrodite, Cerridwen, Diana, Arianrhod, Bride,
and by many other names.

A priestess speaking as the Goddess then continues with the Charge. The first part speaks of how the Goddess's worship shall be conducted.

Whenever ye have need of anything,
once in the month,
and better it be when the Moon is full,
then ye shall assemble in some secret place
and adore the spirit of me
who am Queen of all Witcheries.
There shall ye assemble,
ye who are fain to learn all sorcery,
yet have not won its deepest secrets;
to these will I teach things that are yet unknown.
And ye shall be free from slavery,
and as a sign that ye be truly free,
ye shall be naked in your rites,

and ye shall dance, sing, feast,
make music, and love,
all in my praise.
For mine is the ecstasy of the spirit;
and mine also is joy upon Earth,
for my law is love unto all beings.

The way of the Goddess is a way that is followed not as a duty, but because it gives us joy in the here and now. This is not the joy of hedonism, although earthly pleasures are considered to be gifts of the Goddess, but the *ecstasy of the spirit*, spiritual growth and expansion of consciousness. The goal is an ideal for which we must strive; a quest that leads to immortality.

Next She speaks of what she offers Her worshippers beyond life.

Keep pure your highest ideal:
strive ever towards it;
let naught stop you or turn you aside;
for mine is the secret
which opens upon the door of youth
and mine is the Cup of the Wine of Life,
which is the Cauldron of Cerridwen,
and the Holy Grail of Immortality.
I am the gracious Goddess
who gives the gift of joy unto the heart of man;
upon Earth I give the knowledge of the Spirit Eternal;
and beyond death I give peace and freedom
and reunion with those who have gone before;
nor do I demand sacrifice, for behold:
I am the Mother of all living,
and my love is poured out upon the Earth.

The priest then speaks again.

Hear ye the words of the Star Goddess,
She in the dust of whose feet are the hosts of Heaven;
whose body encircleth the universe.

The Goddess addresses Her worshippers directly, summoning them to know the Divinity that lies at their innermost core.

I, who am the beauty of the green Earth
and the white Moon amongst the stars,
and the mystery of the waters,
and the desire of the heart of woman and of man,
call unto thy soul:
arise and come unto me;
for I am the Soul of Nature
who giveth life to the universe.
From me all things proceed,
and unto me all things must return;
and before my face,
beloved of Gods and of men,
thine inmost divine self
shall be enfolded in the rapture of the infinite.

In the Goddess is found the middle way, the way of balance;
the positive attributes of masculine and feminine which lead to
spiritual and psychological growth.

Let my worship be within the heart that rejoiceth;
for behold all acts of love and pleasure are my rituals.
Therefore let there be beauty and strength,
power and compassion,
honour and humility,
mirth and reverence, within you.

And lastly, She imparts the message which is the key to initiation and confers not mysterious magical powers bestowed by
others, but the way to the Divinity within us.

And thou who thinkest to seek for me,
know thy seeking and yearning shall avail thee not,
unless thou knowest the mystery:
that if that which thou seekest,
thou findest not within thee,
thou wilt never find it without thee;
for behold, I have been with thee from the beginning,
and I am that which is attained at the end of desire.

This is the relationship between Wicca and its Gods.

Notes

1. EA Wallis Budge, *The Book of the Dead: An English translation of the chapters, hymns, etc, of the Theban recension, with Introduction, notes, etc*, pliii-lix, Routledge & Kegan Paul, London, 1923 ed.
2. Carl Jung, *The Collected Works of C.G. Jung*, Vol 9, Part 1: *Archetypes and the Collective Unconscious*, pp284–5, para 513, Routledge and Kegan Paul, 2nd ed, 1968.
3. Carl Jung, *Archetypes and the Collective Unconscious*, p43, para 90.
4. Carl Jung, *The Collected Works of C.G. Jung*, Vol 5: *Symbols of Transformation*, pp86–7, para 130 Routledge and Kegan Paul, 2nd ed, 1967.
5. Carl Jung, *Symbols of Transformation*, pp86–7, para 130.
6. Carl Jung, *Archetypes and the Collective Unconscious*, pp39–41, paras 82–5.
7. Carl Jung, *Archetypes and the Collective Unconscious*, pp113–5, paras 200–5.
8. Carl Jung, *The Collected Works of C.G. Jung*, Vol 11: *Psychology and Religion: West and East*, para 448 Routledge and Kegan Paul, 2nd ed, 1968.
9. Carl Jung, *Symbols of Transformation*, pp86–7, para 130.
10. Carl Jung, *Archetypes and the Collective Unconscious*, p68, para 138.
11. Alice Bailey, *Esoteric Psychology*, Part II, pp67–76.
12. Maxwell Cade and Nona Coxhead, *The Awakened Mind*, p7 Element Books, Shaftesbury, Dorset, 1987.
13. Carl Jung, *Symbols of Transformation*, pp77–8, para 114.
14. Carl Jung, *The Collected Works of C.G. Jung*, Vol 12: *Psychology and Alchemy*, p342, para 444, Routledge and Kegan Paul, 2nd ed, 1970.
15. Vivianne Crowley, 1988.
16. Carl Jung, *Archetypes and the Collective Unconscious*, pp113–5, paras 200–5.

11

The Second Initiation: The Quest Perilous

The second degree initiation marks an important step in the life of a Witch. It is the initiation that makes him or her a High Priest or High Priestess of Wicca. The second degree initiation confers the authority to transmit the tradition and the power to initiate first degree Witches. In most traditions, the second degree is considered a much more important and binding initiation than the first. The commitment of the second degree is considered to have an effect beyond this particular life and must not be undertaken lightly. The initiation is seen as a permanent commitment to the priesthood and to the service of the Gods. This commitment has a deep effect on the Self; whereas the first degree initiation is more an initiation of the personality. There must be a minimum of a year and a day between the first and second degree initiations, but in practice the interval is longer. Three to five years is common; but it can take much longer for someone to feel ready to take the step of becoming a High Priest or High Priestess.

Covens and traditions have slightly different criteria for deciding when someone is ready for the second degree initiation; but this tends to be when the initiate signals that he or she is ready not only to take responsibility for him- or herself, but to take responsibility for leading and/or teaching others. Typically, the individual will be capable of running esbats and seasonal rituals, using magical and divinatory powers wisely, able to give spiritual advice and counselling to those seeking to enter the Craft and be trained within it, and able to teach new initiates. Teaching others requires more than just knowledge of the

Craft; although this is an essential part. It also requires love for and commitment to others and the willingness to nurture and train them in the ways of the Goddess and God.

The nature of the skills the initiate must acquire prior to the second degree will depend on his or her personality and the abilities he or she needs to develop, but also on the coven and its focus. In some covens, this will be healing, in others magic, divination, teaching, spiritual development or craft skills, or some combination of these. Generally, people demonstrate their abilities during the normal course of coven activities. However, some groups will set particular tests or quests for those wishing to take the second degree. These may involve demonstrating their organizational and teaching abilities by taking responsible for some aspect of coven activity; demonstrating their personal qualities through vigils, living in the wild for a time, performing particular rituals; or demonstrating ability in particular techniques.

As with the first degree, the initiation is given male to female and female to male. In some traditions, the second degree is only given by third degree initiators. In other traditions, it may be transmitted by any second degree High Priest or Priestess. In others, it is customary for the agreement of the second degree initiator's third degree High Priest or Priestess to be sought before conferring the second degree. In the 1970s, Alex Sanders gave the second and third degree initiations together. This was to help found new covens quickly and to create leaders for the new generation of would-be initiates who were seeking entry into Wicca and could not be accommodated in existing covens. This practice has now largely fallen into disuse. The problem of there being more would-be Witches than groups to train them remains; but giving the two degrees together is not now generally favoured.

The symbol

The symbol of the second degree is the downward-pointing pentagram, a symbol associated in the popular mind with the Christian Devil. This is not however the symbol of the Christian's 'Evil One', but the symbol of the Horned God, the Dark Lord of Death.

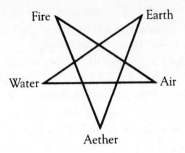

Fire ⟋⟍ Earth

Water ⟍⟋ Air

Aether

Why is the pentagram reversed? The pentagram with its five sides is a very important symbol in Wicca. In terms of spiritual growth, the pentagram is symbolic of the four functions of the personality, together with the fifth or transcendent function, the Self. The five-pointed pentagram shows that the fifth function has emerged, but is not yet transcendent. It lies buried beneath the other four. It is only with the third degree that the pentagram tilts over and attains its rightful upright direction. To turn the pentagram we must uncover that which is hidden, the unknown parts of ourselves.

The inner experience

The first degree is a time for sorting out our material lives and establishing ourselves on our chosen path. Until people can successfully run their outer lives, they are not ready to take charge of other people's spiritual lives. The first degree also takes us on the first stages of fulfilling the command of the Mysteries: *to Know thyself.* To successfully train others, we must come to terms with our own strengths and weaknesses. It is important therefore that during the first degree, we reach some understanding of ourselves and our negative and contra-sexual sides – the *Shadow* and the *Anima* or *Animus*. In order to run a coven, we must have sufficient insight into ourselves to recognize when we are projecting onto others our own desirable and undesirable qualities. We must also have begun to master the irrational likes and dislikes of others which result from such projections. These are not things which are achieved in a few years; but before we take the second degree we must have begun that journey into self-knowledge.

In psychological terms, the second initiation leads to a meeting between two sides of the personality, the bright Ego and the dark unconscious. In one sense these are good and bad. The human psyche is made up of darkness and light, impulses to selfishness and impulses to altruism. In another sense, the encounter of the second degree is a meeting between the male and female. It is as both male/death and female/life that they are portrayed in the *Legend of the Goddess*, the enactment of which is a key feature in the rite.

The rite

The second degree initiation contains many similarities to the first, but the rite also includes a mystery play called *The Legend of the Goddess*. In most traditions, only second and third degree initiates can be present at a second degree rite, but some allow first degree Witches to witness *The Legend*.

The initiate is not blindfolded for the initiation, but he or she is bound with cords in the same manner as before. The same cords as for the first degree can be used, but some traditions use new cords of different colours. The circle is cast in the usual way and the Goddess and God are invoked. The initiate is then bound and taken to the quarters by the initiator who proclaims at each quarter that the initiate is ready to be made a High Priest or High Priestess. At the second degree some people will change their Witch name to one that represents new spiritual aspirations. If so, the initiator will use the initiate's new name to administer the oath of the second degree. This oath is more binding than that of the first degree. The second degree initiation is an initiation into the eternal priesthood and wherever we may incarnate again that mark of the initiate will be upon us. The initiate is called upon to swear: *By my past lives and my hopes of future ones to come.* Given the binding nature of the oath, this is something that we discuss with initiates beforehand to ensure that if they wish to take the initiation they do so with full understanding.

In some traditions, the initiate is given a silver ring, a Witch's ring. In Britain and the United States, this is usually worn on the third finger of the right hand. In Continental Europe, it is usually worn on the third finger of the left hand. It is a ring of betrothal which symbolizes the link that has been made between the initiate and the Goddess and God.

The initiator then kneels and places his or her left hand under the initiate's knee and his or her right hand on the initiate's head to form what is called *the magical link* and says:

I will all my power unto thee.

The initiator wills all the magical power that he or she has so far accrued into the initiate via the base of spine and crown chakras. This is not only the initiator's personal power, but a cumulative legacy of Witch power from all those who have been in the initiatory chain. The old tradition was that the willing of the power was something that a Witch or cunning man did on her or his death-bed – a literal legacy. Here the aim is to make the initiate equal in magical power to the initiator. Some covens then give a Second Instruction that complements the Instruction given in the first degree and also emphasizes the nature of the second degree oath. The initiate is told that:

By this initiation, you will be sworn forever to the Gods, to honour and to serve them, and to make manifest their will upon earth.

The Instruction also speaks of the loneliness of the spiritual path; for at this stage the initiate must undertake the final part of the heroic quest. This is not an exterior quest, but an interior one, the quest for the Grail of the Self. It is at this stage that we can feel most alone. Up until now our initiators have been able to help and guide us. Although this help and guidance will continue, at this stage we will need to rely more and more on the help and guidance that comes from within.

This help and guidance may not appear immediately. An effect of the second degree may be to strip the initiate of his or her belief in the High Priest and High Priestess, who are seen for the first time as struggling human beings with failings. This disillusionment is necessary so that the initiate will turn inward for guidance to find firstly the Animus or Anima, and secondly the Wise Old Woman or Man, the inner High Priest or High Priestess. The Instruction therefore reassures the initiate:

For those who have made this oath,
there can be no loneliness,
for these the Gods love and will ever be with them.

The initiate has said that he or she is willing to suffer to learn and the truth of this is likely to be tested. The path that we must walk from the second to the third degree is a path of sacrifice. What we must sacrifice are the impediments that prevent our entering that last initiatory door, the gateway to the Self.

The true ordeal of your initiation
cannot be inflicted by woman or by man,
but is the sacrifice which you must make
in order to achieve your destiny.

The initiate is released from the cords; for he or she is now bound by something stronger – his or her own oath to the Gods. In some traditions, the initiate is now offered the Cup. The Cup is associated in the psyche with the feeling function and thus with love and humanitarian values. As a weapon of Water, the Cup is a vessel and a container that preserves and cherishes what is sacred. In the *Great Mother Charge*, the Goddess speaks of:

... the Cup of the Wine of Life,
which is the Cauldron of Cerridwen,
and the Holy Grail of Immortality.

Life is a dance of light and darkness, joy and pain. To truly experience life, we must be prepared to embrace all its seasons; its day and night; its bright moments of ecstasy and the dark night of the soul when desolation comes; the warmth of the morning Sun and the peace and rest of eventide. The second degree is a testing ground, a hard path up the steep mountain-side, up through the mists which veil the Sun; but if we are to find that which we seek, we must go forward.

Will you drink therefore of this Cup,
the Cup of the Wine of Life,
which is both pain and joy eternal,

and thus accept the true priesthood,
which is binding both in this life
and those that are to come?

When the initiate has drunk of the Cup, the initiator conse-
crates the initiate in the sign of the second degree, the downward-pointing pentagram.

The initiate is now presented with the eight magical
weapons. This part of the ceremony mirrors that of the first
degree, but with one difference: instead of merely handling the
weapons, the initiate is asked to perform a traditional demon-
stration of his or her mastery of the Craft by using them. In
many traditions, it is part of the work of the first degree that the
initiate makes or buys his or her own set of magical tools.
Making our own magical tools is an ancient tradition and an
important one. The idea is that a part of ourselves goes into the
making. Forging a sword or an athame is beyond the expertise
of most Witches today, but wands and pentacles we can make
ourselves. Making tools can be particularly important and
empowering for women, who are often not taught how to use
hand tools, and also for intellectual men who habitually fight
shy of doing anything with their hands. One of the lessons of the
first degree is control of the material plane. This involves not
only sorting out our everyday lives, but also being able to
manipulate matter. Most groups will insist that people also
make for themselves any robes which are used in the circle
rites. For many male Witches this can be an interesting initiatory experience.

Taking the sword, the initiate casts a circle; taking the
athame, the initiate invokes the quarters; using the white-han-
dled knife, the initiate makes the second degree symbol on a
new candle; with the wand he or she forms the second degree
symbol above the altar; the pentacle is presented to the watchtowers; the censer is used to cense the circle; and finally the initiate is given the cords and the scourge.

The scourge is a tool which it is important that we make and
consecrate ourselves; for it is a symbol of the self-discipline that
is necessary to follow an initiatory path. The teaching given
with the scourge in the first degree was that the initiate should
be willing to suffer to learn. Another important teaching is

given with the presentation of the scourge in the second degree. This is the *Three-fold Law*. In our lives and in magical workings we do not merely reap what we sow: the effect is cumulative. Where we have given good, it shall return to us three-fold; where we have done harm, then we must face the three-fold consequences. If we become teachers and leaders after the second degree, then we enter into a realm where we will have to take responsibility for others. We must then be trebly sure that our practice of the Craft is ethical and true, because we are moving into a realm where our actions can affect other people and influence in turn how they practise the Craft. The effect of our actions becomes cumulative.

The legend of the descent

After revealing the Three-fold Law, the initiator now promises to tell the initiate a further mystery. This is the mystery of *The Legend of the Goddess*. In the *Legend*, the initiate and others enact the descent of the Goddess into the Underworld, the Land of Death. Here she meets with the God as the Dark Lord of Death.

The true purpose of all magic is transformation. This can be transformation of the outer world but, more importantly, it is transformation of the inner world that is the aim. In the Western magical system of Alchemy, the goal was less that of finding physical gold, but more of finding the true gold of the spirit. The rituals, purifications and mental discipline necessary to produce gold bring about a change of the consciousness. The original purpose of the quest then becomes irrelevant. It is the process of seeking that is important. Often the quest involves a descent, for to find that which we seek we must descend into the Underworld of the unconscious.

The myth of the descent of Inanna is one of our earliest recorded religious myths and is over 5,000 years old. The Goddess Inanna, Queen of Heaven, abandons Heaven and Earth to seek knowledge of a third realm – the Netherworld. At the first gateway to the Netherworld the Guardian stops her. To enter she must strip away one of her seven veils at each of the Netherworld's seven gates.[1] This religious mystery has now degenerated into an entertainment – the *Dance of the Seven Veils*. The symbolism of the message in clear: the soul must be laid bare if we are to progress and to understand the mystery.

In Norse-German mythology there is also a legend of the Goddess' descent. This is the descent of the Goddess Freya, whose name means *Lady*. In covens in Northern Europe, Freya may be used for the name of the Goddess and she has some of the same characteristics as the Goddess Aradia. Freya is the daughter of the God of the Sea, Njörd, who sends winds to seafarers and protects them on their journeys. Her mother is the Earth. Freya is the patron and protectress of the human race. In the tarot, her card is the Empress, the Lady of Fertility. Freya's descent is not to conquer death, for in Norse-German mythology she herself rules one of the halls of the dead and half of all battle-slain warriors are hers. Freya's task is to retrieve the necklace *Brisingamen*, which shines like fire.

In some covens, a male initiate will enact a *Legend of the God* rather than the *Legend of the Goddess*. In the *Legend of the God*, the male initiate is the encounterer rather than the encountered; taking the role of the hero who descends to meet the Queen of the Underworld. In the Welsh *Mabinogion*, King Arthur has to enter the Underworld, *Annwn*, to retrieve the Cauldron of Rebirth. Later stories in the Arthurian cycle describe the quest by King Arthur's knights for the mystical treasure of the Holy Grail. The Grail is a Christian symbol, but it evolved from older Celtic legends of the Cauldron of Rebirth and Plenty that contains all blessedness. There is a danger however that if we use a myth of the hero's descent, we will lose one of the important lessons of the Legend for a male initiate, which is to bring him into right relationship with the feminine. For if a man is to make the quest for the Self, he must learn to let go of masculine striving for a goal that is *out there*. The answer is not to be found in books, or in gurus, or in some esoteric group. It is the personification of his unconscious, his Anima, which will bring him the answer.

The message of the esbat and sabbat rites is that the Goddess cannot be found by the hunter. However fast he pursues her she will always escape. It is only when he stops and asks her to come to him that he can win her. A man must learn that, paradoxically, to progress he must stop. Instead of pursuing the goal, he must ask the goal to come to him; for the Goddess has already told him:

> By the well-spring of your being I await you always.
> Behold I have been with you from the beginning.

A female initiate makes the descent into the Underworld, not to become the Dark Lord, but to confront him and solve his mysteries; for he is the keeper of the secret of death. Hers is the journey of Persephone, but here Persephone is not stolen away. She goes willingly into the Underworld. The duty of the priestess is to change and grow and this means that she must seek experience. In doing so, she ceases to be Persephone. After her encounter with the Dark Lord, she becomes the Queen of the Underworld, Hecate the all-wise, keeper of the Mysteries.

In this journey, a woman must take the opposite role to that which society has conditioned her to play. She must not sit at home awaiting the knight on a white charger who will rescue her from the cares of the mundane world. A woman's Animus will not come to save her; she must go and find it and so the Goddess goes on a journey, the *Quest Perilous*.

The Dark Lord is a figure whom many fear and misunderstand; just as many fear to face the unconscious and to see the Shadow that lurks there. The Dark Lord in Wicca is not evil. He is the Lord of the Underworld, the kingdom of the unconscious mind, and in identifying with him a male initiate discovers the Dark Lord's true nature. The dark aspects of the God and Goddess are but the reverse side of the Wise Old Man and Woman who lead us to the Self.

In the tarot, the Dark Lord is symbolized by the card of the Devil, which is but a distorted image of the High Priest/Hierophant, the Wise Old Man which the initiate must become. The Devil is a parody of what the Hierophant should be; but at the same time a clue to what he can become. Both the Devil and the Hierophant are ruled by signs of the Element of Earth, the Element of the Goddess. This provides a clue to the way forward: at this stage a man must pay heed to the Anima and in doing so will find his true masculinity. This is not the stereotyped masculinity of the be-suited city dweller, but the true power of the masculine that is in touch with its feeling side.

Thus the Devil, which is ruled by Capricorn the Goat, becomes the High Priest/Hierophant ruled by Taurus the Bull, the epitome of masculine strength; and one is father to the other.

Enactment of the Legend

The Legend is a mystery play that can be staged simply or elaborately as desired. The initiate takes one of the parts, either the Goddess or the God, and other coven members act as Narrator and the Guardian of the Portal. In the *Book of Shadows*, the Legend is narrated and enacted in mime, but many covens prefer to adapt it so that the principal characters speak their own parts, with the narrator providing linking narrative.

At the beginning of the Legend, the priestess who is to take the part of the Goddess takes off the necklace which female Witches always wear in the circle and lays it on the altar. She is then dressed in veils and jewellery. The priestess waits at the edge of the circle. The priest enacting the God puts on a horned crown, takes the sword and scourge and stands in the God position before the altar. The Guardian waits with another sword by the edge of the circle.

> In ancient times Our Lord, the Horned One,
> was as he still is,
> the consoler, the comforter,
> but men knew him as the Dread Lord of the Shadows,
> lonely, stern and just.
> But Our Lady the Goddess would solve all mysteries,
> even the mystery of death,
> and so she journeyed to the Nether Lands.

The Guardian of the Portal challenges the Priestess with the sword and she removes her seven veils and lays them down at the edge of the circle. The Guardian of the Portal brings her before the God at the altar.

Such was her beauty that Death himself knelt down
and laid his sword and crown at her feet, saying:

> *Blessed Be thy feet*
> *that have brought thee in these ways.*

Here the Priest lays down before the Goddess the symbols of his power and kisses her feet. The sword and crown are seen as symbols of power and legitimate authority. These symbols, the God gives to the Goddess; power and legitimate authority are therefore hers, not his. The symbolic gesture recognizes the reality of male–female relations, however – the fact of the greater physical strength of the male. The woman can only rule if the man permits her to do so. In Wicca, he does.

The Goddess has descended into the Underworld not to seek a lover, but to confront Death and to find the answer to an age-old question. She replies:

> *I love thee not.*
> *Why dost thou cause all things*
> *that I love and take delight in*
> *to fade and die?*

The God seeks to justify his role.

> *Lady, 'tis age and fate*
> *against which I am powerless.*
> *Age causes all things to wither,*
> *but when men die at the end of their time,*
> *I give them rest and peace and strength*
> *so that they may return.*
> *But you, you are lovely, return not,*
> *abide with me.*

The Goddess is not convinced by this argument. She cannot accept the God's role in the scheme of things; that birth implies death, creation implies destruction. The force of life does not wish to yield to the force of death. The force of death wishes to keep the Goddess in the Underworld and not to permit her return to the upperworld, her natural home. The Goddess declares:

> *I love thee not.*

But we cannot refuse the lessons of death. It is age and fate, by which we are all bound. The Lady of Life must submit to the Lord of Death, for each without the other will bring misery and destruction. The forces of creation must be balanced by the forces of destruction else the universe will implode. The Goddess yields, recognizing the inevitability of what must be. She submits to the power of natural law, the law of death. She has passed through the final veil, but at the darkest moment comes rebirth. She discovers the answer to this age-old question which troubles humankind – the mystery of death – and in return she receives a treasure – the Necklace of Rebirth. The mystery play ends as the Goddess wins the necklace that contains the secret of the magic circle that is also the secret of rebirth.

For both male and female initiates, the Legend is a meeting with their contra-sexual side. For a woman, this is a meeting with her Animus and for a man a meeting with his Anima. Jung wrote of the encounter with the Shadow as the apprentice-piece in the individual's development, but it is the encounter with the Anima or Animus that is *the master-piece*.[2] We have not yet reached the point where the Goddess and God will enact the Sacred Marriage; first there must be a period of courtship. We are told that the Marriage will occur, but it is not yet revealed to us. What is revealed is that death on the physical plane is only a stage in the cycle of reincarnation. We are also taught about the death and rebirth that are not physical, but occur within the span of a lifetime – the death of initiation.

In descending to the Underworld the Goddess enters the realm of death, but she does not die. Although she loves and becomes one with Death, and thus overcomes any fear of him, she is also given back the symbol of life, the necklace of rebirth. Her role is not to remain in the Underworld, but to return to the world above, bearing with her the hard-won necklace symbolic of the knowledge she has gained.

The rite of the second degree is complete now except for one last ceremony. The initiator takes an athame in one hand and the initiate by the other and proceeds once round the circle, proclaiming to the four quarters that the initiate has been consecrated a High Priest or Priestess.

Notes

1. See Sylvia Brinton Perera, *Descent to the Goddess, A Way of Initiation for Women*, Inner City Books, Toronto, 1981, for an interesting Jungian interpreration of the Legend of the Descent.
2. Carl Jung, *The Collected Works of C.G. Jung*, Vol 9, Part 1: *Archetypes and the Collective Unconscious*, p29, para 61, Routledge and Kegan Paul, 2nd ed, 1968.

12

The Steep Path

Paganism differs from the monotheisms in its attitude to the darker side of human nature. Christian, Judaic and Islamic theology, together with that of Zoroastrianism, depict dark and light as being in conflict, with light eventually overcoming the darkness. Paganism tends to see darkness and light as being in harmony and necessary counterparts to one another. In Paganism, vices and virtues are not separate classes of entities, but two sides of the same coin. There is no quality which, given unlimited freedom of expression, does not become a vice, and the same is true of any qualities which are suppressed and given no opportunity for expression. Within life we must find a balance between power and compassion, between strength and beauty, between honour and humility, the needs of the self and the needs of others.

Religions that worship the light tend to teach the conscious mind to suppress its negative impulses and to project them onto exterior figures, such as the Devil, the tempter. Paganism encourages people to face their own darkness and to acknowledge and accept it. In the first degree we are taught to face the Shadow and to recognize that:

> When we hate someone we are hating something that is within ourselves, in his image. We are never stirred up by something which does not already exist within us.[1]

Like modern psychologists, Pagans do not believe that the darkness can be overcome by the light. In other words we cannot push the knowledge of our own evil impulses below the threshold of consciousness and pretend that they do not exist. We must recognize, acknowledge and transform them into qualities that are helpful to us and to others.

Negotiating the passage

The titles of *High Priest* and *High Priestess* that we are given at the second degree are heady and fraught with pitfalls. There is a danger that the Ego will succumb to the subtle vanities of these titles and will identify with the persona of the High Priest or High Priestess. This is a psychic falling by the wayside on the journey to the Self. It is succumbing to what Carl Jung described as the *mana-personality*.[2] *Mana* is power, magical power. The male initiate encounters the beautiful Goddess who has descended into the Underworld of his unconscious and, instead of vesting his power in her, he takes her magical powers for himself. He assumes the role of Super-Priest and High Wizard, the Keeper of the Mysteries, the Possessor of the Secret Knowledge. He forgets that he is mortal and has feet of clay. For the new High Priestess, the temptations are equally great. She can fall into the trap of becoming, or rather attempting to become, the Goddess outside the circle and not only within. She strives to become a perfect being, what Jung describes as *The Great Mother*.

> ... the All-merciful, who understands everything, forgives everything, who always acts for the best, living only for others, and never seeking her own interests, the discoverer of the great love.[3]

These are unattainable archetypes, not human beings; but it may take a long time before we realize our mistake. If we start a new coven, our new initiates may be all too willing to see us as the Wise Person of their dreams. Disillusionment can only follow, if we allow the projection to persist; but O how seductive it is to be seen as wise! This leads to the problems of what Jung calls *the second identification*, that of Ego inflation.

The colossal pretension grows into a conviction that one is something extraordinary.[4]

Whilst this phase will wear off, it can be a tricky period to negotiate. The persona of *High Priest* or *High Priestess* can distance us from the other members of our coven and be quite forbidding. This can make it very difficult for the rest of the coven to challenge us when the persona begins to outstrip its usefulness.

An equal danger is what Jung calls a *negative inflation*: the Ego is flattened in what we might call *Ego deflation*. We cannot live up to the image that we have of ourselves as High Priest or High Priestess:

> The impossibility of the pretension ever being fulfilled only proves one's own inferiority ... both forms [of Ego inflation] are identical, because conscious megalomania is balanced by unconscious compensatory inferiority and conscious inferiority by unconscious megalomania (you never get one without the other).[5]

One of the reasons that most groups do not now give the second and third degrees together is because of the amount of psychological upheaval that can accompany taking the second degree, let alone taking the third degree at the same time. In qabalistic terms, the second degree is a joint Hod and Netzach initiation that activates the path of the tarot card of *The Tower.*

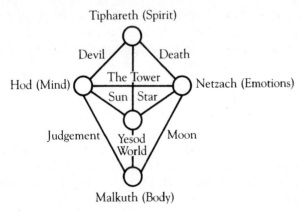

The Lower Tree of Life and Tarot Paths

The second degree can often precipitate psychological trauma. The timing of the second degree is therefore important. It is not a good idea for people to take the second degree when their emotional lives are already under stress.

For those who, after the second degree, undergo a process of Ego inflation (the creation of the towering edifice of the Ego), this will be followed by the destruction of the Ego (falling from the Tower). How painful this process is depends how easily the Ego chooses to relinquish its grip on the psyche.

Some people avoid this trauma. Some have already undergone this transformation through other spiritual, magical or therapeutic work. Others have intelligent Egos, which have learned that it is much better to give in gracefully and to undertake the learning without going through the process of resistance that gives rise to the suffering! However, the majority of us have Egos that resist being unseated from their central position in the psyche. It is important to understand therefore that the process which the second degree precipitates may not always be pleasant. While the first degree initiation is associated with the element of Water, the second degree is associated with a descent to the Underworld in which burns the fire of purgation – *all within you that is unworthy will be burned away* – whether we like it or not. This process can take many years.

Jungian psychologists often see these Ego problems as being symbolized in the Greek poet Homer's *Odyssey* by the twin dangers of Scylla and Charybdis. The hero Odysseus has to descend into the Underworld, the House of Hades. On his return, he is congratulated by the Witch-like Goddess Circe, but his adventures are far from over. Having emerged successfully from the encounter with the Dark Lord, he must face the perils of the rocks of Scylla and Charybdis. On one stands the monster Scylla who devours what passes beneath her. At the base of Charybdis is a whirlpool that sucks down the voyager and drowns him beneath the sea.

Not everyone manages to make the transitions necessary to work the difficult passage through the second degree. Some do not progress beyond the threshold of the second degree and reach a plateau in their spiritual development. They make the descent, but turn back prematurely. The cost of change is too great, the journey too tiring and painful. We give up, preferring to cling to the safety of the known, rather then to venture into the unknown.

To negotiate this tricky passage, we must find a middle way and it is the inner guide of the Anima or Animus that will tell us what to do. Circe warns Odysseus that no masculine solution will help him here. It is useless, she tells him, to put on his armour and gird on his sword, the symbols of his masculinity. He must sail beneath Scylla unarmed and appeal to Cratais, the mother of Scylla, another aspect of his inner feminine, to help.

The encounter with the Anima for a man and the Animus for a woman requires us to integrate their qualities and wisdom into our consciousness. This is not, however, without problems. In the Wiccan journey into the unconscious, we encounter the inner opposite sex figure, both in its negative aspect and at its most benign. The opposite sex initiator is a parental figure, who is both the *bad* parent, the wielder of the sword, and the *good* parent, the bestower of the loving kiss of welcome to a new home. Although in the second degree a man has encountered his Anima and a woman her Animus, there must be a period of courtship before the Sacred Marriage. If we mate too soon with our contra-sexual side there is the danger that instead of successfully integrating it into our lives, we will be swamped by it.

This is the secret fear that the woman has of the Dark Lord; that he will overcome her, rape her, dominate her, hurt her. It is a realistic fear. If we release our inner maleness too quickly, we can become dominated by the Animus. Many women, who in business and politics compete in a masculine environment, succumb to the trap of identifying with the stereotyped behaviour which society advocates for men. They become rigid and authoritarian, parodies of society's maleness, convinced that they are always right. The ability to love and cherish others which should be the prerogative of the feeling part of both sexes disappears. Women must learn strength and power, but it is with the strength and power of the Goddess we must identify, not with a stereotyped image of the male. This is especially important for the Wiccan High Priestess. If as women we have not had the experience of exercising authority, and particularly exercising authority in mixed-sex groups, it is easy to fall into the trap of adopting authoritarian male modes of exercising power.

Whereas until recently, society has denied women an intellect, it has denied men access to their emotions. For a man the feeling realm is usually associated with the feminine, because it is with the mother that his first and most powerful emotional relationship is made. For a man the secret fear is not of rape, but of the devouring vagina which may swallow him whole; for what the mother has given forth she may consume again. For a man, the awakening of the feminine within may arouse the fear that once he lets go and lets himself feel, he will be swamped by his long pent-up emotions.

We must learn to love and trust our contra-sexual sides, before we can fully integrate them into our lives and seek the final unification of the third degree. This is not done in a day, or a year, or even in a lifetime. In Wicca, there is no rush to be perfect, no impetus to leave the world of the material; for the journeying can be just as fun as the arriving!

Leadership

Taking responsibility for others and leading them may be familiar to the new High Priest or Priestess from the world of work, sport or other group activities; but it may be very new. The style of leadership within Wicca is different from what is found in much of outer society. Leadership in a small group situation must be exercised with subtlety and restraint. It requires considerable interpersonal skills, skills which have been traditionally cultivated more by women than by men; although this is changing as men feel free to express their feeling function. Leadership is a matter of group facilitation rather than authoritarian dictates. Unlike outer society, Wiccan covens tend to see women as peculiarly suited to the exercise of authority in a group situation. In many traditions, the preeminence of the High Priestess is considered essential to the success of the group. All this is a new learning experience for many women and men.

The second degree is a period of learning to lead and to guide others. After the second degree, the initiate will usually stay with his or her parent coven for some time and will take on more responsibility within the parent group. This allows second degree initiates to assume responsibility for helping run training groups and running rituals and to learn the skills needed by a High Priest or Priestess. They can thus take on a teaching role supervised by their initiators who can gently guide them through some of the pitfalls of their new status.

To become a High Priest or Priestess, we have to go on an inner journey to find our own power and integrity. This requires self-honesty and being prepared to see ourselves as we are. It also requires the courage to accept challenges, to learn new skills and to put them into practice; in other words to grow. All this makes us a person of power. In finding our own inner sources of energy, we learn self-respect and to know both our strengths and limitations. In achieving this personal inner power, we will find that others naturally turn to us for leadership and guidance. The second degree initiation ceremony alone does not confer the role of High Priestess or High Priestess. The ceremony opens the gateway, but it is a title which we must earn.

When we reach the second degree, it is necessary for us to see our initiators as they really are. As first degree initiates we may put our initiators on pedestals, thinking that they are all-knowing, all-pervading and all-powerful. If we have not already done so, we will now see that this is not the case. Human nature being what it is, we will then swing to the other extreme and think we are just as good at everything as our High Priest and Priestess. Thus the process of Ego inflation begins.

At this stage, the initiating High Priest and Priestess must make a transition in the relationship with the new second degree initiate. In most tarots, the parallels between the images of the High Priest and the Devil are made clear by their symbolism. However, whereas the Hierophant is beneficent and his followers turn willingly to hear him, the Devil binds his followers to him with chains and convinces them that they cannot break free. He looms over them in mastery so that they cannot grow to human stature.

The second degree is a process of spiritual *growing up*. If our initiators bind us too strongly to them, then we cannot develop our own ideas. The card of the Devil is the Shadow side of the guru – the spiritual teacher of the Hierophant no longer in

213

contact with the purpose of his teaching. The role has become an end in itself rather than a route to the spiritual growth of his pupils. The card of the Devil in the Tree of Life is also a Shadow in another sense, the Shadow on the face of the Sun. Only when the Shadow is dethroned can we see behind it the light of the Sun of the True Self in Tiphareth. When initiates have reached the right point of development, the role of initiators is to stand back; to allow them to go forward unaided, even if they must stumble and fall.

It is important that second degree initiates take responsibility for teaching and organizing others. In this way, they develop the skills they need to run their own covens and are given an outlet for their need to assert themselves in their new status. This is not an easy transition for the new second degree person's initiators. It can be threatening to find our assumptions and ideas questioned and to realize that the initiate has ideas of his or her own; ideas with which we may or may not agree. The second degree is a kind of Wiccan adolescence and has all the same problems.

If working in a coven with third degree initiates, the second degree initiate is in a difficult position of being in part an Elder, but also still in the role of pupil. Difficulties can arise between initiator and initiate at this time. Often the new initiate will want to challenge his or her initiators' authority. The initiate may also want to exercise authority and the initiator will need to encourage this, while at the same time stopping the person being unbearably bossy and authoritarian towards everyone else in the coven. The initiators must themselves be mature in order to handle these problems, but a lot can be avoided if the new second degree initiate has specific responsibilities within the group. Power has been willed to the initiate by the initiation and it must be used and given back to aid the Gods, their people on their land. If not, a kind of *psychic constipation* can occur. The initiate becomes bored and frustrated, uncertain where to channel his or her new-found energies.

Initiating others

After receiving the second degree, the new High Priest or Priestess has the authority to give first degree initiation. This

214

authority is conferred by the *Willing of the Power*. To initiate, we must have knowledge of human nature and the insight to determine who is or is not suitable for initiation. No one can get this right every time. Much of this knowledge comes through experience – and through getting it wrong! However, when assessing someone's suitability for the second and third degrees, we will ask ourselves whether we have sufficient confidence in their ability to make sensible decisions about other people's readiness and suitability for initiation.

Initiating is much more than performing a ceremony. It involves building relationships of love and trust with other human beings, so that they will open themselves to us and accept and seek our advice and help. For those setting up a coven, it is important to be realistic about the difficulties involved. After a few months, people often find themselves wondering what on earth possessed them to do it! Far from giving us an exalted sense of being some kind of Wiccan guru, we are likely to find that our delightful and adoring initiates can be self-centred, incompetent, unreliable, selfish, boring, demanding, critical, lazy and conceited. Having engendered in us a total despair of human nature and our own ability to run anything, let alone a Wiccan coven, they will suddenly manifest some completely new spiritual insight and their magical work will fall into place. They will be so brilliant that, losing any common sense we previously possessed, we will probably go and initiate another one.

This sounds a pessimistic picture and coven running can be hard and frustrating work that requires infinite patience. The beauty is when that seed within the individual that you have helped to nourish suddenly blossoms forth and the individual transforms into someone fine, magical and beautiful. It can also be worth remembering, when our initiates are being particularly awful, that we probably made our initiators' lives equally hellish at times.

So why have initiates? I suppose most of us do it because of the joys it brings when the process finally works, but also because we feel that we have been given a great deal and would like to give something back. There is something else. Our initiates become our teachers. Each person we initiate presents us with new and unique problems and challenges. Each will call

upon us to find new resources and knowledge from within ourselves and, as we initiate others, we will find that we are initiating ourselves deeper and deeper into the Mystery. There
comes a point where the only way to learn is to teach.

One of the advantages of a new second degree High Priest or
Priestess *hiving off* immediately is that they can assume their
new role without *treading on the toes* of those who have been
their peers or teachers. However, the disadvantages may out-
weigh the benefits. Where the individual who has been playing
a subordinate role in a coven is suddenly let loose to initiate
others, there can be problems for both initiator and initiated.
Too rapid a transition to hiving off may mean new High Priests
and High Priestesses suddenly find themselves in the heady situation of being surrounded by newcomers to Wicca who treat
their every word and pronouncement on life, Wicca and the
universe as a great and wise revelation.

Here it is useful if the new group leaders have contact with
their peers – others who run groups. Building up a successful
relationship with covens which hive off from us can be difficult
and complex. When starting to run a coven, a new High Priest
or Priestess may well want to turn to their initiators for advice
and should feel no inhibition about doing so. We all go through
a lot of traumas and difficulties when we start to run groups. It
is important that people should be able to ask questions and discuss problems without the fear of losing face or feeling that
they should have to manage everything entirely alone.

If we are in the position of giving advice to the High Priestess
or Priest of a new daughter coven, it is important that we do not
try to tell them what to do or to interfere with the way in which
they run their groups. We can help them find their own solutions
to problems by giving them the benefit of our own experience of
similar situations, but each High Priestess and Priest must find
their own style of doing things. Their initiators are there to provide advice and guidance, not to give out 'orders from above'.

In Wicca, it is the responsibility of others further along the
path to teach those a few steps behind. As teachers, we are nav-
igators, guides and way-showers. We cannot carry another's
burden; for to go forward we must each be strong enough to
carry our own. We cannot push from behind, because each person can only travel as far as his or her own energy will take

them. But we who know the path can help others who would walk it. Our role is to point out the traps and the pitfalls, the rocks where the walker may trip, the precipice where he or she may fall, what to do when night and mist descend. Our role is also to help others to see; to see how far they have already come; to encourage when the going seems hard and unrewarding. Our role is also to help others see the vistas. To point out when their eyes are fixed to the path the beauties of the heights they have achieved and, when they descend into the valleys which are part of all paths upward, to know when it is important to rest, to wait, to endure the dark place of shadows and not to go forward too soon. Our role is also to impart our knowledge, the knowledge that will help them reach the point that we have reached. To be a way-shower requires courage. Sometimes those we teach will outstrip us. Their energy, their vision, their powers will be greater than ours. The role changes and reverses. We know bitterness and disappointment. We must learn humility and to take joy in the fact that we have helped others to stretch their wings and fly.

The journey onwards

Jung[6] describes the journey to our spiritual goal as having four stages. In the first stage, we are in an *Ego-bound* state. It is in this state that we first enter the Wiccan circle at the first degree. Our task is to free ourselves and to find a point of balance within the circle of the four Elements. This gives us the strength and spiritual nourishment to make the second stage of the journey, *the descent of the Ego into the unconscious*, which in Wicca is symbolized by the Legend of the second degree. The result is an encounter in the Underworld which leads to the third stage of the journey, *the conflict and synthesis of conscious and unconscious*. This post-second degree phase is usually the most difficult stage of the journey. However, once the problems and difficulties of the third stage of the journey are overcome, or as Jung puts it successfully circumnavigated:

> This leads to ... a possible synthesis of conscious and unconscious elements of knowledge and action. This in

turns leads to a shifting of the centre of personality from the Ego to the Self.[7]

This shifting of the centre is not easily done. The second degree is an initiation into the mystery of death, and from the perspective of the Ego, giving up its central position in the psyche may equate with death. The annihilation of the Ego was seen by Jung as a crucial stage in the individuation process, but we are all afraid of change. We are afraid of the heights and the depths, of letting go of the solid ground of consciousness and entering the twilight world of the unconscious. We are even more afraid to let go of that centre that hitherto has always been me. This is the point to which our Animus and Anima will bring us. The Dark Lord and the Hag aspect of the Goddess, who is also Cybele the destroyer, lead us to death. This is not the death of the body, but the death of the Ego. This is a death that we seek yet flee; desire yet recoil from.

The Children of Cerridwen

We came then,
the last children of Cerridwen:
Daughters of Light and Darkness,
and Sons of Death.

We sought your presence on the wild hills of the North;
but in the loneliness, we found you not.
We sought your presence in the light of the East;
but in the mists of dawn, we discerned you not.
We sought your presence beneath the sun of the South;
but where shadows shrink, we could not see your face.
We sought your presence where the wind sleeps in the West;
but in the silence, we did not hear your voice.

O Mother of Mystery,
child of my vision and daughter of my dream,
long have I sought you my soul's sister,
O Thou goal of my desire.
When passion sleeps,
I longed for thee;

where death was near,
I pined for thee;
and when the hot breath of the hound was upon my heel,
I longed for that last consummation.
Surrender, death and ecstasy are all thy gifts –
and teeth tearing flesh.

I am the hare which leaps for thee beneath the moon,
I am the fish which glistens for thee beneath the water,
and when at last, in the dark beneath the trees,
in a tremor of stillness I felt your hand upon me,
I knew no other God nor Goddess too –
for all was you.[8]

In the end it is our unconscious urge to grow, to dare, to be, which overcomes our fear and leads us to the last unification with the Anima and Animus, the Sacred Marriage of the third degree.

Notes

1. Herman Hesse, *Demian*, p106, trans Strachan, WJ, Panther Books, London, 1969.
2. Carl Jung, *The Collected Works of C.G. Jung*, Vol 7: *Two Essays on Analytical Psychology*, pp227–41, paras 374–406, Routledge and Kegan Paul, 2nd ed, 1966.
3. Carl Jung, *Two Essays on Analytical Psychology*, p228, para 379.
4. Carl Jung, *The Collected Works of C.G. Jung*, Vol 9, Part 1: *Archetypes and the Collective Unconscious* p180, para 304, Routledge and Kegan Paul,2nd ed, 1968.
5. Carl Jung, *Archetypes and the Collective Unconscious*, p180, para 304.
6. Carl Jung, *The Collected Works of C.G. Jung*, Vol 14: *Mysterium Coniunctionis*, p371, para 523 Routledge and Kegan Paul, 2nd ed, 1970.
7. Carl Jung, *Archetypes and the Collective Unconscious*, pp180–1, para 304.
8. Vivianne Crowley, Autumn 1984.

13

The Third Initiation: The Gateway to the Self

The third degree entitles a High Priest or Priestess to initiate others into the first, second and third degrees of Wicca. Many people do not reach the stage of the third degree and the length of time people take to achieve third degree varies considerably. The third degree is usually given to couples who have attained a level of seniority in the Craft. In some groups and traditions, the third degree is given to couples who are *hiving off* to form their own coven. In others, it is given after a second degree couple have been successfully running a coven or training group and training people at first degree level.

In giving the third degree, we are recognizing that the individual has reached a particular stage of inner growth and development: the centre of consciousness is beginning to transfer from the Ego to the Self. This is accompanied by a sense of inner tranquillity. This is not a serene peacefulness that is never disturbed – we do not live in the security of monasteries – but a sense of inner equilibrium which can endure difficulties, distress and grief – all the problems of human life.

The third degree initiation involves the *Great Rite* or Sacred Marriage. This is an act of ritual sex in which the priest and priestess take the role of the God and Goddess and join together in union and become one. This takes place only privately between couples. The Great Rite can be formed as an actual act of ritual sex, the Great Rite *in true*, or symbolically, the Great Rite *in token*, according to the wishes of the participants. Unlike ordinary sex (if this, one of the greatest of life's mysteries, can ever be called ordinary), the aim of the rite is not to produce a physical child but to produce spiritual twins; the two souls of the participants reborn into the light.

The *Sacred Marriage*, or *hieros gamos* in Greek, is an ancient rite which dates at least as far back as the Neolithic era. It was the ultimate religious experience in many Pagan religions and was reputed to be part of the Greek Eleusian Mysteries:

> Is not there the dark descent, and is not the solemn communion of hierophant and priestess between him and her alone? Are not the torches doused, and does not the great multitude see their salvation in that which is consummated by the two in darkness?[1]

The Sacred Marriage was also the core of the third degree initiation of the Mysteries of Isis and there the male initiate had the power of the God Osiris invoked into him. The imagery of the Great Rite is found in other traditions. The relationship between Goddesses of the land and the holder of worldly power – the king – is an important theme in Celtic mythology. The Irish texts suggest that a king might be married to his tribal Goddess. This would take place as a Sacred Marriage with a priestess or even with the Goddess' symbolic animal. Ronald Hutton of Bristol University, in *Pagan Religions of the Ancient British Isles*,[2] writes that Gerald of Wales in the later twelfth century described how the kings of Donegal mated with a mare and suggests that the number of royal husbands accredited to Maeve Queen of Connaught indicates that she was a Goddess rather than a mortal queen.

The Sacred Marriage is found more commonly in Goddess-oriented religious traditions that conceive of the Divine as both male and female. This brings us back to the theme of balance, which is so important in Wicca – balance between humanity and Nature, between light and dark, between the forces represented by the four elements, between male and female. The balance between male and female is a theme found also in alchemy and in Hinduism. It is not however found in Christianity or Zen Buddhism.

The Sacred Marriage has not been favoured in the West during the Christian era. Christianity has developed a different and more solitary approach to sexuality and spirituality – a mystical tradition in which the physical expression of sexuality is foregone and sexuality is transmuted within the individual to achieve a higher state of consciousness. Sexuality is absorbed into oneself rather than being expressed with another. However, echoes of the Sacred Marriage are found in mysticism – the inner marriage of the soul to the Divine, which is the core of all mystical traditions.

The symbolism

The outer part of the Wiccan third degree involves a uniting of the male and female, of God and Goddess. The Goddess is invoked into the priestess and the God into the priest and their union is considered a reflection of the union of the Goddess and God in the One Divine force. Inwardly, the third degree is a marriage of the two within one person – the marriage of the Ego with the Anima or Animus to give birth to the Self. The Rite is a recognition of the truth of the *Great Mother Charge*.

> If that which thou seekest,
> thou findest not within thee,
> thou will never find it without thee,
> for behold, I have been with thee from the beginning
> and I am that which is attained at the end of desire.

Through sacred sex, sexual ecstasis is transmuted to bring us to a state of unitive consciousness in which there is no separation between Self and other, I and Thou: *I and the other are One.*

The inner marriage is the marriage of soul and spirit, Ego

and Self, and leads to individuation. It is the opening of the *secret way* by the few which will lead to the opening of the way for the many. The unconscious is like a jungle. Its paths must be hacked through with great effort and then kept open by continual use. This is true both on the level of the individual, who having once attained spiritual growth must endeavour to maintain it until the pathways are fixed open for ever, and on the level of the collective mind where those who are in advance of the rest of developing humanity – spiritual leaders, artists, scientists, poets and magicians – must open the paths and byways of the soul and spirit.

The Self is the sum total of our conscious and unconscious minds and is often symbolized by the Sun or by a jewel in dreams and mythology. Our lives can be considered a sacred quest. It is a quest which may have begun in this lifetime or many lifetimes before. It is a quest is to find ourselves: who and what we really are. To do this we must first cease to pretend to be what we are not. We must cast away our *Persona* or mask. We must be prepared to confront the *Shadow*, that which we are and would rather we were not. Only then can we unify our conscious and unconscious minds and so give birth to the hidden Sun – the *Self*.

The stages by which we reach this unity can be aligned to the first, second and third degrees of Wicca. In Wicca the third degree is the gateway to individuation. The Sacred Marriage is only the first part of the individuation process; for only part of what the Self represents can be expressed in anthropomorphic symbols such as the Goddess and God. At the third degree, we become impregnated with the seed of the Self, but there is much to follow. In qabalistic terms, the third degree can be equated to a Tipharetic initiation. Tipharetic initiation takes place in three stages. In terms of the third degree, these are: the *marriage*, which is the ceremony itself; the *pregnancy*, which is usually a period of many years; and then the *birth*. The birth may occur amid greater inner turmoil and pain in our outer lives; for in giving birth to the Self, we are like Prometheus stealing the fire of consciousness from heaven. Such fire is not easily stolen.

Tiphareth is a sephira of sacrifice. To be a High Priest or High Priestess requires a great deal of love. Love implies the setting aside of our own needs in order to serve the needs of others. We sacrifice our own needs and desires to serve the Craft and those whom we initiate. This process begins with the Second Degree, but it is only a beginning. We begin to learn how to think of the needs of others, but it will take a long time before we learn how to serve the greater good, while at the same time knowing when to stop giving and when to receive; when to conserve and restore our own energies so that we may have a sufficient store of inner strength to give to others.

Giving birth to the Self represents a transition in the focus of our consciousness away from the Ego to a new vantage point. This is accompanied by an influx of creativity; for the Self lies on the borders of the collective unconscious and with its birth it is as though the child, the Self, is brought up from the depths of the well of the unconscious to the surface of the waters where it can float between Air and Water, conscious and unconscious, half in each.

To use another analogy, it is as though a birth passage has been made for the Self which afterwards leaves a tunnel from the collective unconscious through which information can flow. The process of finding the Self is akin to digging the tunnel downwards to the cave deep underground where the jewel of the Self awaits us shining in the dark on the central altar. Until this tunnel is wide enough, the Self cannot come to the surface. The work of self-development is making that channel sufficiently wide for the Self to rise into the daylit world.

This centring of consciousness in a new place which is not the Ego has been called by many different names. Magicians call encounters with the Self encounters with the *Holy Guardian Angel* or finding the *True Will*. Jung called this process *individuation*, a process which made a person a true individual, truly unique. He saw the Self as the *wholeness that transcends consciousness*,[5] and the goal of the individuation process *the synthesis of the Self*.

The journey towards individuation involves meeting and absorbing into our own psyches three very powerful archetypes – the Shadow, the Anima or Animus, and the Wise Old Man or Woman. This wise person is our true *Self*. At this stage we must make the final break with all our gurus and all our teachers and cleave only to the wisdom within. This does not mean that we should no longer go and seek new knowledge from others; but in Wicca we no longer have any higher authority, we must make our own decisions, right or wrong.

Coming to terms with the whole of ourselves, with what we really are which is the sum total of the accumulated wisdom of this life and our previous lives is a formidable task. Jung describes the Self as:

> ... that larger and greater personality maturing within us, whom we have already met as the inner friend and companion depicted in a ritual ... The transformation processes strive to approximate them to one another, but our consciousness is aware of resistances, because the other person seems strange and uncanny, and because we cannot get accustomed to the idea that we are not absolute master in our own house.[4]

These *transformation processes* of which Jung speaks are in Wicca the rites and ceremonies of initiation, of the sabbats and of the circle. This is not to say that all those who take the third degree will individuate. Individuation can be seen as a final goal and we are not all aiming to become inner planes adepts just yet. The initiations of Wicca do not give us the experiences which lead to our development on a plate, rather, to quote a phrase from Dion Fortune's invocation to the Horned God, they:

> Open the door, the door that has no key –
> the door of dreams whereby men come to thee.[5]

When the process has been completed, we stand at the turning point, the centre of the circle, and find a new vantage point. The Ego gives birth to the Self. As Jung commented:

> When a summit of life is reached, when the bud unfolds and from the lesser the greater emerges, then, as Nietzsche says, 'One becomes Two,' and the greater figure, which one always was but which remained invisible, appears to the lesser personality with the force of a revelation.[6]

The symbol of the third degree

The symbol of the third degree is an upright pentacle sur-
mounted by an upward-pointing triangle. The triangle of the
first degree was downward-pointing, the alchemical symbol of
Water, the realm of the unconscious. The triangle of the third
degree is upward-pointing, the symbol of the Element of Fire.
The symbolic meaning of Elemental Fire is conveyed by the
Sanskrit word for fire, *tejas*. *Tejas* also means light, spiritual and
magical power, strength, beauty, energy, influence, dignity and
semen; it is the life force itself. The five-pointed star and the
Fire triangle together symbolize *starfire*. In magical and mystical terms, starfire is sacred semen; but this is the semen which
impregnates the soul with spirituality as opposed to the semen
which impregnates the body with child.

The tarot trump which is associated with the Element of Fire
is Judgement, whereby the new-born arises out of the coffin of
death and is reborn into the light. In the third degree symbol,
the Fire triangle is also the triangle of inspiration, the divine
light which we receive into the crown chakra. The Star in the
tarot is one of the cards associated with the Anima and, for a
man, the third degree symbol indicates his marriage with the
Anima. For a woman the Star symbolizes the Star Goddess within her.

The third degree pentagram is in the reverse of the downward pointing pentagram of the second degree. Here the

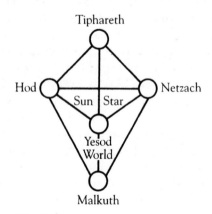

The Lower Tree and the Paths

upward-pointing pentagram symbolizes the Sun God reaching upwards to the outspread thighs of the Goddess. This is the true marriage which gives birth to a third thing which is neither male nor female, but the sun child, the Self.

The star and its crowning triangle are not depicted as united but separated, one above the other. The gap is the abyss which separates the world of the Divine from the world of humanity. After the third degree the gap will still be there, but it can be leaped. It is leaped by the unification of opposites, the unification of male and female.

In the qabalistic Tree of Life, the tarot trump which crosses the abyss between the solar sphere of Tiphareth and the ultimate expression of Divinity in Kether is the card of the High Priestess. Thus, in the third degree, it is the priestess who provides the vehicle for both herself and her male partner to rise to the heights of the Godhead united as One. It is for this reason that in Wicca the woman in a magical partnership is usually initiated first. For a woman, the part which the man will play in the rite is that of the solar hero, the rider in the Chariot, the Midsummer King, and it is the Chariot of her own body which she will offer in order for him to assail the heights.

The rite

The third degree initiation is usually given to a couple who are initiated together. How this is done varies between covens. Often, the High Priest gives the third degree to the female initiate in token and she then gives the third degree to her partner in true. Most working partnerships are likely to be spouses or lovers who will want to consummate the rite. If not, or if an initiate is to receive the initiation without a partner, then the whole of the rite can be performed in token with the initiator.

The circle is set up as usual and, before commencing the initiation, all those who are not third degree initiates leave the circle. The Goddess and the God are invoked into the initiators and, in the first part of the rite, the initiates are in a relationship of human beings to the Gods. In the second half of the rite, they themselves have the Divine forces invoked into them so that the

Sacred Marriage may be performed between the Goddess and the God.

In our Third Instruction, the emphasis is on the unity of the Goddess and the God and their ultimate reconciliation as One.

> Ere time began the One who is all looked inward on itself and beheld itself as though through a reflection in a pool and so came to self-awareness. And in that coming to self-awareness, the One was made two, subject and object; that which looks and that which is looked upon; and it divided from itself. And as the One was made Two, so the ale and the female were made separate.

> And it came to pass that the Two who had come from the One sought to be joined together and made whole again. And so shall the male and the female be joined as One and from that union with the other who is in truth but part of the Self, the doubt and the fear which are the product of the delusion of solitude shall be banished.

Here Jung says:

> ... we enter the realm of syzygies, the paired opposites, where the One is never separated from the Other, its antithesis. It is a field of experience which leads directly to the experience of individuation, the attainment of the Self.[7]

The encounter with the God

Speaking as the God, the High Priest asks the priestess:

Will you pass now through the veil
and the gates of night and day?
Will you be at one with me
who am both death and life?
Will you kneel before me and worship me?

The female initiate affirms and the God continues:

Then I take thee by the hand
and lead thee to the Altar of the Sun.

For a woman, her own inner masculinity is personified by the
Animus, who may appear in a number of forms. The Animus is
the Sun, the Lord of Light, but he is also the Lord of Darkness.
Having taken the initiate to the altar, the God goes to the West,
the quarter of death, and walk widdershins back to the initiate
dressed in a black cloak to address her.

Before the altar of the Sun I say:
look upon me.
I am darkness and the Lord of Night;
to know me is terror, but also rebirth.
Without thee I am divided,
and the light turns its face from me.
Will you come to me, O Lady of Glorious Light, and heal me,
even though it is death to thee?

To gain our life we must be willing to lose it. For in gaining
wholeness and the new and higher centre of consciousness
which is the Self, the Ego lets go its grip on us: in a sense it dies.
Here the God is perceived as Lord of Darkness for, from the perspective of the Ego, he is a bringer of death. If the initiate is willing to accept the Dark Lord, to face the forces of the unconscious,
to accept without fear what to the Ego appears to be death, then
the God can show himself as he truly is. Changing to a gold cloak,
the colour of the sun, the God this time approaches the initiate
deosil from the East, the quarter of morning, the place of birth.

I come to thee then as Lord of Light,
Sun God and King,
look upon me.
I am glorious before all the Gods,
yet am I divided and lost;
for the shadows flee from me
and there is no darkness and peace where I am.
Wilt thou heal me, O Lady of the Moon,
Mother of Mystery, Daughter of Night,
in whom all find their rest?

For a woman, the Animus is Lord of Light, the bright and shining one, the hero who will descend into the underworld to lead her into the light. Now the initiate is ready for the first stage of the transformation. The God continues:

> I shall call into thy body
> the power of the Moon and the Sun
> and thou shalt be Goddess
> and all things to me.

Until now she has known the Goddess as the Moon; now she must become the hidden Sun of the Self, the Goddess Ishtar the Midnight Sun.

The encounter with the Goddess

The male initiate must now assent to union with the Goddess. To seek this healing and wholeness the man must make the journey of the hero. Now we have the reverse of the second degree. Having learned the way of the feminine within him, having ceased his pursuit of Rhiannon of the White Mare and called her to come to him, he can assume a new and integrated masculine role. He must go forth on the Quest into his own darkness and face the dragon, the Hag aspect of the Goddess, who guards the treasured jewel which is the symbol of the Self. The Goddess warns him:

> What you seek is perilous to you;
> for you must journey to my hidden temple.
> Through danger and difficulty
> you must make your way and falter not
> and only then can I reveal myself unto to you.
> Is it truly your will to seek my inner sanctuary?

The initiate must affirm his willingness and then the Goddess will continue:

> Then I shall awaken the Godhead within thee
> and call into thee the power of the Dark Lord
> who opens the way to the light.

The God force is invoked on the initiate. Now the Goddess reveals to him the changing pattern of yin and yang, darkness and the light, the duality within her. He must meet her first not as Isis Urania, but as the Hag, the Spider Woman. Walking widdershins around the circle to the West and putting on a black cloak and veil, she returns widdershins to face the initiate.

> Behold I come before you the Isis the Black;
> look upon me.
> Secret am I,
> and none may penetrate my mystery.
> No force of man will make me open to you
> the gates of my temple.
> Yet will I come to him who woos me,
> to him who seeks me with love,
> who calls to me with desire,
> who awaits me with longing.
> Yet am I fierce and terrible to behold;
> dark is my countenance and stern my words;
> yet fear me not,
> for dark and terrible,
> I am yet thy Goddess.
> Approach me with love
> and I will reveal myself unto you.

If the initiate accepts the Black Isis, then the Goddess reveals herself in her glory. She goes to the East and discards the black cloak and veil for a long white veil and walking deosil approaches the initiate:

> Behold I come before you Isis the Bride;
> look upon me.
> Joyous am I and rejoicing,
> for you have looked upon my face of fear and fled not;
> you have looked upon my face of death and wavered not;
> therefore I shall reveal myself unto you.
> I am the beauty of the green earth
> and the white moon among the stars;
> I am the mystery of the waters
> and the desire of the heart of man;

and I call unto thy soul:
arise and come unto me;
for I am the soul of nature,
who giveth life to the universe
and to know his Godhead a man must wed with me.
But I, Isis the Bride, am the formless fire
and to mate with me unveiled,
would consume your body to ashes
and you would make a journey,
whence no man returns.
But I may be found in many forms,
and there is a secret known to the ancients,
and at the heart of all the mysteries;
for the body of woman is my temple,
and the body of the priestess its inner shrine,
and there within my sacred precincts,
Goddess and man, woman and God.
may be joined as One.
Would you seek me now in my hidden sanctuary?

Once the initiate has affirmed, the Goddess prepares the initiate for the journey to the sacred altar. The High Priestess clothes the male initiate in a black cloak and he girds on a sword and stands behind the crossed sword and broomstick. He is then challenged by the High Priestess:

Thou art a mortal man,
by what right do you enter this,
the sanctuary of the inner Sun,
the Temple of Ishtar the bright,
the Temple of Aradia, the Daughter of the Moon and Sun?

The initiate must then ask for entry on three counts: by his inner power, the power of his sword and the power of love. He must answer a question which the Goddess will pose. If the answer is correct, the High Priestess will welcome him in the names of Love and Trust.

But first you must lay down your sword,
for here a man must come in Perfect Love, unarmed.

And then you must lay down your cloak,
for here both God and man must come in Perfect Trust,
and undisguised.

Returning to the passwords which gave us entry to the circle of the first initiation, the initiate now lays down the sword, his last defence, the symbol of his phallic mastery which kills love and trust, and having cast away the cloak, his last disguise, he is finally admitted into the marriage sanctuary.

The Sacred Marriage in token

The female initiate now lies in the pentacle position with her head to the North, the direction of the altar. The High Priest lights the six candles deosil from the North East to invoke the power of the Sun.

Assist me to erect the ancient altar,
at which in days past all worshipped,
the Great Altar of all things;
for in old times woman was the altar.
Thus was the altar made and placed,
and the sacred place was the point
within the centre of the circle.

The *point within the centre of the circle* is a symbol of the Self and it is also the astrological symbol of the Sun. The High Priest kneels, kisses the priestess's womb, makes a fire-invoking pentagram with the spear or wand and invokes the power of the Goddess into her. Here she is all aspects of the Goddess met as one, but most of all she is Ishtar, the Midnight Sun, the symbol of the Self hidden in the darkness of the unconscious. Bending over her body, with kisses, the priest makes the symbol of the third degree in token upon her body. The token Sacred Marriage is now consummated by the initiate and the High Priest who perform a blessing of wine. The High Priest then draws the priestess into a kneeling position and offers her the cup:

Know then and remember,
in this and in all lives to come,
that I thy God have known thee and loved thee,
and have taken thee for mine own.
Drink now and remember,
and with this wine salute my name.

The High Priest gives the secret name of the God and the initiate drinks and salutes.

The Sacred Marriage in true

If the priestess is taking the third degree with her partner, she will now give the third degree to him. The male initiate is at this point at a halfway stage. He has had the power of the God invoked into him and he has encountered the Goddess in her dark and light aspects. Unable in his mortal form to unite in marriage with the formless Goddess, he will now unite with her priestess who acts in her stead.

In a sense, this is the end of a man's youth. He is turned away by the unattainable *Isis Urania* aspect of the Goddess and commanded instead to seek his true feminine counterpart, Aradia, the Daughter of the Moon and the Sun; Aradia who is the watcher over and protector of humankind, the Goddess come down to Earth and immanent in Nature, the saviour. For woman, her first vision of the Goddess is the immanent Earth Mother, and the last is the transcendent solar Goddess. For a man it is the opposite. For him, the first aspect of the Goddess is the transcendent Isis of the Starry Heavens and the second is the immanent Isis of Nature who is truly his bride. He must marry Earth and not Fire, the real and not the dream.

The priestess lies again in the pentacle position. The High Priestess rings the bell six times. With the spear or wand, the High Priest invokes once more the power of the Goddess upon her; this time using the symbol of the third degree. The Sun has come down upon the body of the priestess. Now the priest must become the Phallic Lord, the Earth aspect of the God, who will be united with the solar Goddess. The priestess is One but the priests are two; for the Goddess is the circle, ever changing, but ever the same, and the God is two – light and dark, death and life. All except the initiates leave the circle. The male initiate kisses the priestess in the pattern of the third degree symbol now given in true; the upright pentagram and triangle joined, the former ascending into the latter. The priestess becomes the temple and then the altar, the hidden sanctuary within; but this time the rite is consummated in reality rather than symbol. The Goddess and the God are united as One.

The journey of the pentagram

Here we have completed the first cycle of the Wiccan journey of initiation and have penetrated the Veil of the Mystery. What lies beyond is between the initiates and their Gods; but before leaving the third degree initiation behind, let us look at the initiatory meaning of that principal religious symbol of Wicca, the pentagram.

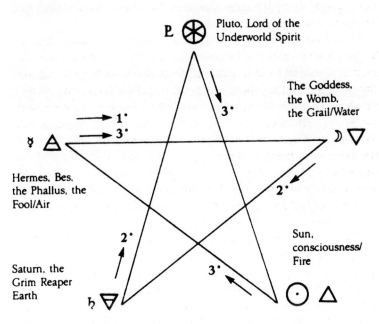

The pentagram of initiation

The pentagram is the friend who travels with us through Wicca; for its five lines symbolize the Wiccan journey of initiation. With the first degree we journey one line, with the second degree two lines and with the third degree the final three. The entry point is the East, the quarter of the youngest of the Elemental Lords, the virgin youth Eurus. At the first degree, we make a journey across the pentagram to the Element of the first degree initiation, the Element of Water.

With the second degree, we leave the Element of Water and journey into the realm of Earth, the realm of Saturn, the grim reaper. With death comes burial. In the Second Degree, we make the descent and enter the Underworld, the realm of the Dead. This is the realm of the spirits, the Element of Ether; for the death of the earthly body is the release of the spirit. Here is the realm of Pluto, Lord of the Underworld, from which spirit must be redeemed. This is the task in which the Greek musician-hero Orpheus failed when he sought to bring his dead wife Euridyce back from Hades.

The work of the third degree is to bring spirit above ground; in other words, to bring into consciousness the newly discovered power of the Self; to journey from darkness to the Element of Fire, the sunlight of the conscious mind. Having entered the realm of Fire, we must become integrated with it. This requires a return to the entry point, the point of Air; for Air is the Element of Hermes or Mercury, the phallic Nature God, whom Jung calls by his Egyptian name *ithyphallic Bes*. Hermes-Mercury-Bes in the tarot is the card of the Fool, which is ruled by the Element of Air. It was as Fools we set off blithely at the first degree into the journey to the unknown, and it is via the Fool we return; for he is numbered zero, the completed circle, the end.

To integrate the Sun of the Self, we must perform the Sacred Marriage, the union of the yoni with the lingam. Here the two are made one and we complete the sixth and sealing line of the pentagram which returns us once more to the Goddess' womb, the point of Water. Here we find not the cauldron of rebirth with which we entered the circle at the first degree, but the Holy Grail of Immortality, the Spirit eternal. Now the six lines can reveal their hidden meaning and the rose-flower of the sealed pentagram can open to reveal the six-sided hexagram, symbol of Sun and Self.

This is the last part of our journey; but at the end we turn once more to the future and find ourselves at another beginning, another round of the Goddess' Spiral Dance. A journey ends and a new journey begins; but here we rest in silence.

Notes

1. Asterius, Bishop of Amasea, *Homilia X, Sanctos martyres* in Migne, *Greek Series*, vol 40, Paris, 1857–66, pp323–4.
2. Ronald B Hutton, *Pagan Religions of the Ancient British Isles*, pp172–3 Basil Blackwell, Oxford, 1991.
3. Carl Jung, *The Collected Works of C.G. Jung*, Vol 9, Part 1: *Archetypes and the Collective Unconscious*, p164, para 278, Routledge and Kegan Paul, 2nd ed, 1968.
4. Carl Jung, *Archetypes and the Collective Unconscious*, p131, para 235.
5. Dion Fortune, *Moon Magic*, p176, Aquarian, Wellingborough, 1989.
6. Carl Jung, *Archetypes and the Collective Unconscious*, p120, para 217.
7. Carl Jung, *Archetypes and the Collective Unconscious*, p106, para 194.

14

Afterword

To talk of religion and Gods in our technological age may seem strange and archaic. Why does Wicca hark back to the past, when we are heading at breath-taking speed towards the future? Interestingly, as we make the transition into the New Millennium, Wicca appears to be thriving. Its long-term future will depend, however, like all other religious and spiritual movements in the world today, on whether there is a place for religion in the modern age. Witches believe that there is; for while large-scale organized religion in the West has gradually declined, at the same time other faiths and spiritual paths have blossomed. Religion and that newer science of the spirit, psychology, have met and are beginning to find common ground as we search for and find the answers to what it means to be human. From these two sciences of the spirit is emerging a new vision of humanity and human potential which shows that to live in harmony with and to understand the spiritual aspect of our humanity is fundamental to human existence and happiness.

Why are Wicca and other Pagan religions reviving and why does Christianity, the established religion of the West, no longer satisfy us? No religion can endure forever. Christianity with its worship of the sacrifice of the self was the religion of the Piscean Age. With the New Millennium, we have entered the Age of Aquarius. Aquarius is the sign of humanity, in which the Divine as God and Goddess will be found in all men and women, not just is one perfect man now long dead. Wicca is growing because religion must evolve to meet the needs of the developing human psyche. Religion must also contain an element of the Mysteries, the unknown. In describing the fate of the Paganism of Greece and Rome, Carl Jung wrote:

> The gods of Greece and Rome perished from the same disease as did our Christian symbols: people discovered then, as today, that they had no thoughts whatever on the subject. On the other hand, the gods of the strangers still had unexhaustable mana. Their names were weird and incomprehensible ... At least one couldn't understand the Asiatic symbols and for this reason they were not banal like the conventional gods.[1]

As consciousness and the needs of humanity evolve, religion must be renewed by going back to its source, the collective unconscious of humankind, finding there new life and vigour. Symbols and myths, whilst containing an essence and force which is eternally true, also contain forms which can become outmoded and outworn; even as can the temple buildings and its ritual implements. When this occurs, the temple must be rebuilt; the implements must be melted down and reforged. It is this which has occurred in Wicca. Taking the myths and archetypes of religion, and in particular those feminine elements which have been neglected by two millennia of Christianity, the cauldron of inspiration of the older faith has given birth to a new child, the religion of Wicca, the worship of the Goddess and the God.

Wicca is not an evangelical religion. It has no need to seek converts; for we do not enter Wicca in response to any human call, but in response to the Horn of Herne the Hunter, which echoes in the deep caverns of our unconscious minds, and in response to the Goddess whose voice like a silver harp-whisper calls us to come to her altar.

> Deep in the recesses of the human psyche, Our Lord the Horned One waited through the centuries until his time should come again. Then he took down from the oak in the centre of the forest his hunting horn not blown for many a thousand year, and sounded three times upon it. He awoke the Goddess from her dreaming sleep and she

spoke in a voice like a silver harp whisper *The Charge of Arianrhod* and said:

I am Arianrhod,
of the spiral castle by the silver sea.
I am the last of my race,
without beginning and without ending;
for before ever time and change began,
my mother the Star Goddess
lay upon the Lord of Darkness
and brought me forth.

I am beyond sound and sight,
I cannot be touched,
I am She who dwells behind the veil of matter.
They ask if I exist
and I answer that I do
and I do not;
but at the end of cycles and seasons,
which some name Death
but those who have lifted my veil name Life,
on the shores of the Sea of Time you will find me,
my head turned to the wind,
walking by the waves of the aeons and waiting,
for your coming and your going.

In truth I was,
I am and I will be,
when all else has faded from your memory.
I am something which you possess,
and something which you seek,
I am the question that is also the answer;
I am that which binds and that which sets free;
I am the beginning of things;
I am the ending;
seek me and know me,
for I am She.

The Goddess and the Horned God have risen from their sleep and call their worshippers, from East and South and West and North, and whispering in the dreams of those who love them:

> Seek us, find us, know us;
> walk the way which lies between the worlds.

Note

1. Carl Jung, *The Collected Works of C.G. Jung*, Vol 9, Part 1: *Archetypes of the Collective Unconscious*, p14, para 26, Routledge and Kegan Paul, 2nd ed, 1968.

Wiccan Resources:
Where to Find Information, Books and Contacts

Below are magazines and organizations which can help you find out more about Wicca. The listings are not exhaustive. There are many different Wiccan contact networks and it is not possible to cover them all. All Wiccan organizations and magazines are run on tight budgets and you should not expect to receive a reply unless you send postage. In your own country, send a stamped addressed envelope and an extra stamp to cover administration costs. To overseas addressees, send two International Reply Coupons. These can be bought in large post offices and exchanged for stamps all over the world. Write your name and address on any letter you send, in case letters and covering envelopes are separated.

If you run a Wiccan group or organization which is not in touch with the major groups listed here, then you may wish to contact them to foster networking and contacts.

Europe

Cauldron, available from Mike Howard, Caemorgan Cottage, Caemorgan Road, Cardigan, Dyfed, SA43 1QU, Wales, UK, is a Pagan journal of the Old Religion and one of the longest-running Craft periodicals.

Circe, Postbus 2191, 3500 GD Utrecht, The Netherlands, provides Wiccan contacts in the Netherlands and also Craft supplies.

Coraen, Moonsstraat 11, 2018 Antwerpen, Belgium, is a teaching coven in Belgium and the Netherlands.

Hole in the Sky, Postlargernd, D-13507 Berlin 27, Germany, provides information on German-speaking Wicca and Wiccan activities and workshops.

Moira, CDD, BP 68, 33034 Bordeaux, France. Pagan/Wiccan magazine and contact point for Wicca in France. Can provide correspondence training in French.

Norwegian Pagan Federation, PO Box 1814, Nordnes, 524 Bergen, Norway. Information network which can assist with Pagan and Wiccan contacts in Norway and other Scandinavian countries.

Pagan Federation, BM Box 7097, London WC1N 3XX, England, is the largest and oldest Pagan and Wiccan body in Europe. It provides an annual conference, local group meetings and contacts across Europe and world-wide.

Quest, BCM-SCL Quest, London WC1N 3XX, England, is one of the oldest Pagan and Craft magazines.

The Wicca Study Group, BM Deosil, London WC1N 3XX, England, is run by Vivianne and Chris Crowley to provide introductory teaching on Wicca through courses, workshops and a correspondence course. The WSG functions mainly in Europe but workshops can be arranged in other parts of the world by request.

Wiccan Rede, PO Box 473, Zeist, NL 3700 AL, The Netherlands, is an English/Dutch Wiccan magazine which can also assist with contacts in the Netherlands.

North America

Circle, PO Box 219, Mount Horeb, WI 53572, is a Shamanic Wiccan Church. It organizes Pagan events, fosters contacts and networking, and publishes *Circle Network News*.

Covenant of the Goddess, PO Box 1226, Berkeley, CA 94704, is a federation of Wiccan covens which publishes a newsletter and holds an annual gathering.

Hecate's Loom, Box 5206, Station B, Victoria, BC, V8R 6N4, is one of the largest and oldest Pagan publications in Canada.

Hidden Path, Windwalker, Box 934, Kenosha, WI 53141, advice on contacting Gardnerian Wicca.

Khaled, PO Box 32 'B', Ottawa, Ontario, K1P 6C3, Canada. Gardnerian and Alexandrian contacts in Canada.

Panegyria, PO Box 73, Index, Washington 98256. Wiccan contacts in the Pacific North-West.

Wiccan Church of Canada, 109 Vaughan Road, Toronto, M6C 2L9 is a network of Wiccan groups in the Odyssian tradition.

Australia and New Zealand

Pan-Pacific Pagan Alliance, PO Box A486, Sydney South, NSW 2000, is the contact organization for all branches of Wicca and Paganism in Australia and New Zealand. Its members' magazine lists groups and contacts.

Bibliography

Adler, Margot, *Drawing Down the Moon*, Beacon Press, Boston, 1986.

Anon, *Das Hexenbuch: Authentische Texte moderner Hexen zu Geschichte, Magie und Mythos des alten Weges*, Goldmann Verlag, 1987.

Avalon, Arthur (Sir John Woodroffe), *Shakti and Shakta*, Dover, NY, 1978 ed (originally published 1918).

Bailey, AA, *Esoteric Psychology*, Part II, Lucis Publishing Co, New York, 1942.

Barret, F, *The Magus*, The Citadel Press, NJ, 1967 (originally published 1801).

Bly, Robert, *Iron John: A Book about Men*, Element Books, Shaftesbury, 1991 (UK Edition).

Budapest, Z, *The Holy Book of Women's Mysteries*, Harper and Row, 1990.

Wallis Budge, EA, *The Book of the Dead: An English translation of the chapters, hymns, etc, of the Theban recension, with Introduction, notes, etc*, Routledge & Kegan Paul, London, 1923 ed.

Burkhardt, J, *The Civilisation of the Renaissance in Italy*, trans SGC Middlemore, New York and London, 1944 (originally published in German, Basel, 1860).

Cade CMC and Coxhead, N, *The Awakened Mind*, Element Books, Shaftesbury, Dorset, 1987.

Campbell, Joseph, *The Hero with a Thousand Faces*, Bollingen Series XVII, Princeton University Press, 1972 (originally published 1949).

Chadwick, Nora, *The Celts*, Penguin Books, Harmondsworth, 1970.

Conway, D, *Magic: An Occult Primer*, Granda Publishing Ltd, St Albans, Herts.

Cronin, Vincent, *The Flowering of the Renaissance*, Pimlico, London, 1969.

Crowley, Vivianne, *Hekserij: Een oude leer voor de nieuwe tijd*, Elsy Kloeg trans, Kosmos, Utrechet, 1990.

Crowley, Vivianne, *Phoenix from the Flame: Living as a Pagan in the Twenty-first Century*, Thorsons, 1996.

Crowley, Vivianne, *Wicca: Die alte Religion im Neuem Zeitalter*, Michael de Witt trans, Edition Ananael, Vien, 1993.

✕ Crowley, Vivianne, *Wicca: The Old Religion in the New Age*, Aquarian, 1989.

✓ Crowley, Vivianne, 'The Initiation', in Jones, Prudence, and Matthews, Caitlín, eds, *Voices from the Circle*, Aquarian Press, 1990.

Crowley, Vivianne, 'Paganism', in Button J and Bloom W, eds, *The Seeker's Guide: A New Age Resource Book*, Aquarian, 1992.

Crowley, Vivianne, 'Priestess and Witch', in Matthews, Caitlín, ed, *Voices of the Goddess*, Aquarian Press, 1991.

Crowley, Vivianne, 'Women and Power in Modern Paganism' in Puttick, E and Clarke, PB, eds, *Women as Teachers and Disciples in Traditional and New Religions*, Edwin Mellen Press, Lewiston, NY, 1993.

de Lancre, P, *Tableau de l'Inconstance des Mauvais Anges*, 1612.

✓ Farrar, Janet and Stewart, *Eight Sabbats for Witches*, Robert Hale, London, 1981.

Farrar, Janet and Stuart, *The Life and Times Of A Modern Witch*, Piatkus, 1987.

⁰ Fortune, Dion, *The Sea Priestess*, Aquarian, Wellingborough, 1989 ed.

○ Fortune, Dion, *Moon Magic*, Aquarian, Wellingborough, 1989 ed.

Fournier, P, 'Etudes Critiques sur le Decret de Burchard de Worms' in *Nouvelle Revue historique de droit francais et etranger*, vol 34, 1910.

∨ Frazer, Sir James G, *The Golden Bough: A Study in Magic and Religion*, abridged edition, Macmillan, London, 1957 (originally published 1922).

Gantz, Jeffrey, trans, *The Mabinogion*, Penguin Books, Harmondsworth, 1976 ed.

Gardner, Gerald B, *High Magick's Aid*, Atlantis Book Shop, 1949.

Gardner, Gerald B, *Witchcraft Today*, Rider & Co, London 1954.

Gardner, Gerald B, *The Meaning of Witchcraft*, Aquarian Press, Wellingborough, 1959.

Gauquelin, M, *The Cosmic Clocks*, Granda Publishing Ltd., St Albans, Herts, 1973.

Graves, Robert, *The White Goddess: A historical grammar of poetic myth*, Faber and Faber, London, 1961 ed.

Guiley, Rosemary Ellen, *The Encyclopaedia of Witches and Witchcraft*, Facts On File, New York and Oxford, 1989.

Hutton, Ronald B, *Pagan Religions of the Ancient British Isles*, Basil Blackwell, Oxford, 1991.

Jarke, KE, *Annalen der deutschen und auslandischen Criminal-Rechts-Pflage*, vol I, Berlin, 1828.

Jones, Evan John, with Doreen Valiente, *Witchcraft: A Tradition Renewed*, Robert Hale, London, 1990.

Jones, Prudence, and Matthews, Caitlín, eds, *Voices from the Circle*, Aquarian Press, 1990.

Jones, Prudence and Pennick, Nigel, *A History of Pagan Europe*, Routledge, London, 1995.

Jung, Carl G, *The Collected Works of C.G. Jung*, Vol 5, *Symbols of Transformation*, Routledge & Kegan Paul, London, 2nd ed, 1967.

Jung, Carl G, *The Collected Works of C.G. Jung*, Vol 6, *Psychological Types*, Routledge & Kegan Paul, London, 2nd ed 1971.

Jung, Carl G, *The Collected Works of C.G. Jung*, Vol 7, *Two Essays on Analytical Psychology*, Routledge & Kegan Paul, London, 2nd ed 1966.

Jung, Carl G, *The Collected Works of C.G. Jung*, Vol 8, *The Structure and Dynamics of the Psyche*, Routledge & Kegan Paul, London, 2nd ed 1966.

Jung, Carl G, *The Collected Works of C.G. Jung*, Vol 9, Part 1, *Archetypes and the Collective Unconscious*, Routledge & Kegan Paul, London, 2nd ed 1968.

Jung, Carl G, *The Collected Works of C.G. Jung*, Vol 10, *Civilization in Transition*, Routledge & Kegan Paul, London, 2nd ed 1968.

Jung, Carl G, *The Collected Works of C.G. Jung*, Vol 11, *Psychology and Religion: West and East*, Routledge & Kegan Paul, London, 2nd ed 1968.

Jung, Carl G, *The Collected Works of C.G. Jung*, Vol 12, *Psychology and Alchemy*, Routledge & Kegan Paul, London, 2nd ed 1970.

Jung, Carl G, *The Collected Works of C.G. Jung*, Vol 14, *Mysterium Coniunctionis: An Enquiry into the separation and synthesis of psychic opposites in Alchemy*, Routledge & Kegan Paul, London, 2nd ed 1970.

Jung, E, *Animus and Anima: Two Essays*, Spring Publications, Zurich, 1957.

Knight, G, *A History of White Magic*, Mowbrays, London and New York, 1978.

Koppana, Kati-ma, *Snakefat and Knotted Threads: A Short Introduction to Finnish Magic*, Mandragora Dimensions, Helskini, 1990.

Koppana, Kati-ma, *The Finnish Gods*, Madragora Dimensions, Helsinki, 1991.

Le Shan, L, *The Science of the Paranormal: The Last Frontier*, Aquarian Press, Wellingborough, 1987.

Leland, Charles G, *Aradia: The Gospel of the Witches*, CW Daniel Company, 1974 ed.

Matthews, Caitlín, *Elements of the Celtic Tradition*, Element Books, Shaftesbury, 1989.

Michelet, Jules, *La Sorciere*, P Viallaneix, 1966 ed (originally published Paris 1862).

Mone, FJ, *Anzeiger für Kunde der teutschen Vorzeit*, Jahrgang 8, Karlsruhe 1839.

Monmouth, Geoffrey of, *The History of the Kings of Britain*, Lewis Thorpe, trans, Penguin, Harmondsworth, 1966 ed.

Murray, Margaret A, *The Witch-Cult in Western Europe: A Study in Anthropology*, Clarendon Press, Oxford, 1921.

Murray, Margaret A, *The God of the Witches*, Oxford University Press, New York and Faber and Faber, London, 1970 ed (originally published 1931).

Peek, W, *Isishymnus von Andros und verwandete Texte*, Berlin, 1930.

Perera, Sylvia B, *Descent to the Goddess, A Way of Initiation for Women*, Inner City Books, Toronto, 1981.

Ramakrishna, *The Gospel of Sri Ramakrishna*, New York, 1971.

Rieu, EV, *The Illustrated Odyssey*, Sidgwick and Jackson, London, 1980.

Ross, Anne, *Everyday Life of the Pagan Celts*, Carousel Books, Transworld Publishers Limited, London.

Scot, R, *The Discoverie of Witchcraft*, 1972 ed, originally published 1584.

Scott, Walter, *Hermetica: The Ancient Greek and Latin Writings which contain Religious or Philosophic Teachings ascribed to Hermes Trismegistus*, Vol. I, Shambhala, Boston, 1985, ed.

Seznec, Jean, *The Survival of the Pagan Gods: The Mythological Tradition and its Place in Renaissance Humanism and Art*, Barbara F Sessions trans, Bollingen Series XXXVIII, Princeton University Press, 1972.

Sprenger, J, and Kramer, H, *Malleus Maleficarum*, Folio Society ed, 1968, London (originally published 1486).

Starhawk, *The Spiral Dance: A Rebirth of the Ancient Religion of the Great Goddess*, Harper and Row, San Francisco, 1979 ed.

Starhawk, *Der Hexencult als Ur-Religion der Grossen Göttin*, Verlag Hermann Bauer, Freiburg im Breisgau, 1983.

Stone, Merlin, *Ancient Mirrors of Womanhood*, Beacon Press, Boston, Mass, 1984.

Sturluson, Snorri, *Edda*, Faulkes, Anthony, trans, Everyman Library, JM Dent London, 1987.

Thomas K, *Religion and the Decline of Magic*, Penguin, Harmondsworth, 1971.

Thorpe, B, *Diplomatrium Anglicum aevi Saxonici*, London, 1865.

Thorpe, B, *Monumenta Ecclesiastica*, London, 1840.

Valiente, D, *Natural Magic*, Hale, London, 1975.

Valiente, D, *The Rebirth of Witchcraft*, Hale, London, 1989.

Wallis, RT, *Neoplatonism*, Duckworth, London, 1972.

Wehr, DS, *Jung and Feminism*, Routledge, London, 1988.

Witt, RE, *Isis in the Graeco-Roman World*, Thames and Hudson, 1971.

Index

Of further interest ...

Principles of Paganism
Vivianne Crowley

Interest in Paganism is steadily increasing and, while rooted in ancient tradition, it is a living religious movement. With its reverence for all creation, it reflects our current concern for the planet. This introductory guide explains:

- what Paganism is
- the different Pagan paths
- what Pagans do
- how to live as a Pagan

Vivianne Crowley is the author of the bestselling *Wicca: The Old Religion in the New Millennium.* She is a priestess, a teacher of the Pagan way and a leading figure in western Paganism. She has a doctorate in psychology and has trained in transpersonal therapy.

A Witch Alone
Thirteen moons to master natural magic

Marian Green

Many witches do not belong to covens but follow a different, solo branch of our magical heritage. Working alone they can connect deeply with nature, talk to the trees, follow the patterns of the sun and moon, and feel the changing energies of the years turning in cycle.

This detailed introduction to natural and folk magic enables everyone to learn something of their magical powers.

The ancient arts and powers are there to be rediscovered, given patience, common sense and a longing to know. You can heal yourself, find peace from stress and discover ways of coping with the turmoil of modern life. You can also do good for others, learn to heal from herbs, see into the future and recover the treasures of wisdom from the past.

Marian Green lectures and runs workshops throughout the world. She is the author of numerous books on natural magic.

'Invaluable to the newcomer to paganism.' – *Mystical Realms*

Witchcraze
A new history of the European witch hunt

Anne Llewellyn Barstow

This rivetting history explores the annihilation of more than seven million women of spirit and intelligence under the guise of the 'witch hunts' of Europe. Barstow's sweeping chronicle examines the persecution of women in order to scapegoat them for the ills of society, investigates their subjugation to sexual violence and death as a message of control to all women, and compares the persecution of women with the enslavement and slaughter of African slaves and Native Americans. Barstow tracks the current backlash against women to its frightening European origins. She leaves an indelible mark on the growing understanding of our violent legacy toward women.

Anne Llewellyn Barstow is the author of *Joan of Arc: Heretic, mystic, shaman* and *Married Priests and the Reforming Papacy.* She is a retired Professor of History and lives in New York City.

PRINCIPLES OF PAGANISM	1 85538 507 4	£5.99	☐
A WITCH ALONE	1 85538 112 5	£7.99	☐
WITCHCRAZE	0 06 251036 3	£9.99	☐

All these books are available from your local bookseller or can be ordered direct from the publishers.

To order direct just tick the titles you want and fill in the form below:

Name: _____

Address: _____

Postcode: _____

Send to: Thorsons Mail Order, Dept 3, HarperCollins*Publishers*, Westerhill Road, Bishopbriggs, Glasgow G64 2QT.

Please enclose a cheque or postal order or your authority to debit your Visa/Access account –

Credit card no: _____

Expiry date: _____

Signature: _____

– to the value of the cover price plus:

UK & BFPO: Add £1.00 for the first book and 25p for each additional book ordered.

Overseas orders including Eire: Please add £2.95 service charge. Books will be sent by surface mail but quotes for airmail despatches will be given on request.

24 HOUR TELEPHONE ORDERING SERVICE FOR ACCESS/VISA CARDHOLDERS – TEL: 0141 772 2281.